STUART BATH

Dedicated to the memory of Stephen Beck, a good friend and a talented illustrator of history books, including seven of my own. This present volume is greatly enriched by several of his imaginative drawings which - as ever - are authentic in historical detail.

STUART BATH

LIFE IN THE FORGOTTEN CITY

1603-1714

JOHN WROUGHTON

THE LANSDOWN PRESS

First published in 2004 by
The Lansdown Press
41 The Empire   Grand Parade
Bath BA2 4DF

ISBN   0 9520249 4 2   (paperback edition)
ISBN   0 9520249 5 0   (cased edition)

Typeset in 11 / 13 Times New Roman
Typesetting, design and origination by
The Lansdown Press, Bath

Printed in Great Britain by
The Cromwell Press, Trowbridge, Wiltshire

Contents

Preface

The story of both Roman Bath and Georgian Bath has been extensively covered not only in the numerous histories which have appeared over the past two centuries, but also visually in the city's impressive museums. Furthermore, buildings and artefacts of those times have survived in abundance for the enjoyment of visitors. It has to be said, however, that the most perceptive of these go on to pose the question...*But what happened in between?* Thanks to the work of the Bath Archaeological Trust and Peter Davenport's excellent book, *Medieval Bath Uncovered* (2002), the 'Dark' and Middle Ages are gradually being brought to life.

Stuart Bath alone, alas, has lacked its own impassioned advocate over the years. Indeed, the seventeenth-century city was initially written about by largely unsympathetic historians - John Wood in the eighteenth century, who wrote in disparaging terms about its buildings and its interiors; and Richard Warner in the early nineteenth century, who ridiculed 'the grossness and simplicity' of its people. Even today, it still finds no place in our museums and galleries. It is as if, for two hundred and fifty years, this period has been gently airbrushed out of our heritage - an age, it seems, which is never mentioned in polite company.

However, in spite of this, many enthusiastic and scholarly individuals were working away quietly on various aspects of the period throughout the twentieth century, so that gradually a great fund of knowledge was being accumulated. The aim of this book, therefore, is to bring together all that research - along with my own published work on civil war, education and religion - in an attempt to resuscitate our forgotten city. What emerges is a city which is both beautiful and ugly, both progressive and traditional, both colourful and squalid - but a city which is always fascinating, lively and controversial; a city which eventually manages to throw off its medieval image to lay foundations for the spectacular rise of the leisure resort under Beau Nash.

Modern spellings have been adopted throughout in the numerous quotations from contemporary sources. The cost of items taken from documentary material has been left in its original 'old money' form. It should be remembered, therefore, that before decimalisation there were twelve old pence to the shilling - today worth five new pence - and twenty shillings to the pound. The dates given are based on the Old Style (or Julian) calendar, which was used in England at the time. This was ten days behind the New Style (or Gregorian) calendar, which was followed on the continent. However, although the year in England began on 25th March, I have taken the year to begin on 1st January for the purpose of this book. It should also be noted that the annual Bath chamberlain's accounts (which are used extensively throughout) covered a period between October and the following September. As it is not normally possible therefore to pin-point whether an entry refers to one year or the next, the earlier date is always taken.

John Wroughton
January 2004

Acknowledgements

The author wishes to thank the following people who have contributed in various ways to the production of this book:

Stephen Beck, a distinguished illustrator of seventeenth-century books, for his imaginative line drawings which accompany the text; Mike Chapman for producing four excellent maps; and Shane Feeney for his original painting of High Street, Bath in 1650, which has formed a superb basis for Martin Latham's striking cover design;

the staff of the British Library and the Public Record Office in London; the Bodleian Library in Oxford; the County Record Office in Taunton; and the City Record Office in Bath - for their courtesy and helpfulness in my research of documentary material;

the staff of the Ashmolean Museum Department of Western Art; the Bildarchiv of the Austrian Nationalbibliothek; the Bath Central Library; the British Library; the Gloucester Folk Museum; the Mary Evans Picture Library; the Museum of London Archive; the Museum of Costume, Bath; the National Portrait Gallery Archive; the Pepys Library, Magdalene College, Cambridge; and the Victoria Art Gallery, Bath - for their patient assistance and expertise in my search for contemporary illustrations;

those who have provided valuable references and illustrations - or who have given permission for the use of copyright material, including the Trustees of St John's Hospital, Bath; the Governors of King Edward's School, Bath; Marek Lewcun and Peter Davenport of the Bath Archaeological Trust; Colin Johnston of Bath Record Office; the Rector of Bath Abbey; Simon Ferguson, Giles White and Marta Inskip, who has provided countless pieces of priceless information from her index of seventeenth-century leases;

those local historians who have placed their own scholarship at my disposal by reading through sections of the book and offering constructive criticism - Peter Basterfield, Kerry Birch, Trevor Fawcett, Roger Rolls and, in particular, Elizabeth Holland, whose detailed knowledge of the people and buildings of the period has been invaluable; Jean Manco, who first took me on a tour of the hidden parts of seventeenth-century Bath; and Rodney Morant for his painstaking correction of the typescript and helpful suggestions - though I would stress that any errors are mine and not theirs.

The copyright source of each illustration is acknowledged within the text.

John Wroughton

January 2004

CHAPTER 1

Nation and City in 1603

England in 1600 was in many ways a country rising in confidence, optimism and prosperity. The exploits of Drake and Hawkins on the Spanish Main, the expansion of overseas trade, the growth of industry and the defeat of the Spanish Armada in 1588 all indicated the emergence of England as a force to be reckoned with in the world at large. The country in general benefited from a growing affluence, which was reflected in the increased comfort of many homes and the fine stone houses which became a feature of most towns. The population (there were some four million inhabitants in England and Wales) was in the main both scattered and rural, agriculture providing the livelihood for the vast majority of people. Nevertheless, by 1600, Bath was one of some six hundred market towns in England with a population of 2,000 or less - and there were probably another hundred larger centres, including London with 200,000 residents. However, in spite of outward signs, cracks were already beginning to appear in the harmony of English society - cracks which eventually would lead in the Stuart Age to division and civil war. Elizabeth's later years were characterised by a population explosion, rampant inflation, a serious growth in poverty and vagabondage, an interminable and costly war with Spain, bitter disputes over religion and increased friction between monarchy and parliament.

Bath from the south: a drawing by William Stukeley in 1723. Note Magdalen's Hospital in the foreground . (By courtesy of the Victoria Art Gallery, Bath & North East Somerset Council.)

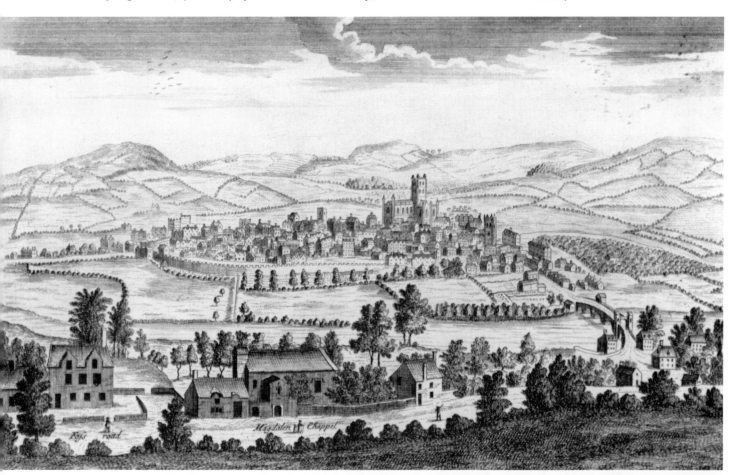

In 1600, Bath remained in most respects a medieval city. Still largely confined to the small area within the old defences (which remained intact), it was surrounded by green fields and orchards which ran up to the very foot of its walls. Throughout the seventeenth century, the population hovered around the two thousand mark, although numbers were increased each year by a seasonal influx of visitors. As one eyewitness commented: ''Tis neither town nor city, yet goes under the name of both; five months in the year 'tis as populous as London *[a slight exaggeration!]*, the other seven as desolate as a wilderness'. Its economy was chiefly dependent on three elements - the cloth industry (in steep decline by 1600), agriculture (freemen of the city still exercised the right to graze their animals on common land) and the health trade. The streets conveyed an air of affluence through what John Leland had described in 1530 as its 'fair and goodly buildings' - the product of the Tudor Age, when the city had reached a peak of prosperity.

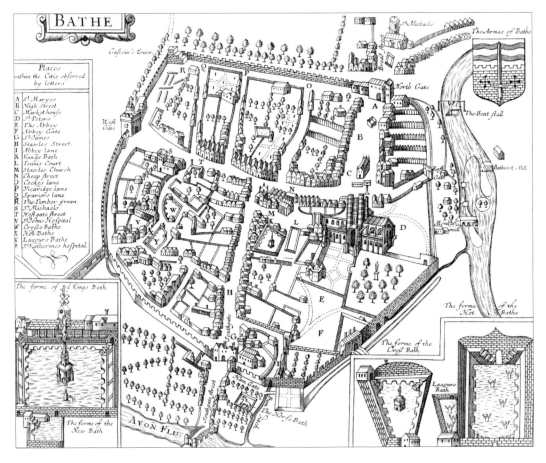

John Speed's map of Bath, published in 1610. (Author's collection)

At the start of the seventeenth century, Bath and its surrounding area were firmly in the grip of the puritan revolution - something that was to dominate its social life and political outlook for the next sixty years. Indeed, religion formed a hugely important element in everyday life with weekly attendance at one of the three parish churches compulsory. The city itself was governed by a self-perpetuating oligarchy of some thirty men, who alone were responsible for electing its two members of parliament. Its powers had been substantially enlarged by a new royal charter in 1590, while its assets had been greatly increased by Edward VI's grant of property in 1552 for the endowment of a grammar school. Among the problems faced by the corporation, as it became more and more conscious of the need to market the city as a health resort, were two eyesores which disfigured its streets - the growing band of beggars, attracted by its comparative affluence; and the unsightly squalor of unhygienic refuse, which rotted away steadily in its gutters.

Nevertheless, Bath had four sizeable assets which added daily to its fame - the hot water springs, an abundant supply of piped drinking water, an impressive new Abbey Church and the city's attractive location. Visitors and residents alike continued to lavish their praise throughout the seventeenth century. Tobias Venner, writing in 1628, called it 'a little, well-compacted city; for goodness of air, nearness of a sweet and delectable river, and fertility of soil, it is pleasant and happy enough'; Henry Chapman, in 1673, admired its backdrop of 'pleasant and fruitful hills full of excellent springs of water'; Thomas Dingley, in 1682, noted that 'this city is besides, without doubt, the prettiest in the kingdom - in a double construction, as it is little and handsome'; and Samuel Pepys, in 1668, appreciated 'the pretty good market place and many good streets and very fair stone houses'.

On the other hand, a few discerning visitors were also quick to notice the city's main disadvantage - namely, its somewhat oppressive atmosphere with high levels of humidity. Celia Fiennes, for instance, on a visit to Bath in 1687, complained that 'the baths in my opinion make the town unpleasant, the air thick and hot by the steam, and by its own situation so low, encompassed with high hills and woods'. Even less flattering was a remark by one visitor, quoted later by John Wood - Bath, he said, 'is a place standing in a hole; in a quagmire; impenetrable to the very beams of the sun; and so confined by inaccessible hills, that people have scarce room to breath in the town, or come at it without danger to their lives'.

Indeed, accessibility was a great problem for the health resort in the seventeenth century, as its economy became more and more dependent on the arrival of a steady stream of affluent visitors. Stage coach travel from London and other major towns, however, was expensive, slow and hazardous. Having journeyed from Warminster in 1687 over 'a deep clay way' which was really 'only made for packhorses', Celia Fiennes discovered that 'the ways to Bath are all difficult - the town lies in a bottom and it is steep ascents all ways out of town'. During her journey, the wheels of her coach became so wedged in rocks that 'several men' were forced to lift it out. As late as 1700, Ned Ward had to endure the painful discomfort of a coach trip between Marlborough and Bath, even though the compartment of the coach was by then slung on leather braces in an attempt to absorb some of the shocks:

> Having dined, we proceeded on our journey, but with a great deal of difficulty: for the road was so rocky and unlevel and narrow in some places that I am persuaded the Alps are to be passed over with less danger;...but we were jolted so cursedly that I thought it would have made a dislocation of my knees: nor would I advise any who have been sufferers in Venus sports to adventure the fatigue of a coach to the Bath, lest it disjoint a member or two.

By the end of the century, with Bath's increasing fame as a major leisure resort, the corporation had begun to realise the importance of improving the immediate access to the city via the hazard of its surrounding hills. Therefore, with the support of its two MPs, it successfully petitioned parliament in 1707 for an Act to establish a

A seventeenth-century coach.
(By permission of the British Library - ref: Roxburghe Ballads, RAX.Rox. I, pt 2, 546)

network of turnpike trust roads into the city. In its preamble, the Act not only acknowledged that the city was 'a place of very great resort from all parts of the kingdom' for its healing waters, but that the roads leading into it were all 'ancient roads' which had been made 'very ruinous and impassable' by heavy goods traffic - so much so, in fact, that they had become 'very dangerous to all persons, horses and cattle that pass those ways'. The Act therefore set up a trust, consisting of local justices, to construct proper surfaces on seven of the access roads (i.e. the roads from Kingsdown, Odd Down, Twerton, Entry Hill, Claverton Down, Lansdown and Locksbrook), totalling twelve-and-a-half miles in all. This at least was a start, although it took several more Acts of Parliament before a decent road was completed between London and Bristol via Bath in 1750.

The economy of the city, however, was also suffering in another way from the problem of its inaccessibility. The condition of the nation's roads (described by Charles Wilson as 'everywhere deplorable and getting steadily worse') gave great advantage in the movement of heavy goods to those cities which were situated on a navigable river. The merchants of Bath and its surrounding area had in previous times made effective use of the River Avon to gain access to the profitable markets of Bristol and its export trade for their supplies of corn, coal, cloth and dairy products. Unfortunately, the Avon had suffered like most rivers from creeping paralysis brought about partly through the gradual process of silting-up and partly through blockages caused by mills, weirs, shallows and fords. By 1619 it was scarcely navigable. In that year, showing a great degree of urgency, Bath Corporation began the process of gaining an Act of Parliament giving them powers to correct that situation. Sadly, however, it was to take over a century before their ambition was finally realised, in spite of frequent but abortive attempts to do so.

As Bath residents entered the new century and greeted the arrival of the new

Stuart dynasty, their outlook was almost certainly pessimistic. North-East Somerset was already in the grip of a recession with the local cloth industry in a state of rapid decline, unemployment high, inflation soaring and food shortages acute. By 1622, the Mayor of Bath had reclassified the place, which had prospered so greatly in Tudor times, as 'a very little poor city'. Furthermore, the powerful impact of the Puritan revolution was beginning to create divisions in local society - divisions that were to widen more openly with the outbreak of war in 1642 and to turn into bitter and factious rivalry in 1661 with the outrageous kidnapping of eleven members of the corporation.

In spite of all these problems, however, the city was to show both resilience and vision in the years following the Restoration in 1660 by adapting most skilfully to the needs of a new consumer society and thus to recover its old prosperity. By the end of the Stuart period, the mood of the citizens was to be one of rising optimism as Bath systematically put in place all the foundations needed for the age of Beau Nash.

SOURCES USED IN CHAPTER 1

1. Printed Material:

Chapman, Henry: *Thermae Redivivae: the City of Bath Described* (1673)

Hart, Roger: *English Life in the Seventeenth Century* (1970)

Morris, Christopher (ed.): *The Illustrated Journeys of Celia Fiennes, 1685-c1712* (1982)

Venner, Tobias: *The Baths of Bath, 1628* (Harleian Miscellany, vol. 2, ed. William Oldys, 1809)

Ward, Ned: *A Step to the Bath* (1700)

Warrington, John (ed.): *The Diary of Samuel Pepys*, vol. 3 (1953 ed.)

Wilson, Charles: *England's Apprenticeship, 1603-1763* (1965)

Wood, John: *Essay Towards a Description of Bath*, vol. 2 (1765 edtn.)

Wroughton, John: *A Community at War: the Civil War in Bath & North Somerset* (1992)

2. Documentary Material

Bath Record Office: Act for Repairing, Amending and Enlarging the Highways, 1707

CHAPTER 2

The Government of the City

The year 1590 gave the citizens of Bath much cause for celebration. Their new charter, granted by Queen Elizabeth I in that year, confirmed in writing - what in reality had been true for several years - that the mayor and corporation had assumed the powers originally exercised by the bishop and the prior. The men who made up the city council were tough businessmen who, once the priory had been dissolved in 1539, had systematically and ruthlessly set about the task of seizing total control of the city. By cleverly petitioning King Edward VI in 1552 to establish a new grammar school by endowing it with property previously owned by the priory, the corporation gained a rich inheritance and a lucrative income - not to mention the power of landlord control. The school's charter of 1552 effectively handed over to the corporation, as trustee, 102 choice properties, mostly situated within the city walls. In taking control of former priory property, it also inherited the prior's general responsibility for the education of the young, the relief of the elderly and the control of the hot water baths.

The Charter granted to Bath Corporation by Queen Elizabeth I in 1590. (By courtesy of Bath Record Office, Bath & North East Somerset Council)

By 1572, the corporation had in addition gained effective control of local religion by purchasing the advowsons (or right of appointment) to the city churches (see Chapter 14). To all this newly-acquired authority, the charter of 1590 added total control of law and order by granting the corporation, for the first time, the right to appoint a coroner and justices of the peace. Furthermore, the bounds of the city were extended beyond the walls to include Barton Farm to the north-west and a large part of Walcot parish, thus providing space for future expansion. The year 1590 was therefore a turning point which launched a gradual transformation of medieval Bath, a somewhat stagnant city, into a bustling new health resort.

Composition of the Corporation

The new charter conferred the government of the city on a 'body corporate' consisting of a mayor (who, in 1640, carried a stipend of £50), between four and ten aldermen and up to twenty common councillors. Bath Corporation, which could elect its own new members for life from amongst the ranks of the freemen of the city (see below), was somewhat smaller in size than that of many other towns in seventeenth century England. Aldermen and common councillors, therefore, sat together as a self-perpetuating oligarchy at meetings of the common council with no great discrimination between them - but with the vast majority of freemen excluded from all say in elections and government. The corporation, which had power to return two members of parliament, was assisted by various officials - a chamberlain (who, by 1640, was paid a stipend of £8), a recorder (£2), a town clerk (£2), two constables, two justices, two bailiffs and two sergeants-at-mace. Apart from the recorder and town clerk, these officers were normally drawn from within the membership of the council on the basis of one year's spell of duty. Refusal to take office could mean a fine or even imprisonment - as Richard Gay, for instance, found to his cost in 1614 when he refused to become mayor. He was duly fined £50 and imprisoned. Similarly, the corporation had the power to expel members for both inappropriate behaviour and non-attendance. In 1668, therefore, James Burton, 'being decayed in his estate and having absented himself from his habitation', was ejected on the grounds that he was no longer able to perform his duties as a councillor. Elections for both new members and office holders took place in September on the Monday before Michaelmas Day with the new mayoral year commencing on the first Monday in October.

The chief officers of the corporation played an important part in the running of the city's affairs. Although he was not a member of the council, **the Town Clerk** was in normal life an attorney who gave legal advice to the corporation. He was also responsible for a wide range of administrative duties as keeper of the city's records, deputy recorder, minuting secretary at council meetings, clerk of the peace and deputy coroner. It was his task to draft documents and petitions, serve writs, attend the county assizes and lobby the government on behalf of the city. Town clerks often gave continuity to the administration by holding office over a long period - John Bushell, for instance, served during the years 1679-1702, years which witnessed dramatic events in the country at large (see Chapter 3). **The Recorder** was also a person who, in the words of the charter, was to be 'learned in the law'. A man of more distinguished status, he usually spent much of his time in London (often as one of the city's two MPs), where he could use his influence to represent the corporation's interests. In Bath, he was responsible for administering the oath of office to the mayor, presiding at the city's court of Quarter Sessions and sitting (when available) as judge at the Court of Record. The actual extent of his involvement in the city's affairs depended very much on the personality of the individual. William Prynne, for instance, played an active and decisive part during the bitter controversy that raged within the council in 1661 (see Chapter 3).

The two **Bailiffs** acted in effect as sheriffs within the 'bailiwick' of Bath, an area which had been freed by royal assent from interference by the High Sheriff of Somerset (the corporation paying in consequence an annual sum of £8 10s 2d to the king 'for the rent of the bailiwick'). The normal practice within the corporation was that the two councillors who had undertaken the onerous and unpaid duties as constables in the previous year should be elected to the highly lucrative posts of bailiffs - for, in addition to their overall responsibility for controlling the gaol and exercising writs, they were also given the profitable task of managing the markets and fairs. For their term

Members of Bath Corporation in procession behind the Sergeants-at-Mace. (Drawing by Stephen Beck)

of office they therefore paid the corporation a rent for both the bailiwick and the butchers' shambles (amounting to an average of £55 by 1690). In return, they were able to hire out the stalls inside the market for personal profit and charge dues to those country traders who came in with baskets of produce. However, they were obliged to use part of these profits to provide a feast for members of the corporation at each of the four Quarter Sessions. In 1684, the council even specified that the bailiffs should 'entertain the corporation with three or four dishes of meat'. Their other duties included the task of transporting prisoners to gaol (in 1631, for instance, they were paid eighteen shillings for 'conveying Edward Hayward to gaol') and attending various courts within the city.

The **Chamberlain** was the treasurer of the corporation, whose task it was to collect the rents of corporation property, the fines imposed for the renewal of leases and the fee charged whenever a freedom was granted; to pay agreed salaries to officers and wages to workmen; to settle the bills of contractors; and to disburse gifts to distinguished visitors as sanctioned by the council. Throughout it all, he was required to keep detailed and accurate accounts, which were presented to the corporation sometime after the ending of the mayoral year. The **Sergeants-at-Mace** fulfilled a number of widely differing functions. Their most public duty was to carry the city's 'maces of gold or silver' before the mayor on ceremonial occasions - maces which had been authorised for the first time by the charter of 1590. Their most profitable duty came from their management of the hot water baths. As the health spa grew in importance, the sergeants-at-mace had responsibility for controlling behaviour around the baths; organising the many guides who assisted the bathers; and supervising the pumping of water (see Chapter 9). Their high profile ensured that they were well regarded by clients, who therefore tended to tip generously at the end of each session. Their most intellectually demanding duty was to act as court attorneys at the Court of Record. Although they were not trained in law, they were always on hand to offer assistance to both sides in any case (and to receive any resulting fees!).

In addition to these major officers of the corporation, there were a number of **minor officials** who carried out important duties in specified areas of city life. The bellman, the watchmen and the beadle were all involved in controlling crime and making the streets safe under the supervision of the constables (see Chapter 4 for an account of their work). The ale tasters, the supervisors of leather, the supervisors of flesh and the supervisors of fish were responsible for checking the quality of food sold in the markets and shops - and for ensuring that accurate weights and measures were used. The overseers of the common, the hayward of the common and the scavenger of the common together ensured that the corporation's regulations for the use of the town common were applied and, at the same time, the city's refuse was properly disposed of in that area.

The Town Hall or Guildhall

The hub of the city's local government and the symbol of its authority was the Guildhall - so called because in medieval times it was the meeting place of the powerful trade guilds, which had largely declined by the seventeenth century. Elizabeth Holland has demonstrated that the medieval Guildhall, which was in use at the start of the Stuart period in 1603, was situated immediately behind the modern building with access gained from the High Street via a narrow passage. It was a timber-framed building with white-washed plaster on its exterior, a tiled roof, glazed casement windows (including one bay) and a stone floor, which was usually strewn with rushes. A meeting hall on the ground floor, with an adjacent kitchen, was used for banquets - the mayor sitting on high table set on a dais which, from 1597, was covered with three yards of green carpet. Guests sat on benches, which were fitted with mats as an aid to comfort in 1611. The council chamber itself was over the kitchen with a small armoury alongside. Oak wainscoting was a striking feature of both the meeting hall and the chamber.

Meanwhile, in about 1552, a separate single-storey market house had been built on the traditional site of the medieval market in the middle of the High Street. By 1625, however, the corporation had decided to combine both Guildhall and market by demolishing the market house and erecting a two-storey structure on the same site - a task which had been completed ywo years later. The old Guildhall was then converted into the 'butchers' shambles' for the exclusive sale of meat, although it was still being referred to in council documents as 'the old Guildhall' as late as 1673.

The new double-gabled Guildhall, which was opened in 1627, consisted of a council chamber/hall and armoury on the first floor, supported by sixteen stone arches. The fishmongers' stalls were situated immediately beneath on a paved area with open sides. Although the windows were in the typical square-headed seventeenth-century style with stone mullions, a large round-headed window was inserted in 1658 to provide more light on the north side - the same facade which also housed the statues of King Coel and King Edgar in niches on either side of the window. The council chamber had benched seating (with cushions from 1638) and a dais for the mayor's chair and desk - the front of the latter boasting the city arms, which were beautifully painted and gilded by Thomas Quilly in 1658. The royal arms were also displayed within the chamber

A map showing the High Street, Northgate Street or Market Place, as surveyed in 1641. Based on a version of John Speed's map of 1610, the map has been re-drawn with added graphics by Mike Chapman. Attributions are taken from a revision of Elizabeth Holland's map of Stuart Bath (1970s).
KEY

1. Tower of St.Mary's Church - the Prison. **2**. Nave of St.Mary's - King Edward's School. **3**. Freehold land, property of the Button family. **4**. Land of John Bigg(s), lease of 1616. **5**. Land of John Pinchin, shoemaker. **6**. Land of Agnes Cray. **7**. Alice Cox, lease of 1640. Previously land of Richard Cox, reproved in 1631 for keeping pigs there. **8**. Land of William Russell, lease of 1631 **9**. The way to the medieval Guildhall. **10**. Held by Walter Chapman. - became Henry Chapman's

Sun Inn. **11**. 'The Horse Head', or 'Corner House'. **12**. The medieval Guildhall, turned into the Butchers' Shambles, 1629. **13**. The house of Governor Bridges in the Civil War (later became the Cross Keys Inn.) **14**. Medieval pillory and stocks. **15**. Once the Market House, built c. 1552; converted to the new Town Hall 1626-1627. **16**. St.Mary's Conduit. **17**. Held by John Parker with a lease of 1635 (later became the site of the Seven Stars Inn.) **18**. Held by John Parker with a lease of 1603 (the corner site later becoming the Greyhound Inn.) **19**. Leased to the Sherstons (once the home of Lady Elizabeth Booth, the Abbey benefactor) **20**. Freehold owned by the Button family (now Northumberland Passage and the Corridor.) **21**. The Katherine Wheele Inn. **22**. Later called the Christopher Inn, though not in the Survey of 1641. The early Christopher seems to have been in Stall Street. **23**. Possible site of George Gibbs' famous herb garden (site formerly owned by John Perman, apothecary).

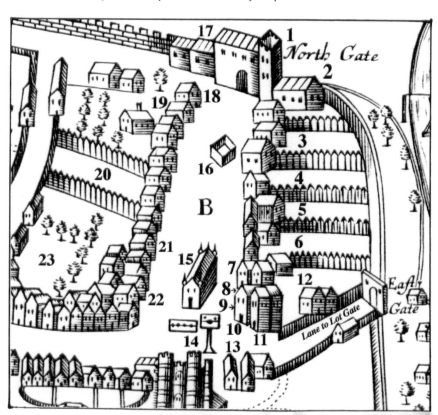

along with heraldic shields of prominent local dignatories. Towards the end of the century, the room was increasingly used for social events, including balls, concerts, dinners and plays. The corporation therefore decided to make the building more fashionable by installing oak wainscoting and modern sash windows - the cost of which was covered eight years later by a gift of £100 from one of the city's honorary freemen, Robert Gay.

The Freemen

In Bath, as in most municipal boroughs in the seventeenth century, there was still a sharp distinction in status between a 'citizen' and a mere 'inhabitant'. This had arisen partly because of the longstanding belief that ownership of property created a sense of responsibility and partly because the influential trade guilds had dominated local affairs for centuries. To become a 'freeman' or 'free citizen', therefore, an inhabitant needed either to serve an apprenticeship for seven years with a master who was already a freeman (after which, he was simply required to pay the cost of his certificate and seal, which varied between 5s 4d and £1 2s 8d); or to purchase his freedom from the corporation by paying the sum of five pounds (although there was growing unease that this method was unfair on the apprentices who had trained hard for seven years). Out of a population of some two thousand people, there were something like two hundred freemen in Bath throughout the century with the corporation electing on average just twelve or thirteen new freemen each year. The free citizens were therefore regarded as the elite - a situation which left the rest of the inhabitants without any civic or political power.

However, the position had been made much more complex by the fact that, over the course of the Middle Ages, this body of freemen had imperceptibly - and almost by default - transferred the government of the city to a smaller group of more active individuals. This small, inner group eventually became known as 'the corporation'.

High Street Bath, looking towards the Old Guildhall. A watercolour by Edward Eyre, c1776. (By courtesy of the Victoria Art Gallery, Bath & North East Somerset Council)

By the sixteenth century (as Richard Warner has pointed out), it was claiming its power and privilege *as a right* based on long usage - a claim which had been frequently disputed by the freemen at large from as early as the fifteenth century. To silence any future such criticism, therefore, the corporation arranged the insertion of a clause in its new Elizabethan charter of 1590 vesting the power solely in the mayor, aldermen and common council.

Consequently, by 1603, **the Freemen of Bath** were in reality divided into two groups - a smaller body numbering some thirty men, who were members of the corporation; and a larger body who, although devoid of power, nevertheless enjoyed a number of privileges. These included their right to graze animals on the Bath Common (see Chapter 7), their exclusive right to open shops inside the city and their annual merrymaking on the Wednesday in Whitsun week after the traditional perambulation of the city boundaries, when the corporation provided beer, bread and cheese in the Guildhall. There was occasionally an additional feast of similar style on midsummer night. Sometimes, too, the corporation offered a special discount to freemen - in 1635, for instance, when it ruled that 'every carpenter or timber man' who was a freeman was only to be charged six pence 'for every tree or timber that he shall lay in the Saw Close', whereas those who were not free were to pay twelve pence. Indeed, outside the various types of freemen, there was a large majority of ordinary inhabitants made up of workmen, apprentices, bath guides etc; and a body of 'strangers' or 'foreigners', who came into the city from outlying districts to set up their stalls or trade from their baskets at the weekly markets or annual fairs - but who were strictly forbidden to open up shop. The corporation pursued vigorously those who defied this ruling - demonstrated by its resolution in 1635 that 'the shops of persons not free shall be shut up until they are free'.

In addition to those who had gained their freedom by serving a master or by outright purchase, there were two other types - the 'honorary freemen' and the 'mayor's freemen'. **Honorary Freemen** were elected from time to time by the corporation as a way of honouring local dignitaries or national figures who would either bring prestige to the city by their association or use their influence on behalf of the city in high places. They were not expected, however, to trade or to compete in any way with the established businesses of ordinary freemen. Their freedom fee of five pounds was normally returned to them. In 1669, therefore, Sir Francis Popham and Sir Thomas Bridges, MP, were elected; in 1674, Lord Berkeley and Sir George Speke; in 1682, the Earl of Nottingham (the Lord High Chancellor) and Sir Edward Villiers (the Knight Marshal); and in 1685, the Earl of Feversham and Robert Strickland (Chamberlain to the Queen). Occasionally, the corporation granted freedom as a reward for particular acts. Henry Wyatt, for example, was made free in 1649 for his generosity in 'taking Roderick Fowler's son apprentice'; while in the following year, Nathaniel Smith and James Stedman - having received their freedoms - had their £5 fees returned to them 'as a gratuity from the corporation in respect of some service done by them to the city'.

A basket trader from the countryside - a familiar sight at the twice-weekly markets in Bath. (By courtesy of the Museum of London)

A custom had also developed that each mayor had the right to 'make a freeman' through personal nomination - and to keep the £5 fee as a perk of office! Initially there were no constraints on the type of person nominated. Thus, in 1667, Stephen Clarke (coachman) had been elected as **the Mayor's Freeman**, followed in the next year by James White (cloakmaker). These nominations by the mayor nevertheless required the approval of the whole council - approval which was sometimes refused, if the person in question was not acceptable. This was the case in 1649, when Mr Morgan, an apothecary, was rejected. Indeed, the growing unease over this type of election surfaced in 1697, when great concern was expressed within the council that the system 'had been a great prejudice to the freemen who had faithfully and honestly served their apprenticeship'. Some of the mayor's freemen on election had apparently set up shop immediately in competition with other traders, even though they had not been properly trained in that trade by a master. The council therefore resolved that in future no person could be elected freeman (including those nominated by the mayor) unless either he had served an apprenticeship or he was classed an honorary freeman, having given guarantees that he 'would not follow any art or trade'. Indeed, the council had already been placing firm restrictions on some of the freemen they had elected. In 1664, for instance, John Oxford of Rode was granted his freedom, having paid the usual fee of £5, 'on condition that he uses no other trade in the city but that of a brazier or pewterer'; while in 1687, John Pocock appointed Barnaby Wilcox as his mayor's freeman on the strict understanding that 'he does not draw teeth or cut hair'.

Once a man had been elected as freeman, he was obliged to swear an oath in which he promised to exercise 'the office, duty and service of a freeman' to the 'profit' of the city; and that he would, according to his 'skill, power and knowledge', maintain and defend the city. Quite apart from the fee payable by those who had purchased their freedom, each newly-elected freeman was required to pay additional small fees to all those involved in his appointment. Applicants who had served their apprenticeship paid a total of 17s 0d to such individuals - including the mayor (6d), the justices (8d each), the chamberlain (6s 0d 'for the chamber'), the town clerk (5s 6d), the under-clerk (2d 'for a copy of the oath'), the crier (4d) and the tithingman (4d) - plus 2s 6d for the parchment paper required for the legal document and the duty to be paid on it. Those who had purchased their freedom paid slightly more (19s 10d) to a similar list of officers with the addition of the sergeants-at-mace (4d each) and the constables (4d each).

As the century progressed, many of the freemen increasingly felt that their original powers had been usurped by the small elite within the corporation - particularly over the right to elect two members of parliament (a right which in fact was to remain solely in the hands of the mayor, aldermen and councillors until 1832). This power was therefore vigorously challenged on several occasions - in 1661, when Henry Chapman summoned all the freemen to hold a mock election in which his own two candidates were 'elected' in opposition to the corporation's legally-elected ones (see Chapter 3); in 1675, when Harry Bridges complained to the Committee of Privileges in the House of Commons that Sir George Speke had been returned as member of parliament for Bath, even though he (Bridges) had been 'elected by the freemen of the city'; and in 1705, when - after the corporation had elected William Blathwayt and Alexander Popham - George Dashwood and Richard Houblin pleaded with the Commons to nullify that election and recognise their own 'by a great majority of legal votes' (i.e. the ordinary freemen). The Committee of Privileges, having examined the 1590 charter, ruled in favour of the corporation.

The Borough Courts

The mayor, the recorder and the two justices (who were elected annually from within the membership of the corporation) had the power not only to apprehend felons, thieves and malefactors, but also to enforce local laws by the imposition of fines and other punishments. They were therefore responsible for the running of several courts within the borough. An ancient medieval court - the Court Leet - was held twice a year on the 'Law Days' before the town clerk to investigate such matters as encroachment of property, illegal fences, water supplies, petty larcenies and the use of false weights and measures. Although by the latter part of the seventeenth century much of this work had been taken over by other courts (see below), one element of the ancient tradition continued. After the court had finished its business, a Law Day Dinner was held - traditionally at the chamberlain's expense - for those freemen who had served on the jury.

It was the borough Court of Quarter Sessions which eventually incorporated the administrative tasks of the **Court Leet**. Meeting four times a year under the presidency of the recorder (aided on the bench by the mayor, the town clerk and the two justices), the court was assisted by a Grand Jury (which determined whether the accused had a case to answer) and a Petty Jury of respectable citizens who heard the trial. The Grand Jury consisted of twenty-three local people, including one representative from each of the eight sectors of the city (i.e. Broad Street, Walcot Street, Northgate Street, Stall Street, Southgate Street, Binbury, Westgate Street and Cheap Street). Regular business consisted partly in taking recognizances from owners of inns and alehouses, who were required to put forward a bond of either £5 or £10 as surety for the sale of ale on the conditions stipulated; and partly in dealing with matters of common assault - including William Ashman in 1693, who had beaten up Mrs Cruck so badly that she was unable to 'help herself' or work. Ashman was ordered to pay her four pence a week until she recovered.

A local court in progress, such as the weekly Court of Record presided over by the Mayor. From J.A. Comenius, Orbis Sensualum Pictus *(1672 edtn.) By courtesy of the British Library - ref: 1607.2351.*

The court also concerned itself with the maintenance of bastard children. In 1683, for instance, Charles Hulbert was ordered to pay 1s 6d a week to Anne Ward for the maintenance of their child until he was eight years old. When Charles died unexpectedly, the court ordered his father to pay six pence a week in maintenance 'to save the city harmless from the said bastard child'. There was always a fear that such children would become chargeable on the city poor rates. Problems over apprenticeships were also investigated, especially when an apprentice wished to transfer to another master - as were problems arising over the illegal establishment of new shops. In 1688, for example, Joseph Davis was summoned to explain 'why he continues upon his shop, not being a freeman'. On another matter, John Aldington, the plumber, was forced to appear in 1690 to explain 'why without authority he had dug up the pitching in several parts of the city' [he had actually been installing water pipes to private houses].

The **Court of Record** met every Monday throughout the year before the mayor, the recorder, the two justices and the town clerk to hear personal suits arising in the borough over matters of debt, contract, trespass and property. A jury was also sworn in to hear the cases. The **Court of Pie Powder** met under a bailiff to try offenders (such as pickpockets) during times of the ancient city fairs. The chamberlain's accounts for 1692-93 provide one small graphic detail of this court at work - William Tagg was paid 2s 6d for 'the victuals he gave the pickpockets before they were sent to gaol'. As this was quite a large sum of money, pickpockets must certainly have been out in numbers at that particular fair!

Although many matters were therefore tried by courts within the city, the corporation was under obligation to refer all serious cases of felony (including murder, rape and burglary) to the **County Assizes**, which met twice yearly (the Winter Assize being in February/March and the Summer Assize in July/August). Prisoners from Bath were escorted to one of the county gaols by the bailiffs and their officers to await trial - and the bailiffs were then able to relay back to the corporation any new assize orders, issued on government instructions, in relation to such matters as the implementation of the poor law by local magistrates. Bathonians certainly did find themselves at the mercy of these courts - such as Thomas Gibbs, who was indicted in 1649 for making a forcible entry in *The King's Arms* at Widcombe, the property of Elizabeth Colthurst.

The Assizes were traditionally held in Taunton, Chard, Wells or Bridgwater - although Bath did provide the base on rare occasions (at least four times before the Civil War and twice after the Restoration). However, with the growth of the city into a prominent health and leisure resort in the second half of the century, the corporation suddenly realised the importance of staging the Assizes to gain both prestige and business (for large numbers of people attended in town for the best part of a week to enjoy what was in part a social occasion). In 1668, therefore, the corporation petitioned parliament for the right to hold the Summer Assizes on an annual basis - with one of its MPs (William Prynne) putting forward eloquent arguments in support of this request. Bath, he said, paid £121 a year in hearth tax, whereas Wells and Taunton paid only £25 and £24 respectively; Bath had been the first town in the west 'to proclaim His Present Majesty', whereas Taunton had been 'the first in opposition'; and Bath was just as convenient a meeting place as Taunton. Sadly, the petition fell on deaf ears. Not to be outdone, the corporation tried again in 1683 in an appeal to the Secretary of State, claiming that Bath was 'a very loyal city and a town that can accommodate both judges and country better than any other in the county'. The request, however, was again refused, because Wells was considered better 'being near the centre of the county and very suitable for entertainment, having a spacious hall'. Furthermore, Bath was inconvenient to reach and the hall was 'very little' in size, while food and accommodation were 'dearer by a third than elsewhere in the shire'.

The Administration of Property

The corporation was responsible for something like four-fifths of the property in Bath, either as owner of the freehold in its own right or as trustee for both the lands belonging to St John's Hospital and the properties contained in Edward VI's endowment of the grammar school in 1552. One of its most important tasks, therefore, was to grant and renew leases, while at the same time ensuring that rents were efficiently collected. All business relating to **leases** was conducted at quarterly meetings of the council. Normally a lease would be granted either for a maximum of three lives (i.e. the lifetimes of three named individuals in the contract - with a ceiling of 99 years, 'if the lives live so long') or 21 years absolute (i.e. a fixed term) - although members of the corporation could be granted 42 years absolute as a privilege. The tenant, having paid a 'fine' or fee for the lease, together with the clerical costs of the 'seal' on the contract, would then be expected to pay no more than a modest annual rent. The fine and seal, depending on the size of the property, could range between £1 and £60 in total.

Under this system, however, the corporation was able to charge relatively large sums or **'fines'** when amendments were made to a lease - a heriot, when one 'life' in the lease died and the next one succeeded (Widow Bondon, for instance, paid a heriot of £3 12s 4d to take over the property in 1620 on the death of her husband); a fine for taking out one name from the lease and inserting a replacement (Mr Warnam was charged forty shillings to do so in 1638); a fine, which could be as high as £80, for renewing a lease after the expiry of the three original lives (a situation confronting Roger Pooke, for example, in 1659 when he paid £10 to renew his contract for another three lives - namely, himself, his wife and his son); a fine for cancelling the current lease (called 'drowning the lives') and replacing it with a new one (as Councillor Shute did in 1683, when he took out a new lease for 42 years on a stable in Vicarage Lane for a fine of ten shillings); and a fine, which could range between six pence and two shillings, for making an encroachment on neighbouring land (a situation which cost William Ball a fine of one shilling for expanding his shop in Northgate Street onto the city waste).

Sometimes an **encroachment** was deemed to be so unacceptable that the offender was simply ordered to remove it. This was the case in 1659 with John Reed, who was instructed to take down the two benches and posts, which he had erected in Westgate Street 'at the door of the house of Widow Poole', because they were obstructions and 'a great nuisance to passengers'. Occasionally the corporation took a more lenient line - as it did in 1668, when it agreed to let Sir Henry Capel 'set up a post at the riverside' for the use of his boat, charging him just 'one peppercorn yearly' for the privilege.

From time to time the corporation, seizing the chance to solve a number of specific problems, added **extra conditions** when a new lease was granted. In the early eighteenth century, for instance, some leaseholders were required to purchase a certain number of fire buckets for general use in the city (see Chapter 4). At other times, householders were instructed to be responsible for particular duties. John Biggs, for example, was required - in return for his lease of 1633 - to act as keeper of the West Gate, to 'pitch the street upon reasonable warning for three-halfpence a yard and to keep the way before his house clean'. The corporation even used leases as a way of exercising disciplinary control over awkward individuals. The lease issued in 1649 to John Fisher, innkeeper of the White Horse, was conditional upon his promise 'not to annoy his wife'. Any breach of that stipulation would immediately render the contract void.

Tenants were responsible for paying their **rents** quarterly at the Guildhall, although the chamberlain regularly found that a fair proportion of the rents remained outstanding at the end of the financial year - £41 in 1661 and £36 in 1669, for instance. One particular property, however, required occasional site visits from the chamberlain in person. In 1663, for instance, he claimed the cost of horse-hire and other expenses 'in going to the coalpits to take their accounts'. As trustee of the lands owned by St John's Hospital, the corporation found itself responsible for much of the coal mining operation in Timsbury, Littleton, Paulton and Hallatrow. In 1640, therefore, it seized the opportunity to exploit these assets financially by granting a lease to Councillor Robert Fisher for 'all the coalworks, coal mines, veins of coal... lying in Timsbury and Littleton' which were under the land occupied by Widow Chilton. Fisher paid a 'fine' of £10 10s to set up the contract, followed by a yearly rent of 6s 8d. Councillors regularly paid visits to the mines - Mayor Masters, for instance, went out to Paulton in 1658 'to see our coal works there'.

An interesting account has survived of mining activity at Timsbury in a surveyor's report of 1610:

> There now be three pits near Widow Blacker's house, the highest about four fathoms, the middle six fathoms, the lowest eight fathoms deep. At these depths they cut out their lanes about four feet high and broad. They need no great store of timberwork for support. The lane we entered was a good quoit's cast in length ... They now work in two pits at once, and have below two or three men and four or five boys, and also three men to wind up the coals. At the end of every lane a man worketh, and there maketh his bench, as they call it ... The wages allowed to the men is to him that hath most four shillings the week, and to the boys 1s 6d. Adding for candles, increase of wages for work by night, ropes, sharpening of tools, baskets, etc., the whole week's charge may arise to £3.

In 1657, the corporation also granted a licence to Francis Jones of Hallatrow 'to mine and dig for coal' on the land in his possession. In return, he was either to give either one-eighth of the coal dug out to the corporation or one-eighth of the profit made 'if the work proves good' - or, if not good, then one-tenth of the coal.

The Corporation's Other Duties

The Mayor of Bath was both the coroner and the clerk-of-the-market, which was held twice a week on Wednesday and Saturday (although much of the active, daily control had been delegated to the bailiffs, and the supervisors of fish, flesh and leather - see above). **The market** was strictly regulated. In 1638, for instance, the council stipulated that no sales of corn were to take place 'before the bell be rung...at the hour of eleven o'clock and not before'. An important task was to ensure that quality was always maintained in all foodstuffs and that customers were not cheated through the use of false measures. Authorised brass weights were therefore obtained from London and offenders were firmly punished for fraudulent practice. No fewer than seven people, for instance, were fined in 1597 for 'engrossing up butter and cheese', while in 1649 a sum of £6 2s 6d was raised in fines partly from 'such as sold ale and beer by small measure' - and partly from 'such as were drunk and such as swore by profane oaths'.

The 1590 charter had given the mayor the right to hold an **Assize of Bread** whenever it was deemed necessary. Although in Bath the price of each type of loaf remained constant, the Assize of Bread enabled the mayor to adjust its weight according to the prevailing price of corn in the Bristol market. The revised, authorised weight of each type of bread was then announced to the bakers and spot-checks undertaken to ensure that loaves were not sold underweight. This, of course, could be somewhat confusing to the housewife who, as a result of grain shortages, suddenly found that the size of her normal loaf had shrunk!

In addition to its other responsibilities, the corporation also had power to issue coins (from the 1660s), to make by-laws and to collect **local rates**. These included the regular poor rates to support the elderly and infirm, a rate to raise the rector's salary by £10 in 1632, a rate to pay the wages of both the sexton and the bellman in 1634, a special rate to help fund the Bridewell in 1634 (see Chapter 11), a rate to pay Prince Maurice's demand for £40 during the Civil War and, from 1615, a rate to help improve the cleanliness of the streets by raising money for the scavenger's wages. Although rates were sometimes collected by parishes, they were increasingly gathered through the appointment of 'tithingmen' to collect on a house-to-house basis within each sector of the city. In 1615, there were six such sectors (although these had been increased to eight by the latter part of the century). It was likewise the corporation's duty to collect in any taxes authorised by king or parliament - such as the ship money in 1635, the subsidy granted in 1641 to pay for the war against the Scots, the subsidy of 1660 to pay off the forces after the Restoration and the hearth tax of 1664-65. Surviving tax returns in the Public Record Office detail street-by-street the payments made by individuals.

In addition to announcing the latest tax demands, the corporation was also required to issue any **royal proclamations** - such as those for 'prohibiting fairs' (1603), 'prohibiting the dressing of meat during Lent' (1622), 'prohibiting the export of wool' (1622) and 'apprehending highwaymen' (1669). There were no fewer than seventeen proclamations in all in 1637 and twelve in 1642. In order to keep itself better informed on national events, the corporation decided in 1672 to subscribe regularly to one of the weekly news-sheets, which had proliferated in London after the Restoration. It was planned that, on delivery, the paper - which cost twenty-five shillings a quarter - should remain available in the mayor's own house 'for public view'. From 1662, communication with the outside world was also speeded up through use of the new postal system (see Chapter 10).

The corporation was also responsible for presenting clergy to serve in local churches (see Chapter 14) and for the management of the baths (see Chapter 9), the Bath Common (see Chapter 7), the grammar school (see Chapter 12) and the hospitals (see Chapter 11). Tight control over St John's Hospital was of course vital, bearing in mind its valuable landed estates. From 1616, therefore, the Corporation adopted the policy of appointing one of its own aldermen to the position of Master of the Hospital - a post which was kept firmly in the hands of the Chapman family until 1655 when, with the appointment of Alderman John Biggs, the corporation decided to strengthen the bond with the hospital even more by linking the offices of mayor and master through a joint annual election. At the Restoration in 1660, however, Tobias Rustat (a member of the royal court) persuaded Charles II to appoint him master, with rights to enjoy the profits of the whole estate, on the grounds that the corporation had illegally seized the king's own right to make that appointment. After a fierce legal battle, the corporation eventually won back its right of appointment from the death of Rustat in 1680, deciding in future to choose clergy for the post rather than lay members of the corporation. However, it took until 1717 to sort out the situation regarding the hospital's property (see Jean Manco's *The Spirit of Care* for a full account of this episode and its consequences).

Corporation Finance

The Bath chamberlain's accounts show clearly the main **sources of income**. In 1640, for instance, £123 4s 4d was raised from annual rents for the corporation's property; and £300 7s 8d from 'casual receipts', which mostly consisted of fines or fees for the granting of freedoms and the renewal or amendment of leases. The expenditure was made up of 'stipends and out rents' (which included the salaries and wages paid to the corporation's officials, including the school master; the annual distributions to the poor at Christmas and Lent; and a rent of £10 paid to the king for the school's endowment property); 'gifts and rewards' (which covered the entertainment of visiting judges etc and the presentation of wine and sugar made to important dignitaries); and 'general payments' (which consisted of bills for fabric repairs, work on the roads, gifts to individual paupers, the mending of water pipes, travel expenses for council officers, improvements to the baths, additions to the armoury etc).

The balance in hand at the end of 1640 was a healthy £56 11s 2d - and this was a striking feature of the corporation's finances until the Restoration in 1660. Even during the four years of civil war, Bath Corporation - unlike those in most other cities - remained impressively in credit (£229 15s 10d in 1646, for example). Bath was after all one of the most affluent cities in the country - an affluence largely based on the properties given by Edward VI in 1552 *solely* as an endowment for the grammar school and the maintenance of ten poor people. [In the eighteenth and nineteenth centuries,

Extract from the Bath Chamberlain's Accounts, 1640, under the heading of 'Gifts and Rewards'. (By courtesy of Bath Record Office, Bath & North Somerset Council). The lines read as follows:

Imprimis for a quart of sacke
Item given to Mr Smith and Mr Popham in wyne * Item given to Mr John Francis in wynne
Item given to Curroner [Coroner]Culpepper in wine * Item given to Justice Crawly in Wyne
Item given to my Lord Chief Justice Bramston in wyne * Item more for bottells
Item given to my Lady Hatten in wyne * Item given to Mr Edward Popham in wyne
Item for entertayninge the Lift Tennants [lieutenants]
Item paid for Turkes [turkeys] given to Justice Crawly * Item for entertayninge the Recorder
Item given to the Earl of Bath in wyne * Item given to Justice Crawly at the hall a potle of white wyne & suger
Item paid to Mr Wintell for the Recorders horse in oate

the corporation was twice successfully charged with the misappropriation of that endowment.] By contrast, the accounts for St John's Hospital, which were kept separately, show that the institution was almost always run at a loss with the shortfall being generously made up by the corporation. In 1640 for instance, whereas the income or rents was £35 18s 2d, the expenditure amounted to £57 11s 2d - leaving a deficit of £21 13s 0d.

However, the corporation was plunged into a serious **financial crisis** in the period after 1660 as the annual accounts slumped badly into deficit. Warning signs of trouble ahead first became apparent in 1651, when the council agreed - in view of the great burden of post-war taxation - that it would not in future grant money to support any wounded soldier who passed through the city (an uncharacteristic move by a hitherto compassionate body). It also admitted that it was actually unable to pay the £55 stipends which it owed to both the previous and present mayors. This problem of cash flow became even more serious in the following year when the corporation, desperate to fund an Act of Parliament to make the Avon navigable between Bath and Bristol, decided to raise money by taking a drastic step. It persuaded the freemen to surrender their right of grazing on the common so that it could be rented out for the

Extracts from the Bath Council Minute Book, No. 2, 23rd March 1664
(by courtesy of Bath Record Office, Bath & North East Somerset Council).

Two questions are here put to the Council for decision. The first one reads:
'Whether for the better bringing this Chamber out of debt The Mayors stipend shall be abated for the future & to what sum it shall be reduced'. *After two votes had been taken (see top item) and various options considered -* 'Agreed the Mayors stipend shall be reduced to xxli And he to keepe but one feast in his yere only at his entrance into his office'.
The second, which deals with the attempt to raise extra cash by changing the terms of leases, reads:
'Mr Edward White by the consent and agreement of Mr John Pynchin bids 35li for 100 yrs in the tenement now in the possession of the said Jo. Pinchin. Agreed a graunte be made to Mr Edmund White for an hundred years absolute for the fine of fifty pounds at rent and usual covenant'.

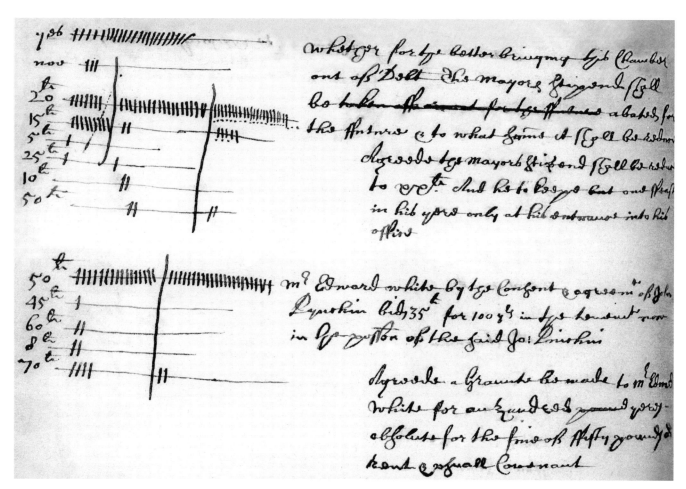

princely sum of over £110 per annum (see Chapter 7 for full details). Nevertheless, at the end of the 1655 financial year - in spite of the above measures - the corporation's credit balance had slumped to just £6 9s 1d.

By 1661, the situation had become critical. Over the next three years, heavy additional expenses confronted an already embattled chamberlain. The cost of lavish celebrations to mark the coronation of Charles II amounted to almost £80 (including fireworks, bonfires, streamers, food, wine and tobacco - not to mention compensation to two householders for the lead on their roofs 'which was melted by fireworks on Coronation Day'); the cost of building the dry pump house to £39; the cost of a 'voluntary present' to the new king to £100; the cost of building a cross in the King's Bath to over £150; and the cost of petitioning parliament to secure an annual meeting of the County Assizes in Bath to £24. The corporation helped to alleviate the situation by borrowing large sums of money - £100 from the account of the Church of St Mary de Stall (on security of the city seal); £100 from William Prynne, MP, to cover the cost of the king's present; and a whole series of smaller loans from members of the corporation. By September 1666, twenty-three loans were still outstanding, ranging from £20 to £300 in size and totalling £2,735 in all. These loans were repaid from time to time - £54 to John Biggs in 1668 and £150 to George Chapman in 1670, for example - although new loans were immediately taken up to cover the repayment!

The corporation also imposed strict economies. In 1664, it decided to cancel the four feasts provided each year by the bailiffs after the Quarter Sessions and the two feasts sponsored by the chamberlain after the Law Days. In return, as a money-making initiative, the bailiffs were to pay £75 for the privilege of office (an increase of £20 on the usual amount) and the chamberlain was to lose his stipend entirely. Similarly, the mayor's stipend was reduced from £50 to just £20 (see extract from the minute book). Furthermore, although the new Master of the Grammar School (Mr Hoyle) was appointed at the usual salary of £30, it was stipulated that *he* was to pay his predecessor's pension of £6 13s 0d for the rest of his life!

Another scheme to improve the immediate cash flow was revealed in 1664. The council agreed to break with the normal tradition of granting new leases for either three lives or 21 years absolute and, instead, to offer them for 100 years absolute 'until such money can be raised as will pay the debts of the chamber'. Several leases of this type were granted with a much larger fine than would otherwise have been received - including one to Edmund White for his tenement (£50 fine - see extract from minute book) and another to the mayor for the prison house and shop (£30 fine). This scheme, however, was not a great success and the corporation quickly reverted to the normal 'three lives' contracts.

In spite of all these efforts, the financial situation remained gloomy for many years to come. A small credit balance in 1662 of £26 17s 6d had been turned into deficits of £65 8s 2d in 1663, £86 10s 7d in 1664 and £79 7s 7d in 1666. Thereafter the accounts mostly showed a modest annual surplus, although by 1701 this was running at just £14 15s 6d - and the corporation was still calling for new loans to pay off specific debts. The tight control, which was experienced under the years of the puritan revolution, had given way to more imaginative (but expensive) policies in keeping with the development of the new leisure resort.

Life as a Councillor

Once elected, a councillor was expected to attend all meetings of the council (usually

The Guildhall from the west. This highlights the area beneath the council chamber, which was used as a fish market, and the later extension of the south side, which was undertaken in 1724-25. Either James or George Vertue drew the original version of this picture in about 1750, although other artists produced later variations. By courtesy of Bath & North East Somerset Library and Archive Service (Bath Central Library).

between six and twelve a year - although sixteen were held in 1643-44, a critical year in the Civil War). Failure to attend without adequate excuse resulted in an automatic fine. In addition to his attendance at meetings, the councillor would eventually be expected to take his turn in filling the various offices on which the corporation depended for its efficient administration of the city (see above). Occasionally he would also be asked to undertake special assignments (see below) - all of which could be extremely time-consuming for a man who had his own business to run.

However, in return, the councillor would not only gain considerable prestige among his friends and neighbours, but would also be given the chance to supply the corporation with goods and services. Many profitable contracts were regularly given to members of the corporation to the exclusion of others. For example, Walter Hickes and his mother (innkeeper of *The Three Swans* in Cheap Street) organised feasts for the corporation at Quarter Sessions and Law Days on no fewer than seven occasions between 1669 and 1671; William Landicke (innkeeper of *The Three Tuns*) provided wine for the king's birthday celebrations in 1665; Benjamin Baber (tailor) supplied cloth for the bellman's coat in 1679; while a number of mercers (Richard Biggs, Richard Abbott, John Bush, Walter Chapman, John Fisher, John Pearce, Robert Penny and Edward White) were called upon at various times between 1647 and 1670 to furnish the corporation with cloth, cotton, bullets, tobacco, pipes, gunpowder, match, shrouds, lead, iron, glass, lime, sugar loaves, buttons and silk.

Two particular examples will illustrate more clearly the tasks which made up a typical councillor's work load. Benjamin Baber, who was a tailor with a business in Cheap Street, was appointed to the prestigious post of Master of the Company of Merchant Tailors in 1666. By then he had already been elected a member of the city council and had survived the government's purge in 1662 after the Corporation Act (see Chapter 3). A man of modest means in 1664 (his house was only assessed for just two hearths in the hearth tax of that year), he clearly grew in affluence over the ensuing years - for he not only rented the butchers' shambles in 1669 and *The Cross Daggers Inn* in Cheap Street in 1679, but was also granted a lease on a brewhouse in the churchyard of St Mary de Stall in 1677. By 1684, he was able to afford the installation of a supply of fresh water which was piped into his house. Baber quickly rose through the ranks in the council to become bailiff in 1663 and 1669, overseer of the common in 1672 and chamberlain in both 1673 and 1675 - the year in which he was also elected alderman. It was therefore almost inevitable that he should eventually become mayor, an office which he successfully held in 1677-78, 1687-89 and 1701-02. In the meantime, he had been given two special assignments - in 1685 (with three other councillors) to carry up to the king in London the city's charter for its renewal; and in 1687, to join the mayor in accompanying the queen, Mary of Modena back to London after her treatment in the hot water baths. He died in 1705 and was buried in the Abbey.

John Pearce, an affluent mercer with a shop in Cheap Street, was assessed for ten hearths in the hearth tax of 1664 - a indication of real prosperity. A moderate supporter of parliament, he was one of the most regular attenders at council meetings throughout the entire Civil War (missing just two sessions in all). He served as chamberlain between 1646 and 1648, before being elected to alderman in that year. He was mayor on three occasions - 1650-52, 1658-59 and 1665-66 (having, like Baber, survived the government's purge in 1662). He was clearly regarded as a solid and reliable character, who could be trusted with a number of special assignments. He was therefore detailed to carry the corporation's petition up to parliament in 1646, begging relief from any further billeting of troops; to undertake a mission, also in 1646, to secure the return of the £100 'which Sir Thomas Bridges extorted from the corporation' when he was royalist governor during the war; to join delegations to parliament in both 1652 and 1654, seeking an Act to make the Avon navigable between Bath and Bristol; to act as supervisor in 1650 for the demolition of the disused church of St Mary de Stalls and the sale of any salvaged materials; and to lobby Lord Protector Richard Cromwell in 1659 to grant the city the next County Assizes - followed by similar missions in 1660, 1663 and 1665. He died in 1672 at the age of fifty-eight.

SOURCES USED IN CHAPTER 2

1. Printed material:
Barnes, Thomas (ed.): *Somerset Assize Orders, 1629-1640* (Somerset Record Society, 1959)
Carew, Thomas: *An Historical Account of the Rights of Elections* (1755)
Cook, Chris & Wroughton, John: *English Historical Facts, 1603-1688* (1980)
Defoe, Daniel: *Tour of the Whole Island of Great Britain*, vol. 2 (ed. Ernest Rhys, 1927)
Fawcett, Trevor: *Bath Administer'd: Corporation Affairs at the 18th-Century Spa* (2002)
Fawcett, Trevor: 'The Stuart Guildhall' in *History of Bath Research Group Newsletter*, 17 Jan. 1992
Haddon, J: *Bath* (1973)
Hamilton, Meg: *Bath before Beau Nash* (1978)
Hart-Davis, Adam: *What the Tudors and Stuarts did for Us* (2002)
Holland, Elizabeth & Chapman, Mike: *Bath Guildhall and its Neighbourhood* (2000)
Holland, Elizabeth: 'The Earliest Guildhall' in *Bath History*, vol. 2 (1988)
Manco, Jean: *The Spirit of Care* (1998)

McInnes, Angus: *The English Town, 1660-1760* (1980)

Page, W. (ed.): *Victoria County History of Somerset*, vol. 2 (1911)

Sydenham, S: 'Bath City and Traders' Tokens during the 17th Century' in *Proceedings of the Bath Natural History & Antiquarian Club*, vol.67 (1905)

Warner, Richard: *The History of Bath* (1801)

Wroughton, John: *A Community at War: the Civil War in Bath & North Somerset* (1992)

2. Documentary material:

Bath Record Office:

Bath Chamberlain's Accounts, 1568-1734

Bath Council Books, Nos. 1, 2 & 3 (1631-1715)

Sessions Books, 1682-1724

The Furman Leases in Furman's Repertory

Freemen's Books (Freemen's Estate), 1697-1775

Public Record Office:

Calendar of State papers Domestic, 1668, 1683

Commons' Journals, vols. 9 & 15

Exchequer Papers - Somerset Hearth Tax, 1664: E.179

CHAPTER 3

Political Life: City and Nation, 1603-1714

Civil War and the Growth of Factions, 1642-1660

King Charles I , 1600-1649. (Author's collection)

The reign of Charles I witnessed a steady growth of discontent in the country at large, particularly during the period of his 'Personal Rule' without parliament (1629-40). Grievances centred on his 'illegal' methods of raising money, his increasingly High Church policies in religion and his belief in the Divine Right of Kings, which seemingly undermined the rights and powers of parliament. Although the city of Bath grumbled as much as most during the 1630s about the economic situation and religious reform, there was - even as late as the spring of 1642 - no hint locally of rebellion or civil war. Indeed, all the evidence suggests that the Bath Corporation dutifully paid its taxes - including the controversial 'ship money', which was extended to inland counties as well as coastal areas for the first time in 1635. The town clerk was therefore despatched to Ilchester 'about the shipping', clutching the city's contribution of £70. Similarly, in 1639, Bath provided its full allocation of fourteen soldiers (together with a sum of £6 9s 4d for their upkeep and ten swords) to join the Somerset contingent in support of the king's war against the Scots.

When civil war broke out in August 1642, it was for local people - above all - a war of religion (see Chapter 14). The strength of puritanism inside the city itself and in the surrounding area ensured that Bath pledged its loyalty to parliament through the war. By sheer coincidence, the County Assizes just happened to be in session when recruiting parties from both king and parliament arrived in Bath in mid-July. The city therefore became the centre of a noisy war of words several weeks before the king finally raised his standard at Nottingham on 22nd August. Alexander Popham of Hunstrete House, one of Bath's two MPs in the Long Parliament and a staunch puritan, worked closely in guiding the corporation over its policy. When, for instance, a royalist petition which was being circulated throughout Somerset reached Bath, he

Alexander Popham (1605-1669) of Littlecote House. Member of Parliament for Bath and commander of the Bath Regiment of trained bands. (By courtesy of the Board of Trustees of the Royal Armouries, accession no. I. 315)

advised the mayor and council 'to nip this in the bud'. The city's other MP was William Basset of Claverton Manor who, after a great crisis of conscience, chose to support the king. He was therefore replaced in 1645 by James Ashe, another strong supporter of the parliamentarian cause.

The early years of the Civil War saw the emergence of three factions or groupings on the city council. Matthew Clift's faction, which demonstrated ardent support for parliament and the puritan revolution; a group of moderate Puritans, who always sided with Clift in any crucial vote (thus giving him a normal majority of around 22 votes to 8); and Henry Chapman's traditionalist faction, which actively supported the royalist cause, mourned the demise of 'Merry England' and resented local domination by a harsh Puritan elite. In spite of their political differences, however, the three groups had one aim in common - namely, to maintain at all costs the livelihood of local people in the face of severe hostilities. As a result, no matter which army occupied the city, the councillors - whenever present - sat together side by side throughout the war keeping open the markets and ensuring the flow of daily life. That became their over-riding priority.

One factor in particular contributed to this local spirit, which brought a degree of stability to life in the city - namely, the close family ties which existed among large sections of the corporation. For instance, Henry Chapman (royalist) was the son of Alderman William Chapman (moderate), brother to Walter Chapman (moderate), cousin to Richard Chapman (moderate), son-in-law to Alderman Robert Fisher (royalist) and brother-in-law to Matthew Clift (parliamentarian). Brothers William Child (royalist) and Robert Child (royalist) were grandsons of Alderman William

Chapman (moderate) and brothers-in-law to John Pearce (moderate). The fact, therefore, that many members of the council were not only business neighbours, but also close relatives undoubtedly helped counter any natural tendency for the body to disintegrate during moments of crisis.

The parliamentarian faction over the next eighteen years drew its members from a wide range of occupations. They included Matthew Clift himself (mercer and draper), John Atwood (baker), John Biggs (innkeeper of *The Unicorn*), John Parker (clothier and draper), Edward Parker (woollen draper), Richard Druce (baker), Anthony Colloby (maltster), George Reeve (goldsmith), John Boyse (postmaster), Henry Moore (?apothecary) and John Ford (?clothier)). Just four of this faction - Clift, Ford, Colloby and Reeve - actually fought at some time for the armies of parliament ; two - Boyse and Biggs - fled the city and took temporary refuge in Bristol when royalist troops seized Bath in 1643; and three - Atwood, Druce and Parker - were imprisoned in 1644 on charges of attempting to starve the king's army by 'refusing to bake bread when required'.

The original members of the royalist faction were Robert Fisher (market gardener) and Robert Sheppard (baker), together with no fewer than five innkeepers - Henry Chapman (*The Sun*), Philip Sherwood (*The Three Tuns*), George Chapman (*The Bear*), Thomas Gibbs (*The Golden Lion*) and Samuel Wintle (*The George*). Later recruits included John Bush (mercer), Robert Child (woollen draper), his brother William Child (shopkeeper), John Fisher (son of Robert, mercer) and Walter Gibbs (son of Thomas, innkeeper of *The Bell*). Centring their activities and discussions on the inns and alehouses of the city, this group commanded a certain degree of popular support in its attempt to resist the excesses of the puritan revolution. Both *The Sun* and *The Three Tuns* became regular meeting places for royalist soldiers during the war, especially between 1643 and 1645 when Chapman, as captain of the Bath trained bands, and Sherwood, as his lieutenant, were responsible for mounting the nightly guard on behalf of the royalist garrison. Three members of the group actually fought against parliament at some time in the war - Henry Chapman, George Chapman and Philip Sherwood; while two others actively assisted the king's cause - Thomas Gibbs, by disarming parliamentarian sympathisers in the Bath area; and Robert Fisher, by supplying royalist armies with food.

The work of the Bath Corporation was put under its greatest strain during the two years of occupation by a royalist garrison (July 1643 - July 1645). Local people submitted themselves to this ordeal with a sullen sense of the inevitable. There was no underground resistance movement, no sabotage and no acts of heroic defiance. The Civil War was not, after all, a total war. Ordinary people, who were not active combatants, therefore regarded the preservation of life as their first priority. Nevertheless, there were other ways of expressing their feelings and their underlying loyalty. Co-operation with the garrison was kept at a minimum; there was resistance to the payment of taxes; and street festivities were designed as a way of 'thumbing the nose' to occupying troops. In 1643 and 1644, for instance, the corporation suddenly revived the tradition of celebrating Gunpowder Treason Day (5th November) and Crown Nation Day (the anniversary of Queen Elizabeth's accession) with bonfires and the ringing of church bells. These anti-Catholic occasions gave local Puritans the opportunity to re-affirm their Protestant faith.

Although the corporation submitted to the demands made on it to strengthen the city's fortifications at its own cost, it bitterly resented an order in 1644 to provide ten barrels of gunpowder at a charge of £50 for the king's forces and to provide storage in its own armoury for powder requisitioned from neighbouring districts. After the occupation had ended, the councillors vented their anger by vigorously striking out the offending item from the minute book (see illustration). Similarly, they exacted their revenge on the former royalist governor of the city, Sir Thomas Bridges of Keynsham. They had deeply resented his high-handed methods, the extravagant expense of maintaining his house, the cost of his linen (£10 a year) and - in the words of the official minute - the one hundred pounds which he 'extorted from the corporation during the time of his being governor here'. Consequently, they not only sued him in 1646 for the recovery of that sum, but did everything in their power to undermine the resistance of the garrison in 1645 when a small detachment of parliament's New Model Army approached the city. Indeed, it had been an earlier street demonstration by large numbers of citizens, crying out to a man 'No Welsh, no Welsh!', that had actually frustrated royalist attempts to reinforce his garrison with Welsh troops from Bristol. His confidence shattered, Bridges meekly surrendered.

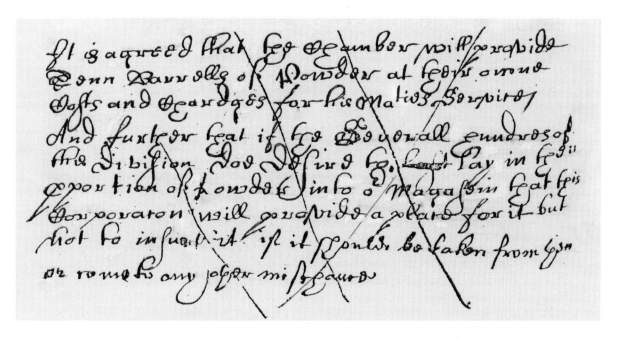

Extract from the Bath Council Minute Book, No. 1, 1643-44 (by courtesy of Bath Record Office, Bath & North East Somerset Council). The entry has later been struck through (see above). It reads:

It is agreed that the Chamber will provide tenn barrells of powder at their owne costs and chardges for His Majesties service And further that if the severall hundres *[hundreds]* of the division doe desire to lay in their proportion of powder into our magasein that this Corporation will provide a place for it but not to insure it if it should be taken from them or come to any other mischance'.

When the war ended, there seemed to be even more reason for sinking political differences and concentrating together on the task of post-war reconstruction. The cost of defence had been considerable, causing fabric to be neglected and a general loss to the quality of life (see Chapter 13). The regular debates of the council, which are recorded in the minute books, give no hint of any intention by the 'parliamentarian' majority to remove the old royalist supporters from their midst. Indeed, for over a year after the ending of hostilities in 1646 the groups continued to sit side-by-side as they tackled vital local issues - while Henry Chapman had even been elected to the

Troops of the royalist garrison in Bath defend the bridge against an attack by cavalry and dragoons
of parliament's New Model Army, 29th July 1645. (Drawing by Stephen Beck).

office of bailiff. Then suddenly, on 27th September 1647, it was decided by a majority of 18 votes to 10 to remove Robert Hyde from his post of Recorder. A member of the well-known royalist family, who had served in person with Prince Rupert during the war, Hyde had held this important office for several years. However, the decision to expel him had been imposed on the council by a parliamentary ordinance ordering the removal of all known royalists from local government. Most councillors were more than happy to forgive and forget - a fact vividly illustrated when, three weeks later, they agreed to quash their original decision. 'There shall be no election for a new Recorder,' they recorded in the minutes, ' but the Sergeant Hyde shall stand'.

The Commons, however, thought otherwise. A few days later, they passed a more precise and forceful ordinance, which put irresistible pressure on local authorities. According to this: 'No person whatsoever that hath been in arms against the parliament, or hath been aiding or assisting the forces of the enemy' would in future be permitted to serve in any office within a corporation. Faced with this ultimatum, Bath Corporation had little choice. On 13th December 1647, they reluctantly agreed to expel the whole of the the royalist group en bloc. Samuel Wintle, Philip Sherwood, Henry Chapman, Robert Sheppard, Robert Fisher, Robert Hyde and Thomas Gibbs all relinquished their places with the first four of these actually present when the decision was taken. This was to prove the first of three purges of the corporation to take place within the space of just thirty-seven years.

Nevertheless, the work of healing continued inside the corporation with the victors showing no signs of vindictiveness towards their former opponents. This was in spite of the fact that Henry Chapman himself displayed little desire for reconciliation. He seized the chance, for instance, during the so-called Second Civil War in 1648, to lead a series of threatening street demonstrations (in defiance of the authorities) centred on two illegal activities - a Prayer Book service *[the Prayer Book had been abolished in 1645 - see Chapter 14]* and a weekly bull-baiting session. On the other hand, the corporation displayed their own charitable nature by not only buying wine from his inn for official events (1655), but also granting him the right to rent both the House of Correction (1648) and the Bath Common (1652). Similarly, Matthew Clift and several other aldermen wrote in support of both Robert Fisher and Walter Gibbs, when they were summoned up to London to face charges of having taken up arms against parliament in the Civil War. They were, argued Clift, unfit to travel. Fisher, he stated, was over seventy-four and 'by reason of his said age, impotence and weakness of body was not any ways able to travel without danger of his life'.

The Restoration and the Revival of Factions, 1660-62

By the time of the death of Oliver Cromwell in 1658 and Restoration of Charles II in 1660, the mood in the country at large, as well as in the city of Bath, had changed most dramatically. For instance, whereas both William Prynne and Alexander Popham (Bath's representatives in the Convention Parliament of 1660) had fiercely opposed Charles I in the Civil War, both had also worked hard to achieve the Restoration of Charles II. It was therefore perhaps not altogether surprising that the city - which had been almost the first in the country to rise for parliament in 1642 - was also the first to proclaim Charles II king (12th May 1660) and the first to offer him a Loyal Address (4th June). The revolution had completed its full circle. John Biggs, the mayor, described the local celebrations in a letter to Prynne:

> The corporation being met at my house, myself and the aldermen being in scarlet (the loud music playing before us) we went about twelve a clock to the usual place of publishing proclamations: where... the proclamation was read, which being done, all men waving their hats or swords over their heads, cried, GOD SAVE KING CHARLES, which was seconded by a volley of shot from 100 musketeers or young men raised within our city for that purpose. By this time our conduit began to run claret, and so continued running claret wine for some few hours: In the meantime we, with the gentry of our city, and divers gentlemen of the country (who came to join with us in this so happy and welcome solemnity) retired into our Guildhall, where with great acclamations of joy, we spent several hours; during which time the bells rung at every church, and in the evening great bonfires were made: so that the whole afternoon was spent in great joy: all men testifying their obedience to their lawful Sovereign.

With the restoration of the king came the restoration of all those ex-cavaliers who had been expelled from municipal corporations in 1647. On 29th June 1660, therefore, Robert Hyde was restored to his

(right) *King Charles II, 1630-1685. (Author's collection).*

position of Recorder, while Henry Chapman, Samuel Wintle and Robert Sheppard resumed their places on the council. Of the others who had originally been expelled, Philip Sherwood and Thomas Gibbs were both dead and Robert Fisher - at the age of 88 - was no longer fit enough to continue in office. The royalist faction had nevertheless been bolstered by a number of more recently-recruited adherents - John Bush, Robert Child, William Child, John Fisher (son of Robert) and Walter Gibbs (son of Thomas) - and there was an expectation amongst them all that their time had finally come. However, in spite of the return of this group to the council, they became more and more frustrated at the slow speed of change. Matthew Clift's parliamentarian faction had been in undisputed control of local affairs since 1647 - and, much to the annoyance of Henry Chapman's group, they were still in control as late as the spring of 1661. Furthermore, Bath was still represented in parliament by Prynne and Popham, who had actively opposed the king in the Civil War. Control of the council held the key, therefore, not only to local domination but also to power over the election of future MPs.

Faced with these dismal facts, Henry Chapman and his followers decided to force the issue by joining forces with Sir Thomas Bridges, who had been royalist governor of the city during the royalist occupation (1643-5). Together they now plotted a remarkable coup. Once Chapman had gained the further distinction of being elected an alderman on 17th August 1660, he launched the first stage of his plan to wrest local power from Clift's faction. Just one month later, therefore, he stood as a candidate for the office of mayor in opposition to Alderman John Ford. The ensuing election (26th September) resulted in a heavy defeat for Chapman by 22 votes to 8, figures which indicated from the outset the size of the Puritan majority against him on the council. It was later alleged that Chapman demonstrated his disgust at being denied high office by one whom he regarded as being his social inferior. Calling him 'a saucy fellow' and claiming that 'he was a better man' than Ford, he openly 'affronted and reviled the said mayor sitting on the bench in open court with very opprobrious and distasteful language'.

However - not to be outdone - when writs were issued for the new 'Cavalier Parliament' in the March of 1661, Chapman decided to counter the corporation's nomination of Popham and Prynne by putting forward two candidates of his own - Sir Thomas Bridges and Sir Charles Berkeley. Unfortunately, the Mayor of Bath, John Ford, declined to show any interest in the claims of these self-appointed rival candidates. Refusing to accept defeat, Bridges lodged a complaint against Ford before the Privy Council, charging him with a history of misdemeanours. His somewhat transparent plan was to get Ford dismissed as mayor in the hope that he himself would be elected to the office and thus gain power to sway the election of the MPs. The scheme failed dismally. When Ford appeared before the Privy Council, he was quickly able to refute the charges and return to Bath in time to organise the election. Prynne and Popham were duly returned to parliament by a majority of 21 votes to 7. Chapman and his faction stormed out of the council chamber in protest.

At this point Chapman, seething with anger, ordered a drummer to beat his drum in every street to summon all two hundred of the freemen of the city to a meeting outside the Guildhall. There, with only thirty or so freemen actually present in support, he held a mock election of his own, declaring Bridges and Berkeley duly elected. According to Prynne, this was conducted 'in a most tumultuous manner' and later ratified next door at *The Sun* (the inn owned by Chapman), 'where they caroused so long that many of them were scarce able to return home'. When parliament eventually met in May, all four candidates arrived to take up their seats! The Commons quickly intervened, ruling that Prynne and Popham were the rightful representatives.

Bridges and Chapman, however, were nothing if not persistent. In anger and desperation, they now pursued their schemes with almost lunatic frenzy. In September, just before the new elections were to take place for the post of mayor, Chapman gained a warrant (signed by Bridges, who was a deputy lieutenant) for the arrest of nine leading members of Clift's faction on the council, described as 'seditious persons of known disloyalty and disaffection to kingly government'. They were taken under escort as prisoners to Ilchester, where they were presented to the sheriff. Chapman's intention was quite clear - namely, to get a sufficient number of his opponents out of the way in order to obtain a majority for himself in the forthcoming election. On the night before the election was due to be held Chapman and his confederates met together in a local alehouse to work out the probable voting intentions of the remainder of the council. To their horror, they concluded that a majority for Henry Chapman was still by no means certain. Early next day, therefore, Chapman himself, as captain of the local trained bands, arrested under warrant two more of the council and sent them under escort to Keynsham, where they were kept overnight in the stables of Sir Thomas Bridges.

Meanwhile, the election proceeded with a depleted council. During the debate, Chapman hurled insults at both the mayor and William Prynne, who sat with the council as its recorder (having been elected to that office by the council a month earlier on the retirement of Robert Hyde). When the question was put, 'who shall be mayor of this city for the year next ensuing?', 8 votes were recorded for John Parker and 11 for Henry Chapman. In a second ballot, with other candidates eliminated, 10 supported Parker and 11 supported Chapman. The result of the election, amid uproar, was duly entered in the minute book in these words: 'Mr Henry Chapman is by the voices present elected mayor of this city of Bath'. By late evening eight of those originally arrested had returned to the city, having been released by the sheriff. Hurrying to the Guildhall under the instructions of Prynne, they cast their votes for Parker and entered them accordingly in the minute book (the different ink is clearly visible). The statement recording Chapman's election as mayor was then crossed out being substituted by the words: 'Mr John Parker is mayor elected for the next year'. In the meantime, Prynne had reported the shameful episode to the Privy Council. When eventually it summoned all the parties to appear, it rebuked the city for its perpetual squabbles which were 'a bad example to to other corporations'; ruled in favour of John Parker; and ordered the dismissal of Chapman as captain of the trained bands.

William Prynne, Recorder of Bath (1648-52, 1661-62) and Member of Parliament for Bath (1660-69). By courtesy of King Edward's School, Bath.

Sir

Comeing this morning to the Citty of Bath to keepe the generall quarter
Sessions on his Majesties behalfe ~~to keepe the generall quarter Sessions~~, who on
wednesday ~~next~~ sennight was acquainted therewith, & wished me a good iourney
thither to discharge that service, Soone after my arrivall there a party of
Sir William Bassetts troope, by your ~~speciall~~ order, seized nine of the
Aldermen & Comon Councill of the Citty, the one a Justice of the peace, another
a Constable, whereby the peace of the Citty was much disturbed, and the
quarter Sessions interrupted, See that I was forced to Adjourne the
same till this day Sennight. The orders to Sr William Bassett to seize
and send them away forthwith this very morning, neare fourty miles of
to the Sherriff to secure them in the Marshalsey there to remaine till
further order without any Cause expressed, or prævious examination
before your selfe, being soe near a neighbour unto them, without proofe
or Conviction of any offences that might demerrit such severe proceedings,
against all rules of law & Justice, is generally interpreted by the Citty
& Countrey, to be a designe (at least in the informers, who engaged you
in these unprecedented proceedings) to interrupt the quarter
Sessions of the Citty this day and the Election of the Major and all
other officers for this Citty on Monday next for the yeare ensuing
(wherein nine of them ought to have their voices) and to put an
affront upon my selfe their newly elected and sworne Recorder
who being by my oath obliged to mainteine their just rights and
liberties to my power & meeting with this high violation of
them beyond expectation I thought it my duty to acquaint you
therewith & to ~~acquaint~~ advise you as your freind and neighbour speedily
to release them, that they may attend the election on monday next
to prevent Complaints thereof to his Majesty & his honoble Councill
by the next post, & unto their Parliament at their next meeting
who how ill they are like to resent such irregular proceedings,
I leave to your owne Judgment to Consider, and in the meane time
Remaine

Your freind & Servant

From Bath this
19th Septembr 1661

Wm Prynne

If you please to acquaint me of the informers against these persons at this
Juncture of time I shall take it as a favour this present ayd to quartr
that might not at Qveens

A letter from William Prynne, the Recorder of Bath, to Sir Hugh Smythe, Deputy Lieutenant of Somerset, 19th September 1661. In it Prynne issues a forthright complaint against the arrest and imprisonment without charge of nine Bath councillors just prior to the election of a new mayor (see above). By courtesy of Bath & North East Somerset Library and Archive Service (Bath Central Library).

In the meantime, the Bath Quarter Sessions (under the chairmanship of William Prynne) heard a number of serious charges against Chapman. Arriving with a retinue of his allies, he treated the court with utter contempt and shouted mockingly at Prynne, 'You ought to have lost your head when you lost your ears' *[in a reference to a punishment sustained by Prynne in the 1630s for writing pamphlets against the court and the bishops]*. When he was later summoned to reappear, Chapman sent back a defiant message that 'he would not appear before such saucy and imperious fellows' - and that they had placed 'a lousy tailor' in the place that should have been his. (John Parker, the new mayor, was a clothier and draper by trade.) Chapman - who was not known as the best of losers - was eventually displaced from his office as alderman and his position on the council. By November, he was also languishing in prison 'for divers great debts'. His attempt to encourage his old soldier friends to rescue him by force even caused the mayor to watch the gaol all night in person alongside the regular guard and some of the 'chiefest inhabitants'.

This, however, was by no means the end of the story. In November 1661, the Corporation Act, which Prynne himself had fiercely opposed in the Commons, became law. Although it required all persons holding office to take the oath of allegiance and supremacy, the local commissioners who were appointed to enforce the Act had powers to remove *all* those regarded as a threat to church or state (even though they had taken the oaths). This gave them almost limitless opportunity to remodel municipal corporations as they wished. When the commissioners (who were composed entirely of local cavalier gentry) visited Bath in October 1662, three members of the corporation failed to attend for the swearing of oaths and were immediately disqualified (including Recorder Prynne). Although all the remainder did in fact take the oath, eleven of them were nevertheless considered unfit 'to continue any longer in their places and trusts' and were therefore ejected for 'the safety of the public'. Those affected in this second great purge were the members of Clift's faction , all of whom had been involved in the election disputes of the previous year and several of whom had dominated the council since 1642 (including Matthew Clift himself, John Parker and John Biggs). The men chosen to replace them consisted of six who were selected by the commissioners themselves (including Henry Chapman) and eight elected later by the remnant of the council. All the replacements were, of course, deemed to be loyal to the king (and, by implication, sympathetic to Chapman).

In Bath, therefore, the Corporation Act had largely achieved in October 1662 what Henry Chapman had striven unsuccessfully to achieve throughout 1661. By November, Sir Thomas Bridges had been given the freedom of the city; by 1663, Henry Chapman had been elected mayor. However, because the new regulations applied only to membership of corporations, William Prynne and Alexander Popham continued to represent the city in parliament until their deaths in 1669.

The Exclusion Crisis and the Revival of Factions, 1678-84

There was at this time in England a deep-seated fear of Roman Catholicism and a suspicion that individual Catholics had managed to infiltrate the highest offices of state. These feelings had been seemingly confirmed when it was revealed that James, Duke of York (Charles II's brother and heir to the throne) had not only subscribed personally to the Catholic faith, but had also taken a Catholic (Mary of Modena) as his second wife. The prospect of a line of Catholic monarchs therefore loomed large. Public passions, however, were stirred even further in 1678 when two clerics - Titus

Oates and Israel Tonge - claimed to have uncovered details of a Catholic plot to murder Charles, install James as king and restore Catholicism to the country by force. Although this so-called 'Popish Plot' (which, allegedly, would have culminated in a foreign invasion inspired by the Pope and Louis XIV of France) was a complete fiction, it was widely believed by a credulous public.

It was therefore no surprise when the election of 1679 returned a substantial majority in favour of the policies advocated by the Earl of Shaftesbury - namely, the supremacy of parliament, freedom of worship for all Protestants and the exclusion of James II from the succession to the throne in favour of the Protestant Duke of Monmouth (an illegitimate son of Charles II). A fierce struggle consequently ensued between Shaftesbury's 'Whigs' (a Scottish term for peasant rebels) and the 'Tories' (an Irish term for cut-throat bandits) - terms of abuse which were to last for some two hundred years. However, attempts by three Whig parliaments in 1679, 1680 and 1681 to gain an Exclusion Bill were thwarted either by the obstruction of the House of Lords or by the king's power to bring about a hurried dissolution of parliament whenever necessary. Public sentiment eventually swung back in favour of Charles, especially after the discovery of a real plot to murder the king and his brother in 1683 (the Rye House Plot). The inevitable counter-attack staged by the government included a successful plan to reduce the power of the municipal boroughs (which returned the majority of members of parliament) by withdrawing and then re-issuing their charters in amended form - a move designed to produce future parliaments more favourable to the king.

In many ways the mood inside the city of Bath reflected the mood of the nation at large. In spite of the fact that the Restoration of 1660 had witnessed the expulsion of Puritan extremists from the Bath Corporation, a fear and hatred of Roman Catholicism still bubbled away beneath the surface. The first outward sign of this came in February 1680, when the corporation found itself forced to displace Alderman Walter Hickes (who was a barber by trade) both as an alderman and as a member of the council 'for speaking scandalous words against His Royal Highness the Duke of York'. Hickes, in a noticeably drunken state at the coffee house run by Mrs Mary Collins, had apparently called the Catholic Duke 'a rogue, a rascal, a traitor, a rebel and a son of a whore'. However, the somewhat stark council minute which recorded his expulsion completely masked the highly complex intrigues which had taken place behind the scene.

In a letter to the Secretary of State (Sir Leoline Jenkins), John Allambridge, who was both a member of the corporation and an attorney, expressed his grave

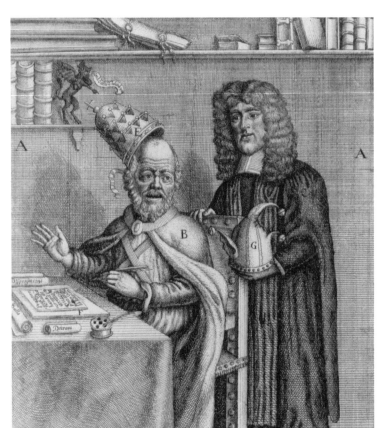

A contemporary cartoon showing Titus Oates (right) in the act of spying on the Pope, who is writing to the Jesuits urging them to support the 'Popish Plot' to murder Charles II. (By courtesy of Ashmolean Museum, University of Oxford).

misgivings about the way in which the case had been handled. The mayor (John Masters) had delayed the enquiry; Allambridge had not been allowed to cross-examine witnesses, the evidence of whom had been doctored by the corporation's attorney, Samuel Hellier; Mrs Collins had been brow-beaten into giving favourable evidence - 'or else', they had said, 'Mr Hickes would be utterly ruined'; and Hickes himself had been seen by the keeper of the Outer Bowling Green 'down on his knees' before one witness, begging him not to inform against him. There is little doubt that the corporation had been doing its level best to save Hickes - a point not lost on the Secretary of State when he replied to Allambridge's letter in March. 'The remissness and connivance' used in this matter, he said, and 'the favour shown to Hickes' would be remembered by His Majesty, whose honour had been 'abominably wounded'. The Attorney-General had therefore issued an indictment against Hickes to appear before the County Assizes. He was later found guilty in his absence, having fled into hiding to escape arrest.

Eventually the dust settled and by June - just four months after his expulsion - Hickes had not only returned unscathed, but had also been re-admitted to his position as alderman. Indeed, such was the speed of his rehabilitation that, four years later, he was elected Mayor of Bath by a corporation which clearly felt that his only error had been in getting himself drunk. The fate of John Allambridge, on the other hand, was (significantly) less fortunate. In May 1682, the corporation found him guilty of 'quarrelling with members without cause' and 'committing other high misdemeanours'. He was duly expelled from his membership of the council. Trouble-makers were clearly not welcome.

Meanwhile, the corporation had felt it expedient in May 1680 to send a loyal address to the king, fearing no doubt that relationships had been soured by the Hickes affair. In it they acknowledged 'the immense benefits' they had enjoyed from his 'most prudent and gracious government' and their utter detestation of 'all tumultuous petitions' (which had recently been circulated in the country at large demanding an immediate recall of parliament). It reassured him that 'not one person in all this city ever set their hands to such seditious and pernicious practices'. Royal support and patronage of the city was of course vital to the growth of the health resort.

The reputation of Bath as a centre of loyal royalist support, however, suffered another serious blow in the August of 1680, when a newsletter reported that 'the Duke of Monmouth was received by the inhabitants of Bath with very great demonstrations of joy and affection, being met out of the city with 200 gentlemen and citizens on horseback' while church bells rang in celebration. Monmouth, who had been adopted by Shaftesbury as a suitable Protestant successor to Charles II (if the Exclusion Bill ever became law), was conducting a 'Progress' through the western counties to whip up

Sir Leoline Jenkins, Charles II's Secretary of State, 1680-84.
(By courtesy of Ashmolean Museum, University of Oxford).

popular support for his cause. The reaction shown to him by many Bath inhabitants was instinctive and very much in keeping with their earlier reaction to the outbreak of Civil War in 1642 - but it merely increased the suspicions at court that there were seditious elements at work in the city.

This feeling was seemingly confirmed by two intelligence reports from local agents. The first in 1680 from an informer, signing himself simply as 'A.R.' *[i.e Amicus Regis - friend of the king]*, warned Secretary of State Jenkins of 'the malicious practices of John Sherston and others against the king and his government by encouraging 'fanatical' ministers in the city to spread rumours from the pulpit that 'the king will let in Popery'. Thus, by stirring up a fear of Catholicism, they tried to 'inflame the people into rebellion'. The second report in 1683 from an anonymous informer living in Bath to a member of the government warned him that, 'although the corporation for the most part consists of honest loyal persons, they are not without some evil members'. He again highlighted the behaviour of John Sherston - 'a most busy, pestilent Presbyterian', who was 'as pernicious to the king's interest as any man in England'. He was apparently working 'tooth and nail' to build up a Whig party within Bath Corporation with the aim of defeating the Tory candidates at the next general election. However, although there was ample evidence against Sherston to have him expelled from the council, the mayor proved reluctant to act. Indeed, such was Sherston's skill 'in making parties' that he had survived not only a presentment by the Grand Jury of local citizens, stating that he was 'a person altogether unfit' to remain in the corporation; but also a letter to the Secretary of State signed by six aldermen urging his dismissal.

His matchless skill at political manoeuvring had therefore saved him - at least on this occasion - from the sustained attacks of his opponents. Two rival factions, however, had clearly emerged during the course of this episode - on the one hand, a group of loyal Tories centred on the hard core of the six aldermen who had complained to the Secretary of State (Henry Chapman, Thomas Gibbs, Walter Gibbs, John Masters, Richard Masters and Francis Pearce); and on the other hand, Sherston's group of Whigs, which was frequently enlarged by moderates - thanks to his powers of persuasion.

This, however, was not quite the end of the story. By 1683, Charles II and his Tory supporters had commenced their national campaign to remove known Whigs from membership of municipal corporations in an attempt to ensure the return of more favourable Tory candidates in future elections. *Quo Warranto* writs were therefore issued demanding that all suspect boroughs surrender their royal charters for legal scrutiny. Once Evesham, Norwich and London had submitted, other corporations had little hope of resistance. Many therefore meekly surrendered their charters in advance rather than incur the heavy legal costs of an appeal. On 10th November 1684, Bath Corporation agreed that their precious charter (granted by Elizabeth I in 1590) should be delivered up to the king in London by four councillors before the end of December. Eleven days later, in a belated attempt to express their undivided loyalty to the crown and at the same time gain favourable terms in the new charter, John Sherston was ejected from the corporation. Shortly afterwards, on 31st December 1684, the king graciously issued a revised charter for the city, which was received with both a feeling of relief and a sense of shock - shock caused by the fact that the legal charges incurred amounted to no less than £230! The impoverished corporation was therefore obliged to take out a loan at 5.10% interest from one of its new members, John Pocock.

The new charter (one of ninety-eight eventually issued in the country at large) confirmed most of the corporation's original powers, while at the same time creating the new position of high steward (a royal nominee) to be superior to both mayor and aldermen. The charter also listed by name the first members of the new corporation (as approved by the king), including High Steward Viscount Fitzharding, Mayor John Bush (a mercer by trade) and all the aldermen and councillors. Furthermore, the crown reserved the right in future to remove any or all of the individuals from membership of the corporation. There were in all eleven aldermen listed (although Henry Chapman, who was by then both old and infirm, never took up his appointment) and twenty councillors. One aldermen and six councillors from the former council were ejected, being replaced by two new aldermen and eight new councillors (mostly the younger sons of trusted Tories already on the council). Walter Hickes - forgiven at last for his drunken lapse - had survived this third great purge.

There is little doubt that the king, closely advised by his Secretary of State Jenkins, knew exactly which members of the corporation to expel. Thanks to a number of intelligence reports from Bath between 1680 and 1684, Sir Leoline Jenkins had been able to build up a detailed picture of the composition of the corporation and the identity of its most troublesome elements. In particular, the letter from A.R. (a local resident - see above) in April 1680 supplied Jenkins with 'the true character' of each individual member - an invaluable survey which Jenkins undoubtedly kept on his desk until the moment of the purge. Indeed, the lists of those retained and those ejected tie in very closely with A.R.'s own assessments.

Those who were confirmed as members of the new corporation, therefore, included John Masters, innkeeper ('a loyal and well-principled man'), Walter Gibbs, gentleman ('a huffish alderman, but a lover of the established government'), Thomas Gibbs, innkeeper ('a furioso, yet well affected to the government'), William Chapman and Richard Masters, innkeeper ('both loyal and jolly fellows'), Francis Clift ('alias Old Rock; firm to the king and his friends') and Edward Woolmer ('a dapper apothecary; in loyalty equal to the best of them'). A group of harmless, but ineffective members, who were also retained, included William Wallis ('an ignoramus: the selling of [a] barrel of ale will make him vote for anything'), Thomas (At)wood, baker ('a chip in porridge') and Robert Chapman, apothecary ('no fanatic; speaks flattering to all parties'). Five of the seven members expelled in the purge had each been severely castigated by A.R. - William Bush, chandler ('a fly fanatic'), John Sherston, clothier ('a damnable anti-monarchical man: a frequenter of conventicles'), John Axford ('Sherston's wholly devoted creature: a frequenter of conventicles'), Benedict Baker, plasterer (A.R.'s comment is illegible) and Matthew Reeve, goldsmith ('a fanatical shatter-headed coxcomb'). Another of those expelled - Arthur Sherston - had joined the council after A.R.'s letter in 1680; while Richard Carwardine, barber ('an old decrepit cavalier') had clearly been excluded on grounds of age rather than loyalty. However, whatever the actual background to the purge, Bath Corporation had now been firmly placed within the tight control of the government.

Factional Rivalry - Common Links in the Purges

The three purges of the council during the period 1647-1684 were essentially all part of the same theme which had divided local people over forty years from the outbreak of civil war in 1642 - a theme which largely centred on religious belief. Although the Puritan faction, which had dominated the council throughout the Civil War and

Letter of Intelligence from 'A.R.' to Secretary of State Jenkins, 5th April 1680, in which he outlines the 'true character of the Corporation men of Bath' - see above. (By courtesy of the National Archives: PRO ref. SP15.42.34)

Protectorate, had been expelled as a result of the Corporation Act in 1662, their spirit had not been extinguished. Matthew Clift, John Biggs and John Parker had disappeared from the scene, but their passionate opposition to Roman Catholicism had been taken up in the 1670s and 1680s, partly by newcomers on the council (such as John Sherston and John Axford) and partly by Matthew Reeve (the son of George Reeve, one of Matthew Clift's closest supporters in the 1640s). Outside the Guildhall, they found active and vocal support from hundreds of 'fanatics' - chiefly Presbyterian - centred on their (illegal) nonconformist conventicles.

Opposing them were the traditionalist Anglicans - epitomised by the remarkable Henry Chapman who, alone out of all those involved on the outbreak of the Civil War, had remained politically active throughout the entire period. By the time of his old age in the 1680s, he was supported in his relentless opposition to Puritan extremists by both Thomas Gibbs, junior, and Walter Gibbs (the son and grandson respectively of his old ally, Thomas Gibbs, senior); and by Harry and Charles Child, who were not only his own great-nephews, but also the sons of William Child, his former associate from the 1640s. However, not all families carried on their old traditions to the same degree. It is noticeable, for instance, that Francis Clift (son of Matthew Clift) and Thomas (At)wood (son of John Atwood) did not show any of their fathers' zeal for the Puritan cause - and were therefore not ejected in the final purge, but gladly retained on Charles II's nominated Council in 1684.

Monmouth's Rebellion, 1685

Shortly after he had granted the city a new charter, Charles II died in February 1685 and was succeeded by his Catholic brother, James II. With the municipal boroughs now firmly under royal control, the general election in April saw the Whigs heavily defeated and the Tories returned with an overwhelming majority. However, the security of the new king's position was immediately threatened by an invasion, launched from Holland, by the Protestant Duke of Monmouth in support of his claim to the throne. Landing at Lyme in Dorset with 150 followers, he saw his ranks rapidly enlarged by some five thousand labourers (many armed with scythes or pitchforks) as he advanced through the western counties - the scene of his highly popular 'Progress' in 1680.

Having failed to take Bristol, the army turned eastwards and appeared outside the walls of Bath (where, of course, Monmouth had been greeted with great enthusiasm just five years earlier). However, Bath Corporation - terrified by the recent experience over its charter, purged of its most active Whig members and fearful that any hint of disloyalty would result in terrible repercussions - firmly shut its gates in the face of the invading mob. Furthermore, it had also taken the precaution of making the atmosphere distinctly unpleasant by hiring workmen to spread the 'night soil' *[i.e. the dung from cess pits]* along the foot of the Borough Walls as a greeting to the rebels. The city itself had been garrisoned by four companies of militia (totalling 500 men) from Oxfordshire,

(right) *James, Duke of Monmouth, 1645-85. (Author's collection)*

Wiltshire and Somerset (the corporation later footing the bill for their thirty-two days' pay, amounting to £86 8s 6d). Breastworks had also been dug in Ham Meadow to strengthen the defences. When eventually a rebel soldier was sent forward to summon the city to surrender ('only in bravado', it was later claimed, 'for we had no expectation of its surrender'), he was shot through the head by one of the guards.

After Monmouth's men had moved on to their inevitable final defeat at Sedgemoor in July, Bath Corporation was, in a message to the king, quick to underline its own faultless conduct throughout the episode. 'Our loyal resolution being so firmly fixed...we had resolved to die at the gates, rather than suffer him to get within them'. It is also worth noting that, whereas 54 men from Frome, 30 from Rode and 18 from Beckington had joined the Duke's army, none had done so from Bath. Nevertheless, Lord Chief Justice Jeffreys (who gained notoriety for his brutal treatment of the rebels during his 'Bloody Assizes') believed that any potential traitors inside the city (which he felt was not above suspicion) needed to be taught a salutary lesson. He therefore instructed the Sheriff of Somerset to issue a warrant to the constables of the city ordering them to organise the execution of four of the convicted rebels - a warrant which underlines something of the brutality of seventeenth-century life and the way in which terror was used as an effective weapon of control. It read:

These are therefore to will and require you immediately, on sight hereof to erect a gallows in the most public place of your said city to hang the said traitors on; and that you provide halters to hang them with, a sufficient number of faggots to burn the bowels of four traitors and a furnace or cauldron to boil their heads and quarters, and salt to boil therewith - half a bushel to each traitor - and tar to tar them with; a sufficient number of spears and poles to fix and place their heads and quarters [on]; and that you warn the owners of four oxen to be ready with a dray or wain; and the said four oxen at the time hereafter mentioned for execution and yourselves together with a guard of forty able men at the least, to be present on Wednesday morning by eight of the clock, to be aiding and assisting to me, or my deputy, to see the said rebels executed. You are also to provide an axe and cleaver for the quartering of the said rebels.

Three contemporary drawings to illustrate the punishment of rebels by hanging (top); drawing and quartering their bodies (middle); and displaying the quarters on poles (bottom). By permission of the British Library: ref - the Roxburghe Ballads, RAZ.Rox, I, pt 2, 491, 488, 490.

After the executions had taken place before the horrified gaze of the citizens of Bath, the various heads and quarters of the victims were distributed around neighbouring villages - as a deterrent - for display on poles at the top of church towers.

Therefore, in spite of the city's longstanding aversion to Roman Catholicism, Bath Corporation found itself pressurised by the state in such a way that it had little choice but to adopt a policy of outward conformity. Eighty faggots were bought out of city funds for great bonfires to celebrate the news of Monmouth's capture, while John Uggins was paid expenses by the mayor 'to give evidence against the rebels' at the Assizes. In 1688, the city sent two addresses of gratitude to the king for his Declaration of Indulgence (which gave freedom of worship to Roman Catholics and nonconformists alike - a great boon to the many Presbyterians and Baptists living around Bath); and then organised an outward show of rejoicing on the birth of his son Prince James Edward (the future Old Pretender). Bells rang in celebration on this 'Prince's Thanksgiving Day', bonfires were again lit, wine flowed freely - and Mayor Benjamin Baber forwarded to the king 'the hearty congratulations' of his 'ever-dutiful and loyal subjects'. There is little doubt that, although this event opened up the prospect of a long line of Catholic monarchs, the city regarded it without doubt as a wonderful advertisement for the effectiveness of its health spa in providing a cure for infertility (for James II had brought his queen, Mary of Modena to Bath in 1687 in the hope of producing a male heir).

(below) The Birth of the Pretender, 1688 by Arnold van Westerhart. The picture shows a court scene in which the baby is being presented to James II by the Papal Nuncio with Queen Mary of Modena in bed in the background. (By courtesy of Ashmolean Museum, University of Oxford).

The Glorious Revolution, 1688-89

The invasion by William of Orange in November 1688 and the flight of James II to France in the following month made possible the Glorious Revolution. This installed William III and Mary II (James II's daughter by his first marriage) as joint sovereigns and restored protestantism to the centre of government. There is no doubt that the citizens of Bath felt a great sense of relief at these events. The corporation quickly restored William Baker to the Mastership of the Grammar School (after he had been displaced by the Catholic Francis Carne a year earlier on the orders of James II); and, anxious to remove all symbols of Popery, it resolved that 'the Crown of Thorns and Cross in the Cross Bath shall be taken down and all other superstitious things belonging thereunto, and the inscription obliterated'. [These symbols had formed part of a large monument, commissioned by the Secretary of State, the Earl of Melfort, to celebrate the royal birth].

To emphasise their heartfelt commitment to the Protestant cause, the Coronation in April 1689 was marked with street celebrations, a Guildhall banquet, a banner inscribed with the words 'God save King William and Queen Mary' and a specially-commissioned song. One verse of this read:

> In praise of him who came with Heaven's high hand
> To drive Rome's priests (these vipers) from our land
> Those locusts who to Lucifer bespoke us
> Whose mock religion is a hocus pocus.

From a political point of view, the remainder of the Stuart period was comparatively quiet in Bath, although there was an occasional suspicion that that the city gave cover to groups of Jacobites [i.e. the supporters of James II in exile and, after his death in 1701, his son, James Francis]. In 1691, for instance, there was a report that a few citizens, meeting in Box, had raised their glasses to the health of James II; in 1693, Mary II was furious that some Bathonians had behaved 'insolently and seditiously' by openly rejoicing at the setback suffered in battle by William III in Flanders; while in 1715, the Privy Council castigated the local authorities for tolerating the gathering of large groups of disaffected people. In the same year, when a regiment of cavalry and dragoons was billeted in the city in readiness for an expected Jacobite rising in the west, its commander (Major-General Wade) discovered a hidden supply of arms and two hundred horses equipped for immediate action. Several arrests were made. The fact of the matter was, however, that would-be conspirators found it all-too-easy to merge into the largely anonymous crowd of visitors to this popular leisure resort. The city itself, with very few resident Catholics (see Chapter 14), remained totally loyal.

SOURCES USED IN CHAPTER 3

1. Printed material:
Cook, Chris & Wroughton, John: *English Historical Facts, 1603-1688* (1980)
Coward, Barry: *The Stuart Age: England, 1603-1714* (1980)
Fawcett, Trevor & Bird, Stephen: *Bath: History and Guide* (1994)
Haddon, J: *Bath* (1973)
Holland, Elizabeth: *The Descent of the Chapman Mayors of Bath in the Seventeenth Century* (1989)
Lamont, William M: *Marginal Prynne, 1600-1669* (1963)
Marlowe, Nicholas: *West Country Boroughs, 1640-62* (unpublished thesis,1986)
Neale, R.S: *Bath: A Social History, 1680-1850* (1981)
Page, W. (ed.): *Victoria County History of Somerset*, vol. 2 (1911)
Peach, R.E.M: *The Annals of the Parish of Swainswick* (1982)
Prynne, William: *Brevia Parliamentaria Redivivae* (1664)
Warner, Richard, *The History of Bath* (1801)
Wingfield, W. MacDonald: *The Monmouth Rebels* (Somerset Rec. Society, vol. 79, 1985)
Western, J.R: *The English Militia in the Eighteenth Century* (1965)
Williams, J.A: *Bath and Rome: the Living Link* (1963)
Williams, J.A., *Post-Reformation Catholicism in Bath*, vol. 1 (1975)
Wroughton, John: *A Community at War: the Civil War in Bath & North Somerset* (1992)
Wroughton, John: *The Stuart Age, 1603-1714* (1997)
Wroughton, John: *From Civil War to Age of Reason: Bath Abbey, 1600-1800* (1997)
Wroughton, John: *Puritanism & Traditionalism, 1620-1662* (in *Bath History*, vol. 4, 1992)

2. Documentary material:

Bath Record Office:	Bath Chamberlain's Accounts, 1603-1734 *passim*
	Bath Council Minute Books, Nos. 1, 2, 3 (1631-1715) *passim*
	Bath Royal Charter (Charles II), 31st December 1684
Public Record Office:	Calendar of State papers Domestic, vols. 1661, 1662, 1677-8, 1679-80, 1682, 1683, 1685, 1693
	State Papers Domestic:
	SP23 204.663-671 (Committee for Compounding - R. Fisher)
	SP29 413.57 (A.R.'s letter to Jenkins, 1680)
	SP29 424.44 (letter from Aldermen to Jenkins, 1683)
	PC2.55 (Privy Council Registers - Council's judgment, 1661)
	Lord's Journals, vol IX, p 430 (expulsion of royalists, 1647)

I am grateful to Elizabeth Holland for identifying the occupations of councillors during the period 1678-1684.

CHAPTER 4

Security

The Trained Bands

The city was well equipped to deal with any physical danger which might threaten. From 1573, Queen Elizabeth had based the country's defences largely on the 'trained bands' of citizens within each county, financed by a 'trained soldiers' rate' - a system which had survived into the Stuart times. Deputy lieutenants were made responsible for calling periodic musters to ensure that the men of this militia were adequately trained. By 1638 the local force in Somerset numbered 4,000 foot and 300 horse with the infantry organised into five regiments, each based on a particular part of the county. Sir Robert Phelps commanded the Bath Regiment of 800 pikes and muskets drawn not only from the city itself, but also from the whole surrounding area of North-East Somerset. Within the regiment, the seven companies were each recruited from a group of neighbouring parishes, which helped to produce something of a local spirit. Bath would probably contribute between twenty and thirty men, whose arms were provided by the city. Their weapons were stored and maintained in the Guildhall, where John Gray, the armourer, was given periodic payments for such items as 'scouring the armour' and 'mending the faults in the armoury'. At the beginning of the century, these soldiers were equipped with caps and blue coats trimmed with lace and silk - all paid for by the corporation.

From a muster roll, dated in Bath on 22nd May 1639, we know that Sir Ralph Hopton commanded a company of two hundred foot soldiers within the Bath Regiment. The structure and organisation are clearly indicated. Hopton was assisted by eleven officers - a lieutenant, a quartermaster, an ensign, four sergeants, a clerk and two drums. The infantrymen, divided into 80 pikes and 125 muskets, were drawn from over forty villages, parish constables being responsible for ensuring that individual quotas for each parish were maintained. The company met for training in Bath once a month after church on Sunday, setting up targets for shooting practice on banks of turf or 'butts' in a close known as 'Butt Hayes' and drilling in a meadow outside the West Gate.

Once a year, the company joined forces with the rest of the regiment for a two-day muster. Although, by mid-century, this usually took place in Wells (where the local regiment met up with the other four county regiments), the location

The armoury in the Guildhall at Bath, containing pikes, halberds, helmets, pistols, muskets and lintocks - together with barrels of bullets and powder. (Drawing by Mark Withers)

until the late 1630s was always Bath. In 1635, for instance, the council gave authority for the colonel to muster his men on the town common and erect a tent for his officers. Then, while the deputy lieutenants were entertained to a splendid dinner, the council provided a large barrel of beer and a good supply of ale for the men. There is little doubt that in peace time membership of the regiment became a somewhat fashionable activity with the monthly training and annual musters regarded as part of an enjoyable social calendar. The Bath Regiment, however, was soon to face the realities of combat. It played an important role in the early months of the Civil War, fighting for parliament under its new commander, Alexander Popham (who was also Member of Parliament for Bath at the time). It became heavily involved in 1643 as the royalist army approached the city and was badly mauled shortly afterwards at the Battle of Roundway Down, near Devizes.

The Bath Regiment of Trained Bands on parade in 1642. (Drawing by Stephen Beck)

The notion of recruiting local inhabitants to maintain a civilian defence force, funded by local taxes, was still much in evidence by the end of the century - even though the name had been changed from 'trained bands' to 'militia'. There was, after all, no standing army or professional police force to offer protection. The Militia Act of 1662, in an attempt to offset any future invasion or insurrection, gave lord lieutenant and deputy lieutenants of each county power not only to raise men, horses and weapons from amongst the community, but also to organise regular training. This was to be conducted for each regiment at annual four-day musters, supplemented by two-day musters held quarterly for individual companies. The cost of providing ammunition and other requirements was to be met by a local rate - as Bath citizens were soon to discover.

Throughout the last three decades of the century, North Somerset supported a militia regiment consisting of three companies (at least one of which was based in Bath). The corporation dutifully collected 'militia money' from the residents to support those who had been recruited through payments to cover their loss of wages during a muster (e.g. £1 15s 0d 'to the trained soldiers at the last day's muster' in 1670; £4 1s 0d 'for the soldiers' at the two-day muster; and £8 2s 0d at the four-day muster in 1683); the cost of gunpowder for use in training; and the expense of repairing or replacing weapons. The local company normally held its quarterly musters on Kingsmead, just outside the West Gate, whereas it joined the rest of the regiment in Frome for the annual muster. With heightened tension in the country at large in 1689-90, the corporation was obliged to find £36 6s 0d for fourteen days pay when the regiment went on alert.

The City Walls

Quite apart from the trained bands, there were other reasons why the city felt reasonably secure from outside attack. Bath, like Chester, Lincoln and other county towns of the period, still retained its old medieval wall as a distinctive and prominent feature. The ancient wall, built of what Henry Chapman was to call in 1673 'a time-defying stone', measured under a mile around its whole circuit - thus making it one of the smallest of all medieval cities with a mere twenty-four acres of land enclosed. According to Richard Warner (writing in 1801), an extension had been built from the south-west angle to the river bank to provide some additional cover for the southern part of the city (which was already protected in part by the loop of the river Avon). However, Peter Davenport of the Bath Archaeological Trust has suggested that this could well have been a wall to mark the western boundary of the Ambury, a meadow previously owned by the monks of Bath Priory. The city wall and its flanking ditch had clearly been kept in good repair throughout medieval times. John Leland, who had visited the city in 1530, remarked that 'it standeth almost all, lacking but a piece about Gascoyne's Tower'. This tower, in the north-west corner had been built by William Gascoyne, a local citizen, to repair 'a little piece of the wall that was in decay' as a fine for being involved in a serious fight within the city.

The city council continued to treat the walls with respect throughout the seventeenth century, constantly repairing and strengthening them as need arose. Samuel Pepys confirmed in 1668 that they had even survived the rigours of the Civil War, for he was able to walk around the whole circuit admiring the walls which were 'good, and the battlements all whole'. As late as the 1690s, the city treasurer was still making periodic payments for labourers to clean out the ditch and for loads of stone and sand to repair the walls. To facilitate this sort of operation, Henry Deverell had been employed in 1669 to provide 'hurdles' for the scaffolding which was erected. The eighteenth century, of course, witnessed the dramatic expansion of the city as a resort and the rapid growth of new buildings outside the the old area. Developers consequently viewed the medieval walls as an obstruction both to their plans and to the inevitable increase in traffic. However, a previous assumption made by many historians that the walls were rased to the ground in order to accommodate all this improvement has in recent times been challenged.

Although it would appear to a modern visitor that only one small section of the wall survives today (i.e. that in Upper Borough Walls - *left*), recent research by the Bath Archaeological Trust has proved that this view is somewhat false. Marek Lewcun has shown, from excavations conducted between 1987 and 1996, that large sections of the wall still exist to a considerable height below pavement level in the areas of Orange Grove, Terrace Walk, Upper Borough Walls, Lower Borough Walls and Boatstall Lane. In the latter example, the wall adjacent to the East Gate has survived in cellars below the modern Guildhall market with even the battlements clearly visible in one place.

These excavations indicate that the wall was between 2.8 and 3.0 metres wide at the base and over six metres high to the top of the battlements. It is thought likely that the wall has survived in this submerged state because eighteenth-century developers found it too difficult to demolish. According to Thomas Pownall, who examined the stretch of wall between the North and West Gates in 1795, the core of the wall (which was Roman at its base) was 'harder than any stone in this country: the workmen could not break it without sledgehammers'; and, although they could easily have removed the facing stones, the demolition of the 'cemented rocky part' was far too labour-intensive and expensive to be of any practical value. According to Marek Lewcun, later house-builders therefore tended merely to remove the parapets and battlements and then to build up 'around and over the wall', encasing it inside the many cellars which were created with the new housing.

The excavations also revealed that the medieval walls had been built upon Roman and Saxon foundations. The second-century earth rampart (with a ditch outside) had been strengthened in the third century by cutting out a terrace, on which was built a stone wall; and by creating a metalled track along the berm (or flat ground) between the wall and the ditch. The medieval defences, which survived throughout the seventeenth century, followed exactly the same plan (see diagrams). Although the ditch (which on average was between 6.5 and 7 metres wide and between 1.5 and 2 metres deep) had become badly silted-up with rubbish and erosion by the fifteenth century, the council frequently paid workers to dig it out particularly during periods of tension. Dudley Carleton commented in a letter to a friend in 1608, for instance, that 'the city ditch is being cleansed'.

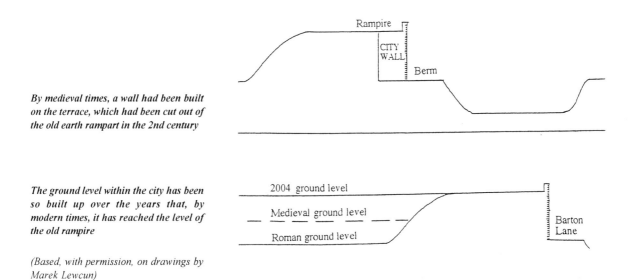

By medieval times, a wall had been built on the terrace, which had been cut out of the old earth rampart in the 2nd century

The ground level within the city has been so built up over the years that, by modern times, it has reached the level of the old rampire

(Based, with permission, on drawings by Marek Lewcun)

The citizens of Bath in the seventeenth century must have felt comparatively secure - if somewhat cramped - within their defensive enclosure. They were also able to look down on the world outside, for the ground level inside the city had risen by some two metres from its original Roman level - thanks to what Peter Davenport describes as 'an accumulation of urban living' within a small, confined area. Even as early as 1530, John Leland had noticed that, although the wall viewed from within the town was 'of no great height to the eyes', when viewed from outside it was 'of reasonable height'. Similarly, Henry Chapman, writing in 1673, also noted that the buildings were 'mounted much higher than in former ages' with the city now standing on a 'batch' much higher than the surface outside the walls. Indeed, as citizens walked along the 'rampire' (i.e. the strip immediately inside the battlements), all they could see was the parapet and the battlements. Then as they peered over the walls, they could view the berm, the ditch and the fields beyond standing some fifteen to twenty feet below. Walking around the circuit was in fact a popular leisure pursuit during the second half of the century - so much so that the council launched a public collection in 1674 to place a rail along the walls 'for the convenience of walking'.

The City Gates

The gateways into the city were strong and well-fortified. The North or Town Gate, over which stood a figure of King Bladud, was three metres wide and four-and-a-half metres high with a smaller postern gate on each side. The statue would certainly be much in evidence by the middle of the century, because Thomas Quilly had been paid six shillings in 1637 'for painting King Bladud'. This main entrance to the town, where important visitors to the city were welcomed by the mayor and corporation, led out onto the London road. The East Gate, giving access to the mill, the river and the ferry, was by comparison quite small. A postern gate, it was a mere 2.7 metres high and 2.1 metres wide. The West Gate, which looked out across the common and meadows towards Bristol, was later described by John Collinson as 'a very large, clumsy pile of buildings'. Over the gate, he said, were 'some handsome apartments, occasionally used by divers of the Royal family and other persons of distinction in their visits to the city'.

The South Gate, which had been rebuilt in 1362, had fine statues of Edward III, Bishop Ralph of Shrewsbury and Prior John Walcote in a niche over the arch. Not far away was the Ham Gate which had given the monks direct access from their priory to their grazing land on the Ham and the Ambury. The South Gate took the traveller out across the bridge up Holloway

An artist's reconstructions of the West Gate (top) and the South Gate (bottom), based on a drawing of a 1630 Plan of Bath and published in James Tunstall's **Rambles about Bath** *(1876)*

and Beechen Cliff onto the Fosse Way. The bridge itself, supported by five stone arches, had a separate gate at the far end flanked on one side by a bear and on the other by a lion, each carved in stone. The bridge also carried at least one shop, rented in 1640 by Nicholas Long; and an oratory chapel dedicated to St Lawrence and maintained by the freemen of Bath, where travellers could pause for prayer as they set off on their journey. The gates were to survive until well into the eighteenth century. Indeed, the importance of being able to lock the gates was still strongly felt in 1693, when the corporation paid 1s 6d for 'a bag to keep the keys of the gates in'. However, the rapid expansion of the Georgian city eventually brought about the demolition of the North and South Gates in 1755 and the West Gate in 1776 as they fell victim to modernisation. The East Gate alone survives to the present day.

An engraving of 1845, showing the East Gate of the city with part of the medieval wall still attached. (By courtesy of the Victoria Art Gallery, Bath & North Somerset Council)

The City Armoury and Extra Security, 1642-46

The city had maintained a well-stocked armoury within the Guildhall from the 1570s. During the latter part of the sixteenth century, the corporation had regularly bought in stocks of bows, arrows, pikes, swords, muskets, helmets, corslets (i.e. back-and-breast plate body armour), powder and match - reflecting a gradual transition in the type of warfare being conducted. This was again demonstrated in 1621 when 'headpieces' were purchased for the musketeers. Twenty years later, they had become obsolete as musketeers sought to lighten the weight of their equipment on the field of battle. As the armoury expanded, money was also spent in 1621 on 'racks to put the pikes on' and 'pins to hang the armour on'. The strength of both the armoury and the city's defences, however, was to be severely tested during the period of the Civil War (1642-46).

As tension mounted throughout the country in 1639, Bath Council - in line with councils in many other places - did its best to safeguard its citizens from attack by 'enemies at present unknown' (or, in the words of the corporation of Worcester, simply 'by reason the times are dangerous'). A period of feverish activity to replenish the armoury within the Guildhall was therefore witnessed. The chamberlain bought new muskets, bandoliers, bullet pouches, a Spanish pike, barrels of powder and 'red cloth for the pikes'; John Gray, the city armourer, busied himself with scouring the armour and repairing two muskets belonging to individual councillors; and money was spent on beer and bread for the 'soldiers that did watch the city'. By 1641, with anxiety fed by rumour, the corporation had realised the vital importance of ensuring that the fortifications were adequate to withstand a siege. In addition to the minor repairs which were undertaken at the North, South and East Gates, they ordered a major rebuilding of the wall in the north-eastern corner of the city, near the prison. This alone cost £36 0s 0d.

Once the war had started, regular attention was paid to outer defences, internal security and weapon supply. During 1642 and 1643, all fortifications were further strengthened, especially at their weakest points. Barricades were erected outside the East and West Gates; breast work dug outside the North and South Gates; the height of the city wall raised at St James's Churchyard and considerable work undertaken on the platform at Gascoyne's Tower. All the gates were repaired - Matthew Clift was paid 'for keys and mending the locks of the city gate', new bars were made for the North and East Gates, whilst a small door was walled up at Westgate House. One of the major difficulties, of course, was to offer a measure of protection to the houses outside the North Gate in Walcot Street and Broad Street. To solve this problem, the council ordered metal chains to be made and erected across of the top of those streets. Christopher Brewer in Broad Street and Thomas Deane in Walcot Street were paid to look after the chains, which could be locked securely in position between wooden posts.

The council also decided on further improvements to its armoury. Old muskets were repaired by Gray, who was paid for 'two new locks and six new cocks and other work to the muskets'; Richard Bleckley was employed 'making staves for musket rests'; three pairs of bandoliers purchased to carry the charges of gunpowder needed by musketeers; and barrels of match, barrels of bullets and stocks of paper 'to make up powder in' placed inside the Guildhall store. Then, in 1643, the city received some 'great guns' and a large powder magazine from Sir William Waller's parliamentarian army. Men were therefore employed in 'drawing up the great guns from the bridge end' to the platform on Gascoyne's Tower, where repair work on the gun carriages was completed. The powder and shot were carried up into the Guildhall, which now housed a sizeable stock.

(below) *Bath Bridge viewed from the east, showing the gate at its southern end and the oratory chapel dedicated to St Laurence in the middle. A drawing by Bernard Lens, 1718. (By courtesy of the Victoria Art Gallery, Bath & North East Somerset Council)*

Apart from these practical improvements, the city authorities also endeavoured to increase the general state of alertness to the danger of attack. An 'extraordinary watch' was started as early as 1642 to supplement the work already being done by the regular nightly patrol. By 1643 three 'courts of guard' were in operation each night in different sectors of the city, one of them certainly based at the South Gate. Once the system had been organised, it cost the council an average of £3 10s 8d per month for 'wood, coal and candles'. Security was perhaps further strengthened by the purchase of 'a drum for the city use'. Even after the ending of the war in 1646 and the restoration of the monarchy in 1660, the corporation continued to maintain its armoury. In 1662, for instance, it authorised a major restocking of equipment with the purchase of 27 swords and scabbards, 12 pikes, 16 muskets, 16 sets of bandoliers, 27 belts and 37 pounds of powder - and, as late as the 1690s, John Ditcher was paid five shillings 'for cleansing of 8 swords and keeping them in repair for two years'.

Peace-Keeping Officers

Before the days of professional police forces and fire services, the corporation was also directly responsible in a more general way for the security of the city, its buildings and its inhabitants. Supervising the operation were two **constables**, who were elected annually by the corporation from among its own members. It was their task to supervise the team of minor peace-keeping officials - the bellman, the watchmen, the crier, the beadle and the parish constables from the three Bath parishes. Working closely with the magistrates, the constables had overall responsibility for apprehending criminals, dealing with beggars and containing public disturbances. They carried painted staves of office and, although unsalaried, had expectations of election to the profitable office of bailiff in the following year.

In peacetime, during at least the first half of the century, the gates were locked at night and the streets patrolled by a **bellman** and two watchmen. A new bell was purchased in 1636 for the bellman (John Davis), who was required by the council to call out the time and raise the alarm on sight of either fire or felon. He was therefore required 'to walk the streets of the city every night from the hours of ten of the clock at night till three in the morning in summer and from the hour of nine of the clock at

night till five in the morning in winter' for an annual salary of ten pounds a year. In his diary, Samuel Pepys described his own experience of such an officer: 'I sat up till the bellman came by with his bell, just under my window...and cried *Past one of the clock on a cold, frosty morning*'.

The **watchmen**, who accompanied the bellman, were sworn not to enter any house until their tour of duty was over, on pain of imprisonment. Although from time to time they were rewarded with gifts of beer by the

(right0 A watchman with his lantern and bell on his nightly patrol of Bath's streets. (Author's collection)

council for their pains, they had the unenviable duty of dealing with disreputable characters - not an easy task in the dark, unlit streets. Nevertheless, Daniel Defoe was scathing about the type of person typically recruited for this position: 'Our streets are so poorly watched: the watchmen for the most part decrepit, superannuated wretches, with one foot in the grave and t'other ready to follow; so feeble that a puff of breath can blow 'em down'.

News of imminent danger, as well as imminent taxation and other disasters, was broadcast locally by the **town crier**. His responsibilities, however, were far wider than this. He assisted in policing the streets, served summonses and attended the city's various courts. For this he was provided with a special 'coat and buttons' (which was regularly replaced) and paid a stipend of ten shillings 'as Crier to the Court of Record' with a further five shillings 'for ringing of the market bell' to signify the hours of trading. Meanwhile, the task of the bellman had been more clearly stated in 1662, when the council appointed George Rogers 'for the better preservation of this city from fire and any other dangers at night'. He was to receive 'a night coat' in addition to his salary. By the end of the century two bellmen were being appointed - one for night patrols and one for daytime duties - with the former largely taking over the function of the watchmen. Some temporary watchmen, however, continued to be appointed for special short-term tasks - for instance, watching the bowling green or the King's Bath when construction work was in progress - or for more traditional duties during periods of national tension (Walter Purlewent, for example, who was paid 'for watching and beer' in 1680; and Mr Short 'for watching' in 1689).

Even by 1700, regular peace-time security was still placed largely in the hands of these local officers - although the council monitored closely their performance and behaviour. John Robins, for instance, was dismissed in 1689 from his post as night watchman for insulting Alderman Baber (though he was later restored after an apology); and James Allen was dismissed in 1696 for 'being negligent in his office' of town crier. Nevertheless, in an act of compassion, the council instructed the new crier (Thomas Tovey) to pay Allen 3s 6d a week out of his salary as a form of pension 'during the corporation's pleasure'. It should be pointed out, however, that Tovey was also the beadle - so his combined salary was much greater than that of a mere crier. Indeed, during the latter part of the century there was an increasing tendency to combine the posts of beadle and crier in view of the fact that some of their duties clearly overlapped.

The **beadle**, a mayor's officer, wore a liveried coat with a laced hat and was responsible for policing the streets, dealing with vagrants and beggars, escorting prisoners to gaol and assisting the justices in court. The city's new by-laws (which had been drafted in 1646 and enacted in 1650) had dealt with the practicalities of apprehending criminals and bringing them before the magistrates. In order to encourage officers such as the beadle, whose task could be both unpleasant and dangerous, it was decreed that every person against whom a complaint was made should pay the officer, who had been sent to make the arrest, the sum of four pence for his trouble. Therefore, although the beadle was only paid a salary of six shillings a week, his office could in fact be quite lucrative. Indeed, by 1681, that council clearly thought that the job was far too lucrative, for it instructed John Russell (who then held the post) to pay two shillings a week 'out of his profits' to specified individuals who were impoverished.

Suspected felons and drunkards, who were arrested during the night, were usually secured in the small wooden '**cage**' or lockup which stood near the North Gate. This had been in use since the sixteenth century, judging by regular payments made for its repair. It was replaced by a new one from time to time - in 1695, for instance (when a carpenter was paid £6 5s 0d for making 'a wooden cage to put unruly rude people in'); and again in 1713 (when the council paid for a replacement in the market place 'for securing night walkers and other disorderly persons'). The corporation rented the cage out at four shillings a year to an individual, who presumably charged a fee for its use in return for maintaining it in good order. Like so many of the minor responsibilities in the city, this task tended to be handed down from father to son (John Deacon rented the cage in 1647, for instance; Benedict Deacon did so in the 1670s).

Convicted criminals or debtors would be housed in the city prison, which was situated in the tower of the disused church of St Mary just inside the North Gate; while those convicted of other offences would be put into the stocks, the pillory or the ducking stool. The **gaoler**, a private contractor, was appointed by the bailiffs to keep the prison clean, to detain prisoners in secure but humane conditions, to supervise visits by friends and to respond to the orders of the courts. Although he received no salary, he could make a living by charging prisoners authorised fees on both their admission and their release - as well as by accepting tips for special privileges granted. Conditions inside the prison in fact distinctly spartan with inmates provided with straw instead of beds - and a tub instead of a privy. Although the prison was cleaned and the tub emptied from time to time by workmen, a special effort was made to do so in 1693 after prisoners on trial at the Quarter Sessions had caused considerable overcrowding of the gaol and overflowing of the tub.

The city **pillory** and city **stocks** both stood outside the Guildhall and are clearly shown on John Speed's map of Bath published in 1610. They were kept in constant repair throughout the century and were used, according to the law, for the punishment of certain prescribed offences, including sex crimes. The pillory was last used in 1727, when a crowd of locals pelted a convicted brothel-keeper. César de Saussure, on a visit to England in 1725, noticed a pillory in use:

Contemporary drawings of the stocks (top - author's collection); the pillory (middle - by permission of the British Library: ref.- Bagford's Ballads, vol. 8, 51); and the ducking stool (bottom - author's collection)

The pillory is a sort of scaffold, surmounted by two strong boards, one above the other, the sufferer's neck being fixed in the aperture of the lower. The low populace, to make this punishment worse, pelts the prisoner with mud, rotten apples, dead cats and dogs - and that with such gusto and enjoyment that sufferers in some cases have been removed in a very exhausted condition.

The **ducking stool**, which stood by the river at the end of Boatstall Lane, was employed to humiliate unruly women or unfaithful wives by giving them a good ducking in the water. Consisting of an old-fashioned arm chair with six iron loops for strapping in the culprit, it was kept in good condition by the council and used periodically over the course of the seventeenth century. It remained intact until at least 1740.

Fire Fighting and Street Lighting

Fires, of course, were even more worrying than miscreants in the days when some buildings were still made of wood and many were still thatched with straw. The council had attempted to reduce the risk in 1633 by making it a condition of any new lease 'that every person that hath thatched house shall not mend his house with thatch or new thatch his house, but shall repair it with tile or slate'. Ever conscious of this hazard, it regularly invested in a supply of buckets, which were hung on hooks outside the Guildhall (though they were moved to a more central position in Stall Street during the Civil War). These copper-riveted leather buckets were only manufactured in the capital - hence the money spent in 1621 on eighteen buckets and 'carrying them from London'. A further twelve were purchased in 1632 and twenty more in 1641 - just before supplies became virtually impossible on the outbreak of civil war. Even so, Bath was noticeably less well-equipped than Gloucester, where over two hundred buckets were available by then. In an attempt to increase the number in use at the start of the eighteenth century, the council periodically made it a condition of any new lease that the applicant should supply a specified number of buckets (each marked with his name). Although the council consequently obtained sixteen by this method in 1705, thirteen in 1707 and four in 1708, it was merely following the practice which was already common in such cities as Hull and Manchester.

'Town ladders' and 'crooks' had also been provided in Bath from the late sixteenth century for use in fires, although the location of these was changed from time to time. In 1671, for instance, they were moved from the Ham Gate back to the Guildhall. Fires, however, remained a serious problem. In the days before the establishment of fire brigades, the council was forced to rely on workmen who

This drawing of 1612 illustrates fire-fighting techniques - a firehook to pull down burning timber, a chain of buckets on the ladder to extinguish the flames and the rescue of a child from a window with a rope. (Author's collection)

were in the vicinity at the time for 'quenching the fire at the *Angel* stables' in 1682 or 'extinguishing a fire' in 1685. Incidents such as these normally cost the council a good supply of beer as appreciation for the men's efforts - not to mention the twelve shillings it cost to replace the water pails lost 'at the fire' in 1692. Even this, however, was nothing compared with the anguish suffered by Elizabeth Doulton, whose house in Southgate Street was burnt to the ground in 1685.

There is little doubt that the city's fire-fighting methods badly lagged behind those in some other cities, which already enjoyed the benefit of 'fire engines'. Described by John Bates in 1634 as being 'drawn upon wheels from place to place for to quench fire among buildings', they were available in London (from the 1630s); Baintree (1634); Exeter (1652); Glasgow (1656); Hereford (1684) and both Stratford and Warwick, where 'water machines', designed by Nicholas Paris, were in use by 1685. Dunstable, too, had by then bought one of John Keeling's fire engines, which he had introduced into London during the 1670s (see illustration). Keeling was one of three fire engine manufacturers in London at the time (Goodwin Wharton and Bernard Strode being the others), who supplied engines to municipalities around the country. It was not until 1694 that Bath received its first fire engine, which was donated by two benefactors, one of whom was William Blathwayt, MP for Bath. Although it is not known which type of engine it was, there is little doubt that the arrival of this machine caused great excitement. The council paid eleven shillings to 'six men that assisted at

(below) John Keeling's fire engine, which was used in London and Dunstable and was probably quite similar to the one donated to Bath Corporation in 1694. (By courtesy of the Pepys Library, Magdalene College, Cambridge)

the unloading of the engine'; and a further two shillings to 'the helpers at the trying[of] the engine'. Sadly, they discovered shortly afterwards that costly repairs were necessary with £1 15s 0d being paid to 'Mr Axford of Bristol for new-casting the barrel of the engine'. A second machine had been added by 1713.

The task of dealing with night-time problems was made all the more difficult by the lack of any **illumination** in the narrow streets of the city. Some light at least was cast on the scene by the new lantern bought for six shillings in 1642 and erected on the front of the Guildhall - although this was frequently out of action through vandalism and was at best little more than a gesture. It was not until 1707 that the corporation took the more radical step of gaining an Act of Parliament to give it greater powers over the matter of street lighting (as well as paving and cleansing). Henceforward, every householder was required, between 14th September and 25th March each year, 'to hang out candles or lights in lanterns on the outside of their houses next the street to enlighten the same for the conveniency of passengers'. The lights were to operate between dusk and midnight. The only alternative was for the householder to agree to mount one of the ten official 'public lamps', which the corporation had purchased at public expense. These 'convex lights' (oil lamps of the type introduced into the capital by Edward Hemming in the 1680s) were bought in London in 1704 at a cost of £1 11s 0d. Guy Miège, who had seen these in use there three years earlier, commented: 'The reflection whereof is so gloriously luminous and of so long a reach that they may be called the little suns of the night'.

SOURCES USED IN CHAPTER 4

1. Printed material

Barnes, T.G: *Somerset, 1635-1640* (1961)
Blackstone, C.V: *A History of the British Fire Service* (1957)
Bath Field Club, vol. IX, pt. 4 (1901)
Chapman, Henry: *Thermae Redivivae, The City of Bath Described* (1693)
Collinson, John: *The History of Somersetshire* (1791)
Davenport, Peter: *Medieval Bath Uncovered* (2002)
Fawcett, Trevor: *Bath Administer'd. Corporation Affairs at the 18th-Century Spa* (2001)
Hill, Dennis: *Bath Fire Brigade and Ambulance Service, 1891-1974* (2003)
Leland, John: *The Itinerary of 1535-43* (ed. L.T. Smith, 1907)
Lewcun, Marek: 'The City Wall of Bath. A Current View of its Survival' (in *The Survey of Bath and District*, no. 10. October 1998)
Saussure, César de: *A Foreign View of England in the Reigns of George I and George II* (1902 edn., ed. Mme van Muyden)
Waller, Maureen: *1700: Scenes from London Life* (2000)
Warner, Richard: *The History of Bath* (1801)
Warrington, John, ed: *The Diary of Samuel Pepys* (1953)
Wood, John: *An Essay towards a Description of Bath*, 2 vol. (1765)
Wroughton, John: *A Community at War: the Civil War in Bath & North Somerset* (1992)

2. Documentary material:

Bath Record Office: Bath Chamberlain's Accounts, 1568-1734
                             Bath Council Minute Books, Nos. 1 & 2
British Library: Add.Mss., 28,273, ff 105-118, Subsidy Assessments and Other
                             Memoranda by J. Locke, 1623-1655 [re Hopton's Company]

CHAPTER 5

Life at Home

House Exteriors

A visitor arriving in Bath from the north would first pass through the impoverished Walcot suburbs, where he would notice many ramshackle hovels built mainly out of wood - although it would also be evident to him, as he neared the city, that the housing in Walcot Street and Broad Street (immediately outside the old medieval walls, where the cloth trade flourished) was of a higher standard with a mixture of timber-framed and stone buildings. Once inside the walled area, the new arrival would immediately become aware of the cobbled streets strewn with refuse, the presence of many horses and other animals and the unpleasant stench, which was at its worse during the humid summer months. A walk around the main thoroughfares - Northgate Street, Cheap Street, Westgate Street, Stall Street and Binbury - would reveal many fine stone houses packed tightly together alongside the city's numerous inns. On the other hand, in Southgate Street (which was liable to flooding) and the small lanes running off Westgate Street and Cheap Street (Bridewell Lane, Vicarage Lane and Cox Lane - now Union Street) he would notice areas containing small workshops, warehouses and less desirable accommodation.

The maps of the period show that, in spite of the initial impression of an overcrowded city, there were many undeveloped spaces, including much of the land just inside the city walls. Usually styled in the council minute books as 'the town waste', it had traditionally been reserved for the drying of cloth (after its final washing) on large racks - some of which can still be seen along Upper Borough Walls on Gilmore's map of 1694. There were also plots of land behind many of the houses, particularly visible in Walcot Street and Southgate Street, where clearly-marked narrow strips ran down to the river. Even in the centre of the city, however, similar areas were available either as paddocks for horses, chickens and pigs or as gardens for herbs and vegetables. As late as the 1680s, the council was still granting leases for 'a tenement and garden' in such widely-spread locations as Lot Lane, Southgate Street, Northgate Street, Cheap Street, Frog Lane, Broad Street, Binbury, Westgate Street and Saw Close.

After the corporation had gained control over the appointment of clergy to the three remaining Bath parishes in 1572 (see Chapter 14), it had also managed to secure control over church property within the city. Towards the end of the sixteenth

(right) A lithograph by Henry Worsley showing the High Street in 1838 - just before the complete demolition of the 17th-century houses, which had been built up to the northern wall of the Abbey. Notice the gabled houses with their mullioned windows and small leaded lights - and the smoking chimneys and open-fronted shop. (Author's collection)

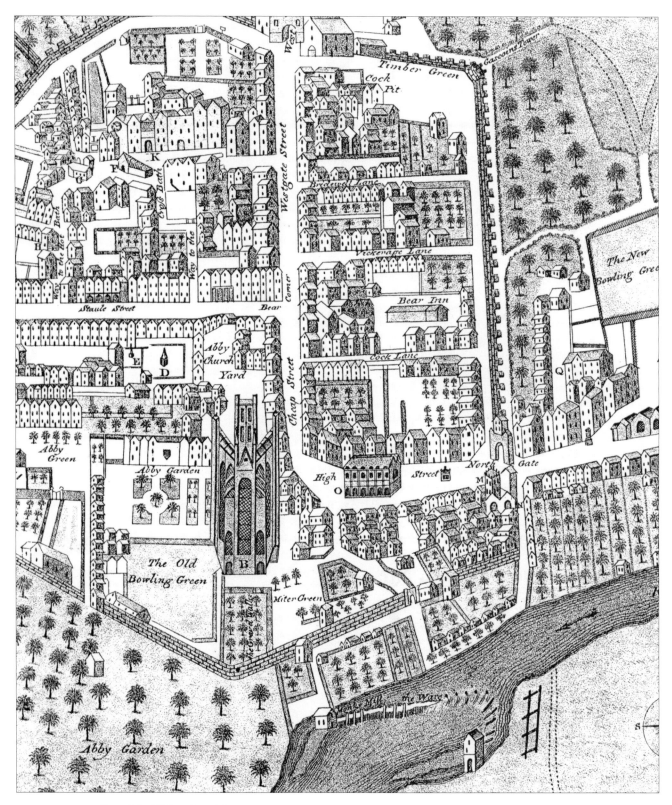

Part of the 1717 version of Joseph Gilmore's map of Bath. This demonstrates not only the houses which had been built right up to the northern wall of the Abbey, but also the open spaces which still remained for the growing of food and the keeping of animals. Note also one of the drying racks used by clothiers in the bottom right-hand corner - see Chapter 8. (Author's collection)

century, therefore, it had begun a policy of building new houses not only over the churchyard of the now-redundant church of St Mary de Stall, but also against the north wall of the Abbey. Even as late as 1648, the corporation, having previously prohibited Richard Abbott from continuing to build his house 'against the Abbey Church', agreed to grant him a 21-year lease for the same property. This whole development was later to cause great problems, because access was effectively blocked off between the Abbey Churchyard and the bowling green area (including the Gravel Walks). This resulted in the north aisle of the Abbey being used as a short cut between the two (see Chapter 15). Indeed, it was not until 1819 that the corporation resolved that no further renewal of leases would be granted for those houses, thus enabling it to commence a gradual demolition from 1823. The other area which witnessed some development early in the seventeenth century was the Abbey precinct to the south of the Abbey. Originally purchased by Matthew Colthurst after the dissolution of Bath Priory in 1639, it was sold in 1612 to John Hall (a wealthy clothier from Bradford-on-Avon), who began building new properties.

By the middle of the sixteenth century, most houses in Bath were timber-framed with wattle-and-daub walls, thatched roofs and small casement windows glazed with leaded lights (or sometimes with just hinged shutters within the frame). They were normally two stories high with the first floor jettied out over the street and the ground floor level built in stone to provide a more solid foundation. From about 1570, however, an increasing number of properties were rebuilt in stone (thanks partly to the increased affluence generated by local clothiers). Constructed in the vernacular style with gabled roofs, mullioned windows and square-headed drip mouldings, they now boasted two further signs of increased prestige - chimneys (as the more prosperous citizens made use of coal from the corporation's own mines at Paulton and Timsbury) and water pipes (which brought fresh water from the city's mains supply).

In an attempt to reduce the risk of fire, the corporation made it a condition for the renewal of any lease from 1633

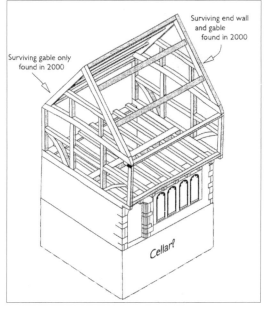

that, when the thatch on a house needed replacement, the roof was to be covered in tiles or slate. Nevertheless, many timber-framed houses survived in the city well into the seventeenth century alongside the new stone dwellings - although Samuel Pepys stressed in 1668 that the town was 'most of stone'. As pressure grew to enlarge accommodation with the development of Bath as a spa and leisure resort, householders were compelled - in view of the lack of space to expand sideways along the already crowded street frontages - to grow upwards by adding on an extra storey. Thus most of the houses depicted on Gilmore's map or Johnson's drawing of the baths are three or four storeys high.

Although at first sight little remains of these seventeenth-century buildings in a city so dominated by eighteenth-century architecture, there is - as Jean Manco has pointed out - far more than one imagines. Abbey Church House, for instance, is the same

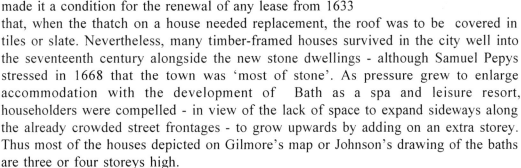

(above) A reconstruction by Peter Davenport, based on the investigations by ASI Heritage of Number 21 High Street. These revealed the remains of a timber-framed house with the ground floor built in stone.

(top left) This picture shows how the 18th-century facade of the **Bunch of Grapes** *in Westgate Street has been stuck on to an earlier building with its rubble side wall and mullioned windows; (top right) The Jacobean plasterwork ceiling on the first floor of the* **Bunch of Grapes;** *(bottom left) The fine 18th-century front of Number 2 Abbey Green; (bottom right) The rear view of Number 2 Abbey Green reveals the outline of an earlier gabled roof and the mullioned windows of its side wall. (Author's collection)*

building which Gilmore depicted on his map as 'Mrs Savil's Lodgings'. Although the house, which was rebuilt in about 1590 by Dr Robert Baker, was bombed during the Second World War, much of the Great Hall on the first floor survived, including the fine Elizabethan fireplace and wooden panelling. Harder to spot are a number of original seventeenth-century properties which lurk behind Georgian ashlar facades with their sash windows. For instance, the rubble side wall of *The Bunch of Grapes* public house in Westgate Street with its stone mullioned windows gives a hint as to what might lie inside - namely, in this case, a spectacular Jacobean plasterwork ceiling on the first floor (one of only two in Bath - the other one being situated in the clergy vestry at the Abbey). A view from the rear of Number 2 Abbey Green (which boasts an imposing mid-eighteenth-century front) not only reveals impressive mullioned windows and drip mouldings along the south side, but also the outline of its earlier gabled roof. Furthermore, on examination, the interior rear or east wall was found to be timber-framed.

Just round the corner, Sally Lunn's teashop (which was built in 1622 as part of a row of timber-framed houses) still possesses inside the low ceilings, timber-framed side wall and small-squared panelling associated with Jacobean buildings - even though its original facade was replaced during the eighteenth century. Just inside the later bow-fronted window can be seen part of the original timber-framing of the house. Perhaps more convincing still is the exterior timber-and-plaster side wall, which has been uncovered at Number 3 Broad Street. Inside the shop is an Elizabethan staircase on the first floor and decorated ceiling beams. A little further up the street (and actually *inside* Number 7) awaits the greatest surprise of all - the outer wall, window, front door and front room of a small stone cottage built in 1593 and inscribed with the initials of its leaseholder in 1640 ('M.B.' i.e. Mary Baber) . This originally formed part of a small courtyard, which was later built over to create the modern shop - with the cottage left inside!

Other buildings of interest in Broad Street include the two-storeyed *Saracen's Head*, which was built just at the end of the Stuart period in 1713; and Number 38 (built in 1709), which is four-storeyed. Both have attractive gables and the sash windows, which were becoming fashionable by the start of the eighteenth century. Green Street, which was developed between 1715 and 1720 to provide better access to the New Bowling Green, offers two good examples of late Stuart

(top) *The recently uncovered timber-and-plaster side wall of Number 3 Broad Street, which belies the impression given by its front facade;* (middle) *The front of the small stone cottage (dating from 1593), which lurks inside Number 7 Broad Street;* (bottom) *The two-storey* Saracen's Head *in Broad Street which, although built in 1713, echoed the style of 17th-century architecture.*

architecture (both with gables and sash windows - Number 3 (built in 1716) with a fine shell-hood over the doorway; and Number 14 with its four storeys. Modern excavations sometimes reveal further clues to seventeenth-century building structure, as Peter Davenport has indicated. In 2000, for instance, a timber-framed side wall on the first floor on Number 21 High Street was uncovered inside its party wall with the adjoining property.

House Interiors

Two typical items of domestic oak furniture from the second half of the century - a simple backstool, c.1680-1690 (left); and a more elaborately carved side chair, c.1680-1685. (Author's collection)

John Wood wrote in somewhat disparaging terms in the eighteenth century about the quality of **fittings and furnishings** to be found in a typical seventeenth-century house in Bath. The wooden floors, he said, were stained brown with a mixture of soot and small beer 'to hide the dirt as well as their own imperfections'; and the chimney breasts, hearths and slabs were constructed out of plain freestone (compared with the marble which became fashionable in the eighteenth century). Furthermore, they were whitewashed daily, in the course of which the brown floors were inadvertently sprayed so that they somewhat resembled 'the starry firmament'; while the furniture, bed linen and curtains were made of low-grade material, which could not compete with the fine mahogany, walnut, linen and brass on offer in Georgian Bath. It was, of course, in the interest of Wood's own reputation to denigrate the Stuart city and thereby enhance the elegance and style of the leisure resort which he had helped to create.

Nevertheless, it is true that furnishings at the beginning of the seventeenth century were plain and simple, although most of the professionals, traders and skilled craftsmen in Bath enjoyed a comfortable standard of living. The inventories of Thomas Chapman (1604) and Margaret Denison (1605), which accompanied their wills, provide ample evidence to support this theory. Thomas Chapman, a glover, occupied a house at the corner of Cheap Street and Stall Street which contained a cellar, a hall, a shop, a room over the shop and a loft. Margaret Denison, who was the widow of a fairly affluent tailor, enjoyed a two-storey house on the east side of Stall Street with a shop, a hall, a back room and a kitchen on the ground floor; and two bedrooms above the shop and the hall. Houses of this type were inevitably gloomy on the inside with small windows (the new Dutch-style sash windows not making an appearance in England until the end of the century). Consequently, people became accustomed to living in dismal conditions, especially as wax candles were expensive and the more affordable tallow variety released a distinctly odious smell. The houses were also bitterly cold. Families therefore tended to go to bed early to save the expense of both light and heat.

The kitchen in such houses would usually feature a broad-arched fireplace with - suspended over the fire - an iron or brass cauldron in which much of the cooking took place (with vegetables placed in net bags and puddings carefully tied up in cloths). Meat could also be boiled in the same container, although many housewives roasted the

joint on an iron spit (by the latter part of the century, the clockwork jack had been
invented as a labour-saving device to turn the spit). Saucepans and frying pans were
also common - although sauces and dishes requiring careful treatment were cooked in
saucepans, placed on a brandreth over a small charcoal fire on the edge of the
fireplace. In addition, the more prosperous homes would possess a small bee-hive oven
for baking bread and pies, while the majority would rely on paying for the use of a
communal oven or a baker's oven. Margaret Denison actually owned a bakehouse in
town, although by 1605 she was leasing it out to someone else. In her own kitchen she
had three cauldrons, three kettles, two skillets *[frying pans with long handles for use
over the main fire]*, two dripping pans, two pot hooks, a 'flesh hook', two chopping
knives, a brass dish and a brass mortar. Most kitchens of the time would also have an
iron fender, a pair of tongs, a poker and a shovel for use around the fire.

Dining room furniture normally consisted of an oak trestle-style table with
either benches or stools for the family to sit on. Cushions were sometimes provided for
greater comfort (Margaret Denison in fact owned nine). In spite of the fact that chairs
were fairly uncommon at the start of the century, some homes boasted at least one for
the master of the house. The table would be covered with a linen cloth and the meals
eaten off pewter plates (although wooden trenchers were still in use in some homes and
pottery dishes were also becoming available). While the food was cut up with knives
(bearing in mind the lack of forks until much later in the century) fingers also were put
to good use throughout the meal. Finger bowls were usually provided for use both
before and after the eating of the various courses. In her back room, Margaret Denison
owned a square table board, seven stools, two chairs, nine tablecloths, twenty-six
napkins, two pewter cups and eleven pewter dishes - plus 69 pounds in weight of other
pewterware. She had a second table with three benches and a small sideboard in the
room over the hall. Thomas Chapman was perhaps slightly more fashionable in this
respect because, in addition to pewter plates, dishes and basins, he owned 'eight pottery
dishes and two saucers'.

Typical **bedrooms** of the period would contain bedsteads of various designs (all but
the poorest families boasted a four-poster bed with curtains hung around for warmth)
and trucklebeds for use by children and servants. These were low beds on wheels, which

*An early 17th-century supper party. Note that the men, who wear their hats, are sitting on stools with cushions. The table is
covered with a cloth and the men are drinking out of both tankards and glasses. (By permission of the British Library: ref -
Roxburghe Ballads, RAX.Rox 1, pt. 1, 18)*

A Jacobean four-poster bed in oak with heavy curtains for warmth and a tapestry coverlet of the type owned by Margaret Denison. (By courtesy of the Museum of London)

could be pushed under the larger beds for storage as a space-saving idea. Margaret Denison owned a total of six bedsteads, two trucklebeds, two feather mattresses, four flock under-mattresses, six bolsters, nine pillows, ten pairs of sheets, four pairs of blankets, four yarn coverlets, one tapestry coverlet, five towels and three chamber pots. The latter item, made of pewter or porcelain, was sometimes placed in a portable 'close stool'. This was essentially a box with a lid, which opened to reveal a (sometimes padded) seat with a hole cut out, thus giving access to the pot on a shelf below. In larger houses, these stools could be stored in 'a house of office' just off the bedroom, although the chamberpots were normally stored downstairs in the scullery and brought up as required by servants. Those families without a close stool would simply place the chamber pot, together with a candle, next to the bed on a 'back-stool' (i.e. a stool with a back). [The term 'house of office', which was also used for public conveniences, derived from the French equivalent, *lieux d'aisances* or, simply, *lieux* - hence our modern word 'loo'.]

To make life more comfortable Margaret Denison owned one rug and eight red-and-green curtains. At the start of the century, the latter were normally used as draught excluders on doors, although later it became fashionable to use them also around windows. Even so, most were single curtains - the idea of dividing them into two halves was not generally recognised until the final quarter of the century. Although her eight candlesticks provided whatever light was needed once the sun had set, she did not possess a looking glass as her descendants probably would have done some ninety years later. Thomas Chapman, on the other hand, was the proud possessor of 'a green carpet and three cushions' - not to mention his three flower pots. His carpet was probably quite small and more like a rug, because the custom in most households of the period was to leave the oak floorboards completely uncovered. Indeed, small carpets were often placed on the tables! Larger carpets to cover much of the floor area were generally not introduced until the eighteenth century. On the other hand, the main rooms were usually furnished with oak chests (for the storage of bedding and linen), cupboards and trunks, while the walls were panelled with wainscot (which, according to Wood, was seldom painted). With the spread of new ideas on internal decor from France after 1660, this wood panelling slowly gave way in more fashionable houses to 'hangings' of cloth and tapestry - or even wallpaper.

Family Life

Family life centred in part around the dining table. Most of the citizens of Bath living in the better quality houses inside the the city walls would start the day with a breakfast of cold meat, bread, cakes and ale. Much later in the century the more affluent people would possibly treat themselves to a drink of tea (normally served weak without milk in view of its high cost), coffee or chocolate - imported respectively from China, Turkey and the West Indies. The main meal was **dinner**, which was served at midday and consisted of two or three courses. Joints of beef, pork and mutton (or, alternatively, fish) with appropriate sauces, accompanied by soups and salads, would be followed by custards, jellies, candied fruit, cheese and gingerbreads (this course often being referred to as 'the banquet'). Supper was a much lighter meal with a selection of cold meats served with bread and ale. The men in the family by custom wore their hats during the meal and smoked their pipes afterwards. On the other hand, poorer families would live on an unchanging diet of coarse brown bread, cheese, beer and the cheaper cuts of meat such as offal.

Middle class families therefore consumed great quantities of meat (often forming up to 75 per cent of each meal) - hence the bustling meat market situated in the 'butchers' shambles' just behind Northgate Street. Henri Misson, a French visitor to England in 1698 commented: 'I always heard they were great flesh eaters, and I found it true. I have known several people in England that never eat any bread and universally they eat very little. They nibble a few crumbs, while they chew the meat by whole mouthfuls'. This habit largely accounted for the high degree of suffering experienced by many in the seventeenth century from both gout and constipation. One problem facing the housewife, in the days before refrigeration, was the need to keep the meat as fresh as possible - hence the practice of putting the joint into a barrel of salt water until it was required. As Maureen Waller has pointed out, some commentators were also appalled at the lack of table manners exhibited in many homes. Misson, for instance, noted that 'belching at table...is a thing about which the English no more scruple than they do coughing and sneezing'. Hannah Woolley in 1682 besought her reader not 'to fill your mouth so full that your cheeks shall swell like a pair of Scotch bagpipes'; not to blow on your soup to cool it, 'to smack like a pig' or to pick your teeth with your knife; but rather 'to close your lips when you eat' and avoid talking 'when you have meat in your mouth'.

Vegetables and herbs were frequently grown in private back gardens - a great mixture of onions, carrots, cabbage, peas, beans and parsnips - although they were not

A family meal in the early 17th-century. Note the use of stools at table; the simple wooden bowls and plates for food; the use of spoons (not forks) for eating; the windows with leaded lights, but no curtains; and the lack of floor covering. (By permission of the British Library: ref - Roxburghe Ballads, RAX.Rox. 1, pt. 1, 228)

particularly enjoyed or appreciated as a separate dish. Consequently, they were chiefly used in the making of soups. In spite of the fact that potatoes were in theory available in England by the seventeenth century, they were still comparatively rare in everyday cooking. On the other hand, local orchards over the river in Widcombe and Lyncombe helped to keep the inhabitants of Bath well supplied with apples, pears, cherries, strawberries, plums, gooseberries and raspberries. Indeed, by the start of the Stuart period, most of the main types of food available today were already on offer in English markets.

Cookery books (such as *The Accomplisht Ladys Delight*, *The New Booke of Cookerie* and *The Compleat Cook*) were also being published to encourage the housewife to experiment with new dishes, which were sometimes flavoured with imported spices. From the middle of the century, too, a more plentiful supply of sugar was becoming available (imported from Barbados), thus enabling cooks to increase the quantity of homemade jams, biscuits, cakes and sweet deserts. 'Ah, what an excellent thing is an English pudding', wrote Henri Misson in 1698 - particularly those boiled in a pudding cloth. Most housewives would have the skill and technique to ensure that a sufficient quantity of food was preserved for consumption during the winter - including dried beans and peas, salted pork (from the pig fed by the family in the back garden) or pickled fish.

Ale and small beer provided by far the most common drinks for all members of the family, especially in view of the fact that wine was expensive and water was often contaminated (though less so in Bath - see Chapter 6). Ale was made in most homes by mixing together boiling water with malted barley and then adding yeast to bring about fermentation in the barrel. Sometimes thyme or rosemary would be added to provide extra flavour. Beer was brewed in a similar fashion, but with the additional ingredient of hops, which acted as a preservative enabling the liquid to be stored for up to two years. The same portion of malted barley would in fact be used in three successive brews - the first to produce a strong beer, the second to provide a medium strength drink and the third to create 'small beer'. The latter had a very low alcohol content and was used for everyday drinking (most people consuming at least a gallon a day). Some individuals were of course tempted to make a profit by selling their home brew to family outsiders, although this practice was strictly forbidden by Bath Corporation in 1613 on pain of a ten shillings fine for each pennyworth sold. Citizens wishing to purchase ale or beer for consumption at home were instructed to do so 'from the common brewers appointed to brew in this city'. This was often obtained in an eight-gallon firkin for storage in the house. A few years earlier, Richard Humphries had in fact been fined 5s 0d 'for selling ale without a licence' and James Appowell 2s 6d 'for brewing without a licence'. In 1641, at least three licensed brewhouses were mentioned in the survey of corporation property - John Perman's, situated behind Northgate Street, Thomas Murford's in Stall Street and the brewhouse belonging to the *Hart Inn*.

Another task undertaken by many housewives was that of providing **homemade medicines** for the family - a skill passed on from mother to daughter. In the still room, water would be distilled for use in the production of herb-based salves, infusions and syrups (as well as scented rosewater for personal washing). If mother's own treatment failed to cure the sickness, the patient would then be taken on to one of the growing number of apothecaries, surgeons and physicians - many of whom were of course associated with the hot water spa. In that sense, Bath residents were in a fortunate situation. However, their health was put at risk by the amount of pollution generated through the burning of coal in domestic fires - not to mention the smoke from kilns, soap-boilers, brewhouses and tanneries. This was, of course, a national problem. As one observer commented in London: 'a multitude of chimneys arose - and there did arise so many dusty clouds in the air as to hide the light of the sun'. John Evelyn, who visited Bath in 1654, lamented 'the horrid smoke, which fouls our clothes and corrupts our waters, spots and contaminates whatever is exposed to it'. He greatly lamented that London, 'this glorious and ancient city should wrap her stately head in clouds of smoke and sulphur, so full of stink and darkness'. Bath, too, had a growing number of chimneys.

(below) *Frontispiece from Hannah Woolley,* **The Queene-Like Closet**, *1681. Notice the cooking of delicate sauces over a small fire (top); the distillation of herbal medicines and the baking of bread (middle); the spit-roasting of meat and boiling of vegetables over a large fire - and the baking of pies (bottom). By permission of the British Library: ref- 1037.e.16.*

Personal hygiene was probably much more important in the seventeenth century than was at one time believed. It consisted in part of the frequent washing of hands and face with home-made soap, plus an occasional wash of the body using a linen cloth soaked in scented rosewater. The servant would normally carry the water and washbasin up from the scullery to the bedroom for this purpose. Teeth were cleaned simply by rubbing them with salt or the toothpaste sold by apothecaries - tooth brushes had not yet been invented. Although it was originally thought that clothes were only washed in 'the great wash' at a stream or in a large tub every two or three months, Alison Sims has shown that the Stuarts were much more particular than that. This applied especially to the linen undergarment (the shirt or chemise, as it was called), which everyone wore - garments which were regularly washed. There was of course an abundant supply of clean water for this purpose at the city conduits (see Chapter 6).

The housewife would make her own soap for use in both washing clothes and personal washing by boiling animal fat (which had been saved from the meat) with lye (a strong alkaline solution made when water or urine is passed through wood ashes). This produced 'black soap', which was like a jelly in texture. Dirty linen clothes (including bed linen as well as shirts) were carefully placed in a 'buck tub' and soaked in lye before being rinsed in clean water. They could then be made whiter after washing by using a homemade bleach consisting of a mixture of lye and lime. Drying clothes would sometimes present something of a problem in town centres, although it was common practice to spread out sheets and other bedding on bushes in the fields outside the city. It is highly probable, however, that Bath citizens would also use the ready-made drying racks erected for clothiers, which existed along the line of the city walls (see above). The housewife would then endeavour to iron the clothes as best she could. Margaret Denison owned a 'pressing iron', which would either have been the flat type, which was heated in the fire, or the hollow type, which drew its heat from a piece of red-hot coal plucked from the fire and placed inside. Tight-fitting outer garments were often kept sweet by using various scents to hide the odour of stale perspiration. Thomas Chapman listed in his 1604 inventory two shirts, an old cloak and breeches, an old gown, two petticoats, two waistcoats. He was clearly not a leader of local fashion!

Boys in a middle class family in Bath would eventually be sent to the grammar school and then possibly on to university for **careers** in the church or the professions (see Chapter 12). Otherwise they would learn a trade locally through the apprentice system (see Chapter 10). Those from less affluent homes would find employment either as labourers in the fields or as part of the large workforce needed to service the health resort as coachmen, grooms, footmen or guides. Girls, on the other hand, would receive little formal education, but would rather be taught at home by their mothers in the art of being both a housewife and a mother. Those from poorer families, after a period at home learning basic skills, would often be sent out to serve in the bigger houses as cooks, chambermaids and scullery maids. The design of city-centre houses ensured that their work was hard, involving endless use of the narrow stairs to transport coal, food, water, chamberpots and washbasins up from the basement to the family rooms above - and then to carry down the debris.

Most female servants were under twenty-five years of age - and most looked forward thereafter to a happy **marriage**. However, as Alison Sims has shown, a marriage was arranged by parents almost in the form of a business deal with the size of the girl's dowry as an important factor. Once a contract had been settled by the families and vows exchanged in front of family and friends (the 'spousals' or witnesses), it was assumed that the marriage had effectively taken place. The arrangement was therefore binding in the eyes of ecclesiastical law. It was therefore felt perfectly acceptable for the couple to sleep together from that point on - even though the actual church ceremony would probably not be scheduled until some time later. Nevertheless, the church service was still important because, in the eyes of common law, future property rights were dependent upon it.

Once married, the husband would legally own all his wife's property and other wealth. It was not usual in the seventeenth century for people to marry at a very young age - men on average did so at 27 or 28, women at 25 or 26. It is estimated that a typical family would produce three or four children, sixty-six per cent of whom survived into adult life. Under the powerful influence of Puritanism (particularly in such areas as North-East Somerset), extra-marital sex was regarded with strong disapproval. As a result, the illegitimate birth rate was low - probably no more than about three per cent. Local communities and church courts alike put considerable pressure on individuals to conform - partly, of course, because bastard children and their mothers usually turned to the parish for financial support and relief. These feelings were well demonstrated in Bath in 1618 when, amid great consternation, John Crook was paid three shillings to lead a posse of citizens in the traditional 'hue and cry' in pursuit of 'a wench that fled and left her bastard behind her'.

SOURCES USED IN CHAPTER 5

1. Printed material:

Beer, E.S.(ed.): *Memoirs Illustrative of the Life and Writings of John Evelyn* (1955 edn.)

Borsay, Peter: 'The English Urban Renaissance', 1680-1760' (in *Social History*, 1977)

Brears, Peter: *Food and Cooking in Seventeenth-Century Britain* (1985)

Davenport, Peter: *Medieval Bath Uncovered* (2002)

Erickson, Amy Louise: 'Family, Household and Community' in *The Oxford Illustrated History of Tudor & Stuart Britain* (ed. John Morrill, 1996)

Hamilton, Meg: *Bath before Beau Nash* (1978)

Hart, Roger: *English Life in the Seventeenth Century* (1970)

Hart-Davis, Adam: *What the Tudors and Stuarts did for Us* (2002)

Holland, Elizabeth: *Citizens of Bath* (1988)

James, P.R: *The Baths of Bath in the Sixteenth and Early Seventeenth Centuries* (1938)

Mainwaring, Rowland: *Annals of Bath in the Sixteenth and Early Seventeenth Centuries* (1838)

Manco, Jean: 'Bath's Lost Era' (in *Bath City Life*, Summer 1992)

Manco, Jean: *Guidelines*, no. 44 (1992)

Manco, Jean: 'Bath and the Great Rebuilding' (in *Bath History*, vol. IV, 1997)

McInnes, Angus: *The English Town, 1660-1760* (1980)

Misson, Henri: *Memoirs and Observations in His Travels over England* (1719 Eng. edn)

Neale, R.S: *Bath: A Social History, 1680-1850* (1981)

Picard, Lisa: *Restoration London* (1997)

Sims, Alison: *Pleasure and Pastimes in Tudor England* (1999)

Sims, Alison: *The Tudor Housewife* (1996)

Waller, Maureen: *1700: Scenes from London Life* (2000)

Warrington, John (ed.): *The Diary of Samuel Pepys*, vol. 3 (1953 ed.)

Wood, John: *Essay Towards a Description of Bath*, vol. 2 (1765)

Woolley, Hannah: *The Gentlewoman's Companion* (1682)

Wroughton, John: *A Community at War: the Civil War in Bath & North Somerset* (1992)

2. Documentary material:

Bath Record Office: Bath Chamberlain's Accounts, 1568-1734

                                        Bath Council Books, Nos. 1, 2 & 3 (1631-1715)

                                        Furman Bundle 18 (10): Inventory of Thomas Chapman, 1604

CHAPTER 6

Public Health

Faced with the task of marketing Bath as a nationally famous spa, the corporation became increasingly conscious throughout the seventeenth century of the need to maintain a healthy image for the city. There were three crucial areas which needed attention - the safe disposal of refuse and sewage; the establishment of a reliable supply of clean drinking water; and the control of any deadly disease which could rapidly spread within the narrow confines of a walled city.

The Cleaning of Streets

At the beginning of the century, the condition of the streets was appalling. Foul-smelling rubbish accumulated on every footpath to rot away slowly in the still and humid air of Bath. The open channel or culvert, which ran down the centre of the main streets, was often blocked by ashes, rubble and other unpleasant debris, while horses, cattle and other animals (often on their way to market) left behind them a trail of manure and urine. Although the city's revised charter of 1590 had given the corporation powers to make by-laws over such matters as street cleaning, it was not until 1646 that these were taken up. During the first half of the century, therefore, the streets were only cleaned at very irregular intervals. Payments were made occasionally by the chamberlain for 'shovelling up the dirt in Westgate Street', 'cleansing the way by the Bridge', or 'cleansing the way by the borough walls'. Even as late as 1654, John Evelyn described the streets as 'narrow, uneven, and unpleasant'.

However, Samuel Pepys, writing after a visit in 1668, seemed to hint at a radical improvement when he referred to the town as being 'clean, though the streets generally narrow'. Nevertheless, all the evidence suggests that the street-cleaning operation remained totally unsystematic throughout the century with the Corporation responding either to a particular crisis of accumulated filth (e.g. 'cleansing Cox Lane and Vicarage Lane' in 1672; and 'shovelling at the Borough Walls' in 1682) or to a

visit by a distinguished guest (e.g. 'cleaning Southgate when the Queen came' in 1687). Earlier, in 1602, the corporation had found itself in a state of undisguised panic when rumours swept the city of an impending visit by Queen Elizabeth. The streets were in such a deplorable state that messengers were urgently dispatched to Tetbury, Cirencester, Frome, Bristol, Sodbury, Warminster and Chippenham 'to get paviours against the Queen's coming'. Emergency repairs were then quickly undertaken by these experienced reinforcements in both High Street and Westgate Street - although the rumours eventually proved to be false!

(left) *A contemporary drawing, which shows workmen on their way to repair the streets.*
(By permission of the British Library: ref - Roxburghe Ballads, RAX.Rox. II, pt. 2.383)

However, as the century progressed, the streets were normally well cobbled and kept in reasonable repair - a fact which undoubtedly aided the cleaning process. Sometimes it was only a matter of employing workmen 'for mending the highway at Holloway' or for 'pitching at Southgate', although occasionally whole stretches of road were completely remade. In 1648, for instance, the council resurfaced 268 yards of Westgate Street and 'under the gate', a task which required thirty-four loads of stone. Fourteen loads of 'rubbish stone' were carted away by the workers who spent in all a week on the job. There were no pavements as such until one was specially laid in front of the new shops on the edge of the Gravel Walks between 1702 and 1705. Previously the area intended for pedestrians at the side of the road had simply been marked out with a series of wooden posts (see the drawing of the High Street by Edward Eyre in Chapter 2).

As early as 1633 the corporation had tried to impose standards of behaviour on its citizens in relation to the streets, particularly over the matter of the drainage channels. Councillors therefore ruled that 'everyone that doth sweep the street before their doors and put it [i.e. the dirt] into the channel shall pay 12d for each offence'. The measure met with limited success. However, the new by-laws, which came into force in 1650 (having been first drafted in 1646), made a determined effort to tighten up on a number of abuses, which had crept in over the course of time. The householder was henceforward strictly forbidden to throw 'any soil, dung or filth in or near any open street, which shall be offensive to such street'. He was also required 'to sweep and make clean the street before his house every Saturday morning' or face a one shilling fine for neglect. Fines were to be put towards the cost of repairing and cleansing the streets. Then, in order to reduce the amount of animal droppings, the city's first-ever parking restriction was introduced. No-one from henceforth was 'to tie or feed, or suffer any kind of beast to stand in any of the said streets above the space of one quarter of an hour'.

A few years earlier (in 1631), Dr Edward Jordan had observed that 'the butchers dressed their meat at their own doors, while pigs wallow in the mire' and that the streets were no more than 'dung hills, slaughter houses and pig sties'. Indeed, in the same year, after complaints about the problem of pigs, three councillors were detailed 'to view the annoyances in Mr Cox's garden next the [butchers'] shambles'. Two years later, when Cox was in the process of renewing his lease, the corporation actually made it a condition that he was 'to remove his pigsties'. The by-laws therefore attempted to tackle the whole question of hygiene in the preparation of food, aiming to prevent butchers from adding to the filthy state of the streets and to ensure that only meat in good condition reached the market. Part of the problem was that cattle and sheep were often brought into Bath 'on the hoof' for slaughter by butchers in the spaces behind and around their shops. This practice not only contributed to the general stench, but also added to the whole question of waste disposal.

It was consequently stipulated in the new by-laws that 'no butcher should kill any calf, sheep, swine or any other cattle in any of the open streets, nor hang out any flesh newly killed so as to soil or annoy the said streets'. Furthermore, pig owners were strictly banned from allowing their animals to wander around the streets in search of discarded waste - a practice which had clearly been prevalent before. In an age long before refrigeration, the corporation also imposed restrictions on the sale of pork and mutton during the hottest months of the year. Fines for all these food offences were to be devoted to the care of the poor. Nevertheless, John Wood was to claim in 1765 that, even at the end of the seventeenth century, the streets were still the same as

Jordan had described them with pigs foraging for scraps and horses being fed 'at almost every door from small racks or mangers'.

The existing health regulations were somewhat strengthened by a resolution of the council in 1663, which also tackled the problem of children's behaviour in the streets. Anyone in future who did 'lay or deposit any manner of coal, ashes, dirt or soil whatsoever in any of the streets, lanes or ways within the city, or let forth their child or children to do their easement or ordure [i.e. excrement] in any of the streets' would be liable to a fine of 3s 4d (with half going to the informer and half to the poor). There is some evidence that this tougher line was implemented. In 1677, for instance, the council ruled that Edward Taylor was to be prosecuted for establishing his own 'mixon' or rubbish dump 'in the highway'; while in 1683 the borough Quarter Sessions ordered Richard Edgill 'to carry away the soil and horse dung' that he had dumped in the Outer Bowling Green - or face a fine of ten shillings. Air quality was also important in a health resort - hence a decision by the council in 1698 to prosecute Thomas Rosewell 'for the nuisance to this city' caused by his lime kiln; or an earlier ruling in 1646 that 'no inhabitant was to brew or dry malt by night between nine o'clock at night and four o'clock in the morning or light any fire' on pain of a five shilling fine. Pollution, however, remained a serious problem, thanks in part to the work of the tanners, chandlers and soap-boilers - in addition to the brewers and lime-kiln operators.

(above) *A contemporary drawing of a typical street scene. Note the piles of refuse, which the scavenger is belatedly loading into his cart; the central drainage channel, which has become an open sewer; the child using the street as a toilet; a pig wallowing in the dirt; and the chamber pot being emptied out of a first-floor window. (By permission of the British Library: ref - Roxburghe Ballads, RAX.Rox. I, pt. 2.547)*

Nevertheless, in spite of the efforts of the corporation to improve cleanliness within the city, corrective action still tended to be just as irregular and spasmodic at the end of the century as it had always been. Indeed, it was not until 1707 that the corporation, after many complaints from visitors to the spa, gained an Act of

Parliament giving them authority 'to pave, cleanse and light the streets and lanes of the town' in a systematic manner. In particular, the Act enabled the mayor and justices to appoint 'surveyors of the streets' in each parish 'to have the care of the cleansing of the said streets'. Furthermore, it required every householder to sweep the street in front of his house three times a week (on Tuesday, Thursday and Saturday) in readiness for a collection by the scavenger. In addition, the citizen was strictly forbidden to throw any filth, rubbish or dung into the streets, but to keep it inside his house or yard until the scavenger's visit. Of even greater significance was the stipulation that each householder would on occasions be directed 'to pitch or pave' the street in front of his house up to the middle of the road. Failure to comply with any of these regulations would result in a fine ranging from 3s 4d to 10s 0d.

Bath High Street in 1650, illustrating the general squalor of the streets with accumulated filth being collected by the scavenger, animals wandering freely, cobbles being replaced at random and beggars menacing the citizens. (An original painting by Shane Feeney)

The Disposal of 'Night Soil'

The sanitary arrangements were probably no better and no worse than in most cities at this time. Some of the people living in Southgate Street had privies at the bottom of their gardens, which drained into Bum Ditch (see below). These can clearly be seen on Joseph Gilmore's map of Bath in 1694. Most of the people who lived in the more cramped conditions inside the city walls would have been far less fortunate, being faced by a serious problem over waste disposal. If they had no space in a back garden or yard to site an earth closet and cesspit, they would be obliged to rely on the use of chamber pots and close stools (see Chapter 5). The servants would often dispose of the contents of these receptacles by emptying them into the channel in the middle of the street, where they were churned up with other refuse by passing traffic. The more idle servants would simply threw the contents out of an upper floor window - hence the fact that pedestrians tried hard (or even struggled forcefully) to walk as close as possible to the walls of houses under cover of the overhanging storeys above. Samuel

(below) A section of Joseph Gilmore's map of 1694, which shows thirteen individual privies situated at the bottom of gardens belonging to the houses in Southgate Street. These drained into Bum Ditch, which itself drained into the river. (Author's collection)

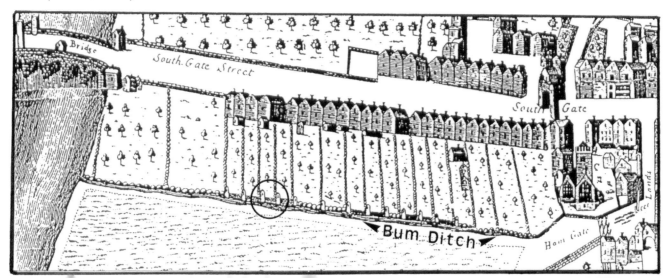

Pepys describes in his diary for 1664 how two men, who were 'jostling for the wall' in a London street, killed each other in a furious brawl over this issue. [As there was no toilet paper in the seventeenth century, ordinary folk would be obliged to rely on bundles of grass, moss or leaves.]

The alternative, which was taken in some houses, was to store the sewage into a vault in the basement. However, vaults such as these - and cess pits, too - needed to be cleared periodically by digging out the contents - an unpleasant task undertaken by 'night-soil men'. Failure to do so could often bring unfortunate consequences. Pepys, for instance, describes how the vault in his neighbour's cellar in London had not been emptied on a regular basis with the result that the contents overflowed into his own basement. Going there one day, he stepped 'into a great heap of turds', which alerted him to the fact that 'Mr Turner's house of office is full'. It had been usual practice in many towns for this dung or 'night soil' (as it was called) to be dumped haphazardly outside the city or flung into the river, either by individuals or by the night-soil men themselves.

Such behaviour was however banned by the Bath Council in 1613, when a **scavenger** was appointed to collect the refuse. Consequently, each citizen was ordered to 'send his dust [i.e. sewage] to the scavenger's cart ... in some vessel to be emptied into the said cart'. The scavenger then carried this refuse outside the city, where it was mainly deposited in mixons (or rubbish dumps) outside the South and West Gates - although there was also one outside both the East Gate in 1634 and the Ham Gate in 1615. This situation undoubtedly contributed to the stench which so upset visitors to the city in summer. In a determined effort to enforce this new order, the corporation instructed the beadle and each tithingman within his tithing (or sector) to inspect each week 'the common annoyance of casting of soil over the town walls'. They were then to present a list of offenders to the town clerk each Monday for punishment in court.

A drawing taken from a leaflet advertising the services of a 'Night Man' or Scavenger in London, who specialised in emptying 'cesspools'. It shows the two men carrying out of the house a large tub of sewage, which has been dug out of the pit. It is then tipped into a cart capable of holding 'two tons'. (By courtesy of the Museum of London)

As the century progressed, other locations were also used for the disposal of night soil. In 1632, for instance, the new 'scavenger of the common' (to give him his full title) was instructed 'to collect soil in the city and suburbs and to spread it on the common according to the overseers' orders'. Even so, no consistent policy seems to have prevailed. In 1689, for instance, the council paid workmen for 'cleansing the soil abroad in the town'; and in 1685 for 'throwing soil over the borough walls'. At least they no longer threw it into the Avon, where water-borne diseases such as typhoid could thrive amid the pollution. It should also be remembered that the spread of germs from sewage was largely responsible for the high mortality rate in infancy (with possibly one in five babies dying in the first few months - many from diarrhoea).

In order to limit the scale of this problem, the corporation had built 'a common privy' or **public convenience** in 1575, paying a labourer for 'digging a dyke' *[ditch]*, constructing a timber frame and tiling the roof. In 1623, 'a house of office' (or public convenience) was built near the Ham Gate, situated over the stream which eventually ran into Bum Ditch. Payments were occasionally made thereafter for 'cleansing the Ham privy' - but whether this was abused by vandals or merely over-used by visitors, the chamberlain sealed its fate in 1636 by paying money for 'walling up the privy door and 2 sacks of lime'. However, other such conveniences were established from time to time - such as 'a house of ease' (also called 'the house of office') at the bowling green in 1681. Examples of these public privies found elsewhere suggest that they usually consisted of an oak bench with a row of holes (but with no partitions between) and a pit below. Those detained in the tower of the former church of St Mary's by the North Gate were not so lucky and were forced to endure even more primitive conditions when the corporation purchased 'a tub for the prisoners' easement' in 1685. At least they were spared the modern-day task of 'slopping out', for Michael Holder was regularly paid for 'emptying the tub in the prison'. A great step forward was made in 1707 when a more elegant-sounding convenience - a 'pass house for the use of ladies frequenting this city' - was erected near the Abbey.

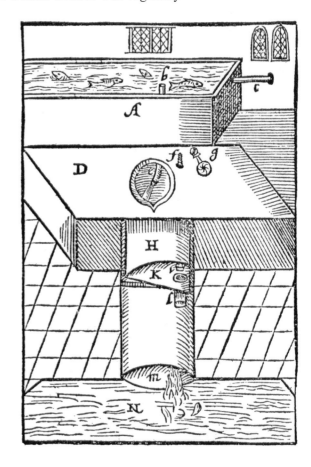

In this connection it is worth mentioning that a local man, Sir John Harington of Kelston (who also owned a town house in Bath), had already invented a flushing toilet in 1596 and had issued a do-it-yourself manual for others to follow his example. No-one did. A contemporary, who was present when the device was demonstrated, described how it worked:

(above) *Sir John Harington, 1590-1654* ; (right) *Sir John Harington's design for a flushing toilet from his book,* **The Metamorphosis of Ajax** *(1591).*
A = the cistern; D = the seat; H = the 'stool pot'; and M, N = 'the vault into which it falls'. In his key, Harington adds: 'always remember that at noon and at night, empty the vault and leave it half a foot deep in fair water. And this being well done, and orderly kept, your worst privy may be as sweet as your best chamber'. (Author's collection)

A man I met at Raleigh's, John Harington, Bess's *[Queen Elizabeth's]* godson, had invented a privy that could be drained by water. You pulled a little handle and water gushed from a cistern above. He had scented water for the ladies. But people won't be clean. They think he's mad or merely dirty-minded

Harington, who installed one of these toilets in his own house at Kelston, was somewhat obsessed with cleanliness. In his book, *The Metamorphosis of Ajax*, he wrote in detail about 'how unsavoury places may be made sweet, noisome places may be made wholesome, filthy places made cleanly'. The reality, however, was that Bath - like all other cities - suffered from a persistent and highly unpleasant stench, made worse of course by its high level of humidity and its location in a hollow. One French visitor put it like this: 'Bath, situated - or rather buried - in deep valleys in the middle of a thick atmosphere and a sulphureous fog, is at the gates of Hell'. Even as late as 1716, the Duchess of Marlborough complained: 'I never saw any place abroad that had more stinks and dirt in it than Bath'. Daniel Defoe was much more specific after a visit to the city in 1722. Bath, he said, 'was more like a prison than a place of diversion; scarce gives the company any room to converse out of the smell of their own excrements, and where the city itself may be said to stink like a general common-shore'. As a result, the corporation - ever conscious of the city's reputation as a health resort - always did its best to ensure that a good stock of sweet-smelling herbs was available for the personal use royal visitors (e.g. James II in 1686; his queen, Mary of Modena in 1687; and Princess Anne in 1692).

The Water Supply

Bath had one vital asset which helped to protect its citizens from the terrible hazards to health which affected most cities at the time - an abundant supply of fresh water. Even as early as 1530 John Leland had noticed on a visit that Bath 'is environed on every side with great hills, out of the which come many springs of pure water, that be conveyed by divers ways to serve the city. Insomuch that, lead being made there at hand *[i.e. on the Mendips]*, many houses in the town have pipes of lead to convey water from place to place'. This remarkable situation meant that Bath was never obliged to rely on the polluted waters of the Avon and thus was able to maintain its reputation as a healthy place (unlike Bristol, for instance, where typhoid and plague from the rat-infested port frequently swept through its densely-packed population).

The city drew its water from two springs - the 'upper water' on Beacon Hill drawn from St Swithin's Well (which had been granted to the corporation in 1552 as trustee of the endowment of King Edward's School); and the 'lower water' on Beechen Cliff (for which a rent was paid to the Bruton almshouse, owner the site). The water was carried down into the city by a variety of underground lead pipes and stone watercourses. Even wooden pipes seem to have been used in Walcot Lane, which were similar in design to those on display in Gloucester (see photograph). The pipes were each ten feet long, made from elm tree logs and bored out using successively larger iron auger bits. They were then fixed together by cone-and-socket joints, reinforced with iron bands and sealed with tallow. However, the system was not without its problems. All the various pipes tended to leak and therefore required constant attention and repair. Furthermore, the supply was not constant - a situation which forced some householders to store the water in cisterns down in the cellars. Consequently, the water they used was not always strictly fresh.

The council, which was responsible for the system, made frequent spasmodic payments for such items as 'mending water course at Becknall', 'mending the pipes at Walcot', 'opening the ground in Blind Lane to mend the pipes' etc. As the expense involved in this was considerable, the council started a more systematic policy from 1647 by employing a plumber under contract to maintain and service a specific part of the network. Thomas Burford was therefore paid £2 a year to look after the important watercourse from Beechen Cliff to Southgate. By 1664, this idea had been extended with William Aldington receiving £12 a year for controlling the more extensive array of pipes leading from the upper water . However the council, which was by then heavily in debt, decided to reduce its own costs by reaching a deal with the plumber. If Aldington agreed to surrender his pay and at the same time to continue repairing the pipes, he would be granted the right to sell any 'surplus water' directly to private houses. This would be done by installing lead 'feathers' (or small-bore branch pipes) taken from the corporations's mains. Aldington agreed.

However, serious problems with the new system quickly emerged. After many complaints in 1667 that the supply of water at the public drinking fountains had become unreliable 'by reason of the many feathers', the council immediately ordered the feathers to be cut off - and when, in the following year they appointed William Aldington, junior, to succeed his father as plumber, it reverted to its old policy. Aldington would be paid £11 a year - and the council would control the sale of feathers at an annual charge of ten shillings. The problem, however, would not go away and, during the 1670s, feathers were always liable to be cut off in various sectors of the city in an

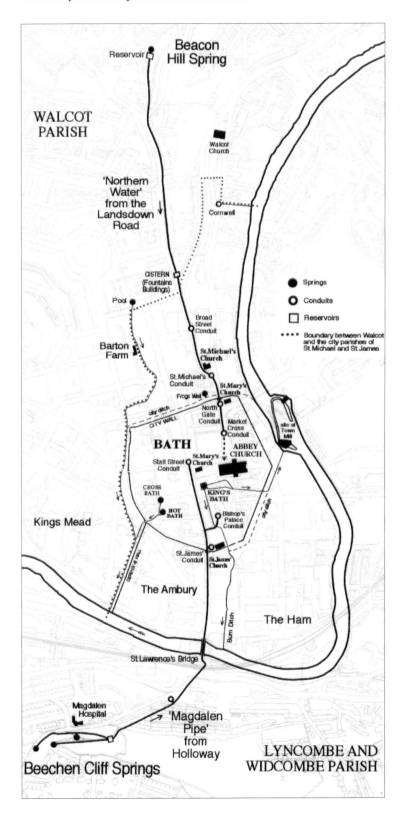

(below) *A map by Mike Chapman to illustrate the system of water supply in Bath during the seventeenth century. Spring water from the two sources (the upper or northern water on Beacon Hill and the lower or southern water on Beechen Cliff) was carried in underground pipes to the various conduits or drinking fountains in the city. Note also the drains, which carried away waste water from the baths into the river.*

attempt to maintain pressure elsewhere.

By 1676, the council had confirmed its own permanent control of the feathers by appointing two new plumbers - one to service the upper water for £12 a year and the other to look after the lower water for £2. Twenty years later, an historic decision was taken in council that 'every person shall have the water in their houses' - members of the corporation to pay five shillings a year for the privilege and other people ten shillings! It is worth remembering, however, that that whereas Bath had had a piped water supply to individual houses by the time of Leland's visit in 1530, York had no permanent system until the later 1670s, Bristol until the 1690s and Liverpool until 1720. In London, on the other hand, Hugh Middleton had constructed a 'New River' in 1609 to bring water from a spring in Hertfordshire (thirty-eight miles away) to a reservoir in Islington. This served 30,000 London homes.

People who could not afford the luxury of their own piped supply were able to obtain fresh water from several conduits or **drinking fountains** erected at points around the city. These were often lavishly decorated with elegant stone work. St Mary's Conduit stood in the middle of the High Street in front of St Mary's Church just inside the North Gate. It was, according to John Collinson, 'a handsome quadrangular reservoir of water, built in the Dorick Style and decorated with pinnacles at the angles'. The mayor and corporation traditionally made their grand processions to this conduit, which famously ran with claret wine in 1661 (when the city celebrated the coronation of Charles II). Not far away, near the Market Hall and the Abbey, was the High Cross Conduit (or the Conduit of St Peter and St Paul), which was actually built in the form of a cross. Stall's Conduit was placed on Bear Corner at the junction of Cheap Street with Stall Street. At the end of this street, just outside the South Gate, was St James's Conduit which was supplied by the lower water. St Michael's Conduit was situated outside the North Gate near the church. Its tower was crowned with an hour glass and water gushed out on all four sides of its base. Around the corner stood the Broad Street Conduit in the middle of the street and the Carnwell Conduit in Walcot Street 'within an alcove surmounted by a lofty turret of Gothic workmanship'.

The new by-laws of 1646 acknowledged the vital importance of maintaining the cleanliness of these conduits by tightening up on abuses which had gradually crept in. Citizens were therefore banned in future from watering their horses and other animals there or allowing them to come within twenty feet of the conduits (although

(above) *A section of a 17th-century wooden water main found in Gloucester and similar to that used in Bath. Lead branch pipes (or feathers) supplied individual houses from the main. By courtesy of the Gloucester Folk Museum;* (left) *Two of the public conduits or water fountains illustrated on Joseph Gilmore's map of Bath in 1694 - one situated outside the North Gate and the other in the centre of the High Street. (Author's collection)*

this regulation had lapsed somewhat by 1693, when a horse trough was erected 'at the conduit' at a cost of seven shillings). The inhabitants were also forbidden, on pain of a shilling fine, from laundering their clothes or washing 'any other noisome or unfit thing' there. Previously it had almost become customary for housewives to take their tubs of family washing to the fountains, although this practice had always been frowned upon by the corporation. There had been, for instance, a short-lived purge in 1630 when both Widow Godwin and Jane Long had each been fined one shilling 'for washing at the pipe' *[the conduit]* - and George Goldsmith a similar sum 'for washing at his door'. By the end of the century - with an increase in the supply of water to private houses together with the need to widen streets - the elaborate stone structures of the conduits gradually disappeared. John Wood lamented in his description of Bath in the next century that many had been reduced 'to a single cock for water' fixed to a neighbouring wall. They had all disappeared by 1755.

There was one further problem - namely, the **drainage of waste water** from individual properties. In medieval times (as Peter Davenport has shown), a drain had been constructed to remove excess water from the King's Bath, taking it under the city wall to turn the Isabel Mill (dating from 1135) by the Ham Gate before it disgorged into Bum Ditch. The latter was in effect an open sewer, which ran behind the gardens of the houses in Southgate Street and into the river Avon near the bridge. Householders nearby were occasionally permitted to install their own drains, taking their water through holes in the city wall and into Bum Ditch. One other main system had been established in medieval times to convey the large amount of waste water from the Priory eastwards through a covered drain and under the city wall, where it fed into an open watercourse before feeding into the river near Monks' Mill.

However, in the seventeenth century, very few private houses enjoyed the luxury of a plumbed-in drain for the disposal of waste water. Furthermore, in view of the cramped nature of their premises and the lack of sizeable gardens inside the city wall, it was virtually impossible for the majority of citizens in Bath to establish 'sinks' (or stone-lined drainage holes) outside their homes - as was often the case in the countryside. Most people were therefore obliged to rely on the open channels (or 'kennels'), which ran down the middle of the main streets, for the removal of waste.

This accounts for the preference of most housewives (until this behaviour was finally prohibited in 1650) to do their washing outside in the streets near one of the conduits - a practice which also saved them burdensome task of carrying water into the house. It was not until 1718 that the first proper sewer was constructed. Built privately by Thomas Atwood and Walter Chapman, it served the area around the Gravel Walks taking away both surplus water and sewage from the adjacent 'house of ease'. By the 1720s, Bath residents in some parts of the city were able to pay an annual fee for the privilege of having their homes connected to a main sewer.

(right) *The conduits were used by those householders, who did not enjoy the luxury of their own piped supply for cooking and washing. Until the practice was banned by the new by-laws of 1650, many people also watered their horses there. (Drawing by Stephen Beck)*

Control of Disease

There is no doubt that Bath Corporation adopted a most responsible policy towards
maintaining the health of the local community. It gradually set tight controls over the
cleanliness of the city, the disposal of night soil and the purity of its water supply.
With all its public drinking fountains fed by clear spring water and a well at the North
Gate (which safeguarded the city's supply during time of siege), Bath was spared many
of the anxieties and problems over health which affected most cities at this time.
Health hazards in Worcester, for instance, were alarming with the river constantly
polluted from the dyers' vats as well as refuse of all kinds. Outbreaks of bubonic plague
- the scourge of most towns - were also frequent. Norwich suffered six epidemics
between 1579 and 1665; Bristol lost a sixth of its population on three occasions
between 1565 and 1603; Newcastle witnessed a mortality rate of a third during the
epidemic of 1636-7; and over two thousand died in Chester during the attack of 1647.

The filthy streets and densely-packed houses of the large cities provided an ideal
environment for the black rats on which the infection-bearing fleas bred. Although
bubonic plague was in itself a disease of rats, when the host rat died the infected fleas
attacked humans (if another rat could not be found). As Roger Rolls has pointed out,
the disease - indicated by swollen lymph glands (buboes) in the neck, groin and armpits,
a high fever, delirium and red blotches all over the skin - was highly infectious. Bath by
comparison remained largely immune from threats of this kind within the community.
Its main problem was to ensure that a city, which actively encouraged visitors to flock
in numbers to sample its healing waters, did not at the same time encourage the
importation of plague. Precautions, however, did not always work. Sir Thomas
Seymour, for instance, admitted in 1605 that - as the plague had struck down two
people in his house in London - he had forsaken the capital and was living in Bath. In
an attempt to counter this unwelcome form of intrusion, the corporation had (as early
as 1583) paid two watchmen, Oliver and Green, 'for seeing that none should come into
the city from Paulton and other places which were infected with the plague'.

A much more serious crisis, however, arose in 1604 when the plague actually
struck inside the city. The extent of this is graphically described in a number of letters
to Robert Cecil, James I's Secretary of State, who was planning a visit to the baths to
gain relief from his chronic ailments. Dr John Sherwood, a leading physician at the spa,
advised Cecil to delay his visit until the plague had passed its peak. By 21st July, he
said, twenty-six people had died and seven or eight houses in various parts of the city
had become infected. Revised figures were given in August by Captain John Winter of
Dyrham in a further letter to Cecil. He reported that, although fifty people had died
between 6th May (when the epidemic began) and 18th August, the disease was by then
confined to four houses, including the *White Swan* in Westgate Street (where two
people lay sick and a further six had already died). Winter, however, was forced to
admit in September that a further three houses had become infected, although much of
the city was by then completely clear.

Cecil in fact decided in the end to postpone his visit. Although Sherwood had
given the Secretary of State an honest assessment of the situation at the end of August
(seventy-two dead and twenty-four houses infected), many local people were furious
with him for discouraging the visit of such an eminent person - someone who could
have used his influence 'to renew their old charter with more immunities'. Sherwood
was disgusted at such selfish attitudes, which failed to heed 'the health and safety of
others' - especially when it later transpired that one of Cecil's own cooks, who would

(below) The frontispiece of John Taylor's book, The Fearfull Summer *(1636 edition), in which he describes the suffering experienced in London and other cities from outbreaks of the bubonic plague. Note in the picture the portrayal of death; the woman (bottom left) with the tell-tale blotches on her skin; and the people on the right who are prevented from fleeing elsewhere by armed soldiers. (By permission of the British Library: ref - c30.d.31)*

The Fearefull Summer:

OR,

Londons Calamitie, The Countries Difcour-tefie, And both their Miferie.

Printed by Authoritie in *Oxford*, in the laft great Infection of the Plague, 1625. And now reprinted with fome Editions, concerning this prefent yeere, 1636.

With fome mention of the grievous and afflicted eftate of the famous Towne of New-Caftle upon Tine, with fome other vifited Townes of this Kingdome.

By IOHN TAYLOR.

have been preparing his food in Bath, had been staying in one of the newly-infected houses. The prospect of this, commented Sherwood to Cecil later, was 'a thing of terror to those that truly love you'. On occasions, therefore, commercial interest could even cloud the judgment of a city so totally committed to the health of its community.

In human terms, the impact of this outbreak is vividly illustrated by a bill of mortality for the city dated 20th September. This revealed that no fewer than eighty-eight people had died within the city during the four months from the middle of May - including seventy-two 'of the plague', eleven 'by the ordinary visitation of God' and five whose deaths were 'uncertain'. These deaths were in stark contrast to the average *annual* death rate for Bath of just fifty-four during the period 1603-1620 . The plague victims (who mostly lived in the parishes of the Abbey and St James) included eight people each from the houses of Goodwife Moore and John Adye; eight from the *Swan Inn*; five from the home of Dr Richard Bayly; and four from Walter Misam's house. In addition eight people, who had been 'carried from the town' in a sick condition, eventually died of the plague in the specially built 'pest house' on the common. Nevertheless, although Bath seems to have escaped quite lightly (unlike Bristol which lost over 2,000 victims during the same epidemic), such was the anxiety within the city that even many of the doctors had moved away in fear. Lord Zouche, in a letter to the Secretary of State (Lord Cecil) at the end of July, commented that he had been informed that 'the sickness is at the Bath dispersed so much as the physicians be fled from thence'. A week earlier, Dr John Sherwood (one of the city's most reputable physicians) had admitted in a letter that he was actually writing from Tockington 'where, for preventing the worst, I have for a time reposed my poor family'.

Disturbing stories often reached the ears of the corporation and terrified many local people as rumours abounded. In 1625 and 1626, when plague again threatened the area, one local observer commented: 'The contagious sickness did so much affright the inhabitants of Widcombe that they were fearful to come into other people's company'. It was at a time when cities throughout the country were again being devastated by the disease - thousands died in Exeter, while 20 per cent of the population were swept away in both Norwich and London. It was hardly surprising, therefore, that alarming news quickly spread from Frome of a man called Phillips, who had returned from London with his wife and child, having been exposed to the 'infection of the plague'. The authorities in Frome ordered them to be locked up in a house outside the town and placed under strong guard at the door. This remained in position until the family eventually died.

Bath did not escape completely from this outbreak, although the numbers affected never reached major epidemic proportions. Under the circumstances, the corporation felt impelled to take decisive action by again isolating those who were ill by building three special houses 'for the sick folks' on the common - but also showed a little more compassion than was shown in Frome by ensuring that they were kept well supplied with food (at a cost of £13 1s 8d). When the crisis was over, workmen were paid for dismantling the temporary buildings and, in the words of the council minute, 'bringing the pest-houses home' (presumably for use on a future occasion). The burial registers show that, whereas the parish of St James remained largely unaffected, the parish of St Michael's took the brunt of the distress. In just four months (February to May, 1626) there were thirty-one burials (almost twice the annual average for that decade) - including those of Walter Robence and four of his children; and four sons of John Fowler. On the other hand, the Abbey parish (with thirty-three burials in 1625 as opposed to a normal average of twenty-three) suffered by far the most traumatic experience when Edmund Tucker lost his wife, his two sons and two daughters; and James Smith lost his five daughters and two sons. In all probability, the four families mentioned above were among those billeted in the 'pest-houses' on the common.

The year 1635 witnessed another distressing outbreak of disease in Bath - a disease which particularly affected children living in the parishes of St Michael's and the Abbey. A clue to the nature of this illness is given in Sir William Brereton's account of his visit to the city in the July of that year where, he said, 'the **smallpox** had raged exceedingly'. The problem was most acute in St Michael's where twenty-four children died in nine months from July 1635 to March 1636 - against an annual *total* average (including adults) of just eighteen for that particular decade. The Allins lost three children, while the Sherstons, the Englands and the Lockwoods each lost two. Families living in the Abbey parish lost twenty-five children during a sixth-month peak period between June and November 1635 - a total which would normally have represented the number of all deaths (including adults) for one whole year.

As a result of this experience, the corporation decided in October 1636 to look at the possibility of 'building of houses in the common for persons infected with the plague and for appointing of persons to attend them and for maintenance of them during their sickness'. The implication is that these would be held in readiness for future attacks. It has to be said, however, that most people - living, as they did, at a time when religion dominated every aspect of life - viewed sudden epidemics such as these as God's punishment upon a sinful community. For instance, John Taylor, writing in 1625, spoke of 'our heinous sins' which had provoked 'God's just indignation' and brought about 'this heavy visitation and mortality'. Furthermore, these outbreaks had become such regular events that they were generally accepted as part of the normal hazards of life (along with bad harvests, unemployment and inflation).

A much more alarming crisis hit the city in 1643 - quite apart from the Battle of Lansdown which was fought on its doorstep. The burial registers all recorded by far their largest total of deaths for any one year in the first half of the century - 72 for St James (compared with an annual average of 22 for the previous ten years), 109 for the Abbey (compared with an average of 35) and about 92 for St Michael's (compared with an average of 21). [An allowance has been made here for additional entries made on a full page which has been torn out of the registers.] Families again suffered terribly with at least seven of those living in St Michael's parish losing two or more of their members. It is highly unlikely that any of the people who died were casualties of the battle. Civil War soldiers killed in action were almost always buried speedily in great pits on the battlefield by local villagers in an attempt to prevent the spread of disease. Indeed, contemporary accounts refer to the royalist dead being loaded into carts and buried on Tog Hill and the wounded being carried away with the army in wagons as it retreated to Devizes. Commanders always tried hard to transport their sick and wounded to one of the war hospitals, which had been set up in various cities such as Bristol and Oxford.

Nevertheless, the soldiers were - in all probability - largely responsible for this outbreak. In 1643 the armies of both king and parliament were ravaged with what was known at the time 'camp fever', 'gaol fever' or **typhus** - an illness which had already killed one-fifth of the population in the garrisoned city of Oxford. This virulent disease (the symptoms of which were a purple rash and a high fever) was transmitted by lice, which found a productive breeding ground in the bedding and clothing of

Many householders suffered from the dreaded, but compulsory task of billeting soldiers during the Civil War - soldiers who not only plundered their houses, but also introduced infection into the crowded and insanitary conditions. (Drawing by Stephen Beck)

soldiers crowded into insanitary billets. It was inevitable that large numbers of these troops were accommodated in the homes of local citizens whenever a besieging army captured and garrisoned a city. Typhus speedily took root, therefore, among the civilian population. One eyewitness in Bristol, following the fall of the city to royalist forces in 1643, noted that twenty or thirty men were packed into quite ordinary houses, 'causing men, women and children to lay upon the boards, while the cavaliers possess their beds, which they fill with lice'. The disease rapidly spread throughout the entire place, a parliamentarian agent noting that 'there die a hundred a week of the new disease at Bristol'.

Bath had also suffered from a heavy military presence during the summer of 1643 in the weeks prior to the Battle of Lansdown, as parliamentarian forces waited to intercept the march of the royalist army from Cornwall. Many were billeted inside the city. Once Bath had been captured for the king in mid-July, a royalist garrison was installed - with soldiers from the Bristol garrison! It is perhaps not surprising, therefore, that the typhus outbreak in Bath was at its peak between August and November that year. It is also not surprising that when, two years later, the plague was again ravaging Bristol, the citizens of Bath objected strongly to a decision by Prince Rupert (the royalist governor of Bristol) to send a detachment of Welsh troops from that city to strengthen the Bath garrison. Local people turned out of their houses *en masse* to stage a noisy street demonstration, calling out to a man, 'No Welsh! No Welsh'.

Further panic hit the city of Bath in 1665, when the notorious **Great Plague of London** - carried over from Amsterdam - threatened to spread nationwide. It is estimated that, at one stage in the epidemic, a thousand people were dying each day in the capital - with the death toll eventually reaching a hundred thousand. News was quickly circulated by travellers and merchants of plague-stricken homes with red crosses daubed on doors (as a sign of the plague within) - homes guarded by watchmen with halberds to prevent the escape of the family; of handcarts being wheeled through the streets to the cry of *Bring out your dead*; of corpses being thrown into great pits - some fifty at a time - and buried in haste. The words of the Reverend Thomas Vincent also reverberated: 'Now death rides triumphant on his pale horse through our streets and breaks into every house where any inhabitants are to be found'.

There was inevitably a great stampede out of London by citizens desperate to escape this threat to their lives - a stampede which brought terror to other places. During the earlier outbreak in 1625, John Taylor had described a similar situation in *The Fearful Summer*:

The name of London now both far and near
Strikes all the towns and villages with fear
And to be thought a Londoner is worse
Than one that breaks a house or takes a purse.

The council in Bath urgently debated the crisis and the worrying information that many people from London were daily attempting to reach Bath 'to the great danger of our city'. It was therefore resolved that no citizen was to receive into his house any people from the plague-ridden areas on pain of a £10 fine. Furthermore, the night watchmen were instructed to prevent any strangers from entering the city between ten o'clock in the evening and five o'clock in the morning - or risk being fined £5 for each offence. On this occasion at least - judging by the low number of burials - the city survived unscathed. The 1665 outbreak of plague turned out to be the last - partly because this disease (which was normally imported by black rats on board ships) was gradually contained through stricter controls at the ports. As the black rats disappeared, they were replaced by brown rats, which may have been immune to the plague bacterium carried by fleas.

(above) *A contemporary drawing to illustrate the attempted flight from London by many fearful citizens during the Great Plague of 1665. Notice how Death waits to ambush them at every turn, indicating with his hourglass that, for them, the sands of time are running out. (Author's collection)*

Treatment of Patients

As the century progressed, both the local community and the visitors to the health resort were served by an ever-increasing medical fraternity. The **physicians**, some of whom were members of the College of Physicians, had studied for up to fourteen years in Europe's best universities. They were, therefore, highly regarded and were accorded the status of gentlemen - although, as Roger Rolls has pointed out, many of them were theoreticians, steeped in dogma and given to star-gazing. On the other hand, the **surgeons** or barber-surgeons, who had each served a seven-year apprenticeship without attending university, were the practical hands-on and clinically-based practitioners. Therefore, although they did not enjoy equal status with the physicians, they were nevertheless greatly respected and in great demand for such surgery as the removal of stones from the kidney and bladder or superficial tumours on the breast and limbs. They also specialised in the cutting of a disc from the skull to release pressure -

recommended when 'hot humours flew to the head', causing headaches or confusion. Nevertheless, most of their everyday work was concerned with blood-letting, dressing wounds and ulcers, incising abscesses and reducing fractures. Patients undergoing such treatment, of course, were forced to endure not only the risk of infection during the operation, but also the pain of surgery which could not be eased by anaesthetic. Alcohol or opium were therefore used to dull the senses.

The **apothecaries**, who likewise served a seven-year apprenticeship, had originally been grocers before, as an organised group, they had gained permission to dispense medicine - and many of them, indeed, continued to sell other goods in their shops (including tobacco, for instance, in Bath). In many respects, the apothecaries performed the function of a modern general practitioner and, like the surgeons, were practical in their approach. They not only made up prescriptions for the physicians, with whom they worked closely, but also undertook their own diagnosis and treatment for customers. The **medicines** they prescribed could well have included some of the growing number of proprietary remedies, which were coming onto the market (such as Daffy's Elixir or Anderson's Scots Pills) - although, during the seventeenth century,

most of their treatment was based on traditional herbal medicine. When, in 1634, Thomas Johnson visited the herb garden of the Bath apothecary, George Gibbs, he was able to list about one hundred and twenty plants - many of which Gibbs had brought back from Virginia. Recent research by Elizabeth Holland has revealed that the probable site of this garden (which measured approximately 75 feet by 50 feet) was right in the heart of the city, lying between Cox Lane and the High Street.

Physicians and surgeons worked in the belief that illnesses were caused when the **four vital 'humours'**, which flowed through the body, got out of balance. In

(top) *A contemporary drawing of a typical barber's shop, which was a far more than a place for haircutting and shaving. Note in the backgound a barber-surgeon blood-letting his pateint's right arm. (Taken from J.A. Comenius,* Orbis Sensualiun Pictus, *1672 edtn., by permission of the British Library: ref - 1607.2351)*

(bottom) *A drawing to illustrate the three main sources of medical treatment - the Physician (top left) studying his papers; the Surgeon (top right) examining a sample of his patient's urine; and the Apothecary (bottom) mixing up herbal medicines in his shop. (Taken from J.A. Comenius,* Orbis Sensualiun Pictus, *1672 edtn., by permission of the British Library: ref - 1607.2351)*

order to restore the equilibrium, it was essential first to diagnose which humour had significantly increased in volume and then to draw off the excess. This was achieved by blood-letting, purging (through a laxative), vomiting (through a 'vomit'), blistering (through the application of certain ointments, which caused the flesh to blister and then to expel the 'pus' from within), or cleaning out the bowels (through the injection of a 'clyster' or enema). The most frequent complaints - apart from smallpox, typhus and the plague - were dysentery and diarrhoea (caused chiefly by contaminated food and water), together with 'consumption' (i.e. tuberculosis) which thrived in squalid conditions.

An idea of how all this worked in practice is given by a number of **case studies** relating to Bath. In 1612, a physician named Mr Luke had treated Thomas Pope for 'a tumour in his legs, who by application of his medicines was excoriated [i.e. had part of the skin removed by abrasion] and ulcerated with much pain and inflammation to the discontent of the patient'. He was therefore referred into 'the hands of William Priest, surgeon, who hath through his endeavours not only taken away the said tumour and inflammation, but also hath skinned and sealed the same and set the said Thomas free of that pain'. The treatment, which lasted for twenty-four days, cost £6 13s 4d - no small sum in 1612! The certificate, which confirmed that the man had been healed, was signed by four eminent local doctors - John Sherwood, Ralph Bayly, Walter Chapman and Thomas Ireland.

Towards the end of the century, a few high-calibre physicians (such as Dr Thomas Guidott and Dr Robert Peirce) were beginning to record carefully the cases they had undertaken and the treatments they had recommended. This gradually led to the development of a more scientific approach to medicine. Dr Peirce, who practised in Bath between 1653 and 1705 (having first been responsible for a large 'riding practice' in the area around the city), was physician to Bellott's Hospital for over forty years. He believed that 'a catalogue of eminent cures should every year be printed...not to instruct physicians... but to direct patients where and how to seek for remedy'. Dr Guidott, who had found refuge in Bath in 1665 from the Great Plague which was raging in London, became an eminent physician in the city for the next four decades. He eventually drew up a 'Register' of some two hundred cases which he had undertaken in Bath. The case he cites of John Cosens (aged 50) of Huntingdonshire in 1682 illustrates the combined use of medicines with the waters of Bath. Although Cossins had been 'seized with a numbness' and a lack of mobility in his limbs, he had 'never used much physic' and was reluctant to take more than one 'purging potion' to clean out his system. However, perseverance in using the baths and being treated with 'a corroborating lotion when out of the bath in his bed' brought about his full recovery.

Arthur Sherston (aged 50) from Wiltshire in 1685 suffered from the seizing-up of his hand, knee and foot. Guidott first of all tried 'bleeding him once or twice in the arm' and prescribing medicines to take 'inwardly' and ointments to apply 'externally'. Although the treatment restored his mobility and reduced the inflammation, the pains continued as 'the remaining humours' settled on his nerves, muscles and tendons. He therefore committed the patient 'to the moderate use of the temperate Queen's Bath in the winter season'. He fully recovered. On the other hand, some patients were cured simply by drinking the waters. In 1686, George Kelly of London (32 years old) had been 'long troubled and almost worn out by extreme tormenting pains in his stomach and guts' - and was now showing symptoms of consumption. He was therefore prescribed to drink the waters of the King's Bath for a month, taking between three and eight pints a day. He was restored to 'a perfect state of health'.

Peirce, who often accommodated his patients in his own home adjoining the King's Bath, strongly believed in the effectiveness of bathing and drinking the waters. He did not set any great store by the large quantities of medicines - 'the baskets of physic' - brought with them by some of his patients (although he realised that his views had not endeared him to apothecaries living in Bath). In 1675, he treated an elderly servant of Lord Digby - a man 'horribly decrepit, not able to use hand or foot as he should, all rendered useless by gout and stone. The gout had knotted all his joints...[while] the stone urged him to a perpetual desire to make water and that with great sharpness and pain'. Peirce advised him to drink the spring waters to wash out the 'gravel' and to ease 'his painful pissing'. The result was that 'he daily discharged vast quantities of gravel and with it some small stones of the bigness of coriander seeds'. A course of bathing followed, which gradually made the nodules on his toes, fingers and knees much softer. 'Some of these tumours later opened of themselves, others were laid open [by a surgeon] with an instrument', thus making all the joints much more pliable. It was only at this stage in the man's recovery that Peirce recommended some 'arthritic pills' and 'cordials to support him in his faintness'. It was his firm belief that the cure had been largely achieved by the waters of Bath.

SOURCES USED IN CHAPTER 6

1. Printed material

Brereton, Sir William: *Travels in Holland etc* (ed. Edward Hawkins, Chatham Society, 1844)

Beer, E.S. (ed.): *Memoirs Illustrative of the Life and Writings of John Evelyn* (1955 edn.)

Chapman, Henry: *Thermae Redivivae, The City of Bath Described* (1693)

Collinson, John: *The History of Somersetshire* (1791)

Davenport, Peter: *Medieval Bath Uncovered* (2002)

Defoe, Daniel: *Tour of the Whole Island of Great Britain* (Everyman edtn., vol. 2, 1927)

Fawcett, Trevor: *Bath Administer'd. Corporation Affairs at the 18th-Century Spa* (2001)

Fawcett, Trevor: 'Bubonic Plague at Bath in 1604' (in *History of Bath Research Group Newsletter*, no. 20, January, 1993)

Guidott, Thomas: *The Register of Bath* (1694)

Guidott, Thomas: *A Collection of Treatises relating to the City and Waters of Bath* (1725)

Historical Manuscripts Commission: *Salisbury Papers* (9 Salisbury, 16-17; includes the bill of mortality, 1604)

Hart, Roger: *English Life in the Seventeenth Century* (1970)

Hart-Davis, Adam: *What the Tudors & Stuarts did for Us* (2002)

Johnson, Thomas: *Mercurius Botanicus* (1934)

Jordan, Edward: *Discourse of Natural Baths and Mineral Waters* (1631)

Leland, John: *The Itinerary of 1535-43* (ed. L.T. Smith, 1907)

Lynch, John: *For King and Parliament: Bristol in the Civil War* (1999)

Neale, R.S: *Bath: A Social History, 1680-1850* (1981)

Page, W (ed.): *Victoria County History of Somerset*, vol. 2 (1911)

Peirce, Robert: *History and Memoirs of the Bath* (1713 edn.)

Picard, Lisa: *Restoration London* (1997)

Rolls, Roger: *The Hospital of the Nation* (1988)

Rolls, Roger: 'Bath cases - care and treatment of patients at the Bath General Hospital in *Bath History*, vol. 2 (1988)

Stoyle, Mark: *From Deliverance to Destruction* (1996)

Sims, Alison: *The Tudor Housewife* (1998)

Taylor, John: *The Fearful Summer: or London's Calamity* (1625)

Waller, Maureen: *1700: Scenes from London Life* (2000)

Warner, Richard: *The History of Bath* (1801)

Warrington, John, ed: *The Diary of Samuel Pepys* (1953)

Wood, John: *An Essay towards a Description of Bath*, 2 vol. (1765)

Wroughton, John: *A Community at War: the Civil War in Bath and North Somerset* (1992)

2. Documentary material:

Bath Record Office: Bath Chamberlain's Accounts, 1568-1734

Bath Council Minute Books, Nos. 1 & 2

Act for the Repairing, Amending and Cleansing of the
    Highways, 1707

Transcripts of the Burial Registers for the three Bath parishes.

Public Record Office: Calendar of State Papers Domestic, 1663-4

I am grateful to Elizabeth Holland for statistical information relating to burials in 1604 and 1643; and to Roger Rolls for his expert medical knowledge relating to this period.

CHAPTER 7

Agriculture

Citizens as Farmers

A glance at Joseph Gilmore's of 1694 quickly emphasises the fact that the small community of Bath was surrounded by fields and meadows, which ran up to the very gates and walls of the old medieval city. It is hardly surprising, therefore, that many of its citizens still partly involved themselves in agricultural activities - whatever their urban occupation or trade. This was not uncommon in the seventeenth century. The smell of the countryside was still strong, even within the confines of a walled city like Oxford, where animals were regularly kept. Leicester, like Bath, enjoyed its orchards and gardens within the walls, whereas Barnstable could even boast some arable land. The fact that many of the inhabitants of Bath owned animals throughout the century, for instance, is underlined by the continued existence of the 'common pound', used for securing straying sheep, cattle or pigs. Situated in 'Timber Green' (or Saw Close), it was rented in 1649 by Benjamin Beacon, who was given authority by the council to replace the existing one with a new construction built of 'timber and pitched stone'. He made a profit by charging fees to owners when they reclaimed their strays. As the century progressed, the corporation became extremely anxious, in the interests of public health, about the importance of controlling the number of animals within the city walls (see Chapter 6). In 1631, for instance, it was furious with Henry Nor(ro)way for feeding 'sheep and cattle' in the Litton, the former churchyard of the Priory situated right in the centre of town. He was warned that, if he offended again, he would be 'put out' and the ground rented to someone else. Similarly, Richard Cox was censured for keeping pigs in his property in Northgate Street in 1632.

In addition to keeping animals and chickens or growing vegetables for personal use, many of the wealthier and more enterprising citizens of Bath were quick to exploit the real opportunity of making money by growing for profit. The demand for food in local markets, created by a rapidly rising population and the growing numbers of a landless workforce, offered lucrative bait even to those whose prime interests lay within the city. For instance, Councillor Henry Chapman was innkeeper of *The Sun* in Northgate Street, but he also rented a five-acre close in the neighbouring parish of Widcombe where he raised geese, hens and turkeys and grew apples, pears, cherries and other fruit for the market. Similarly, Councillor Samuel Wintle, innkeeper of *The George* in Lower Borough Walls, was the tenant of a fourteen-acre close in Widcombe which he used to rear geese, horses and cattle. His near neighbour, John Biggs used his thirty acres of meadow, pasture and orchards in Widcombe to produce food for sale in Bath. It was estimated that he harvested in 1652 between thirty and forty bushels of apples and about fifty-seven loads of hay worth twenty shillings a load.

Councillor John Atwood, a baker with property in Stall Street, also rented an orchard and three plots of pasture ground in the northern suburbs of the city. Alderman Robert Fisher, a mercer by trade, not only rented a property in Stall Street near the

South Gate, but also operated the Corporation's 'coal works' at Timsbury. In addition to all this, he was the tenant of three orchards and other land in Widcombe which, according to witnesses, were highly profitable in 1653. His market gardening operation enabled him to keep four cows and four calves and to produce one hundred bushels of apples at 12d per bushel; £10 worth of garden fruit (including forty quarters of strawberries at 5d per quarter - plus plums, cherries, gooseberries, raspberries, cabbage, carrots and peas); a small quantity of hops and £12 worth of teasels from his two-acre crop. All these - and many others - found that such diversification of interests could prove extremely profitable. Furthermore, it provided a cushion against recession in the cloth industry or a decline of visitors in the health resort.

The Bath Common - its Original Use

One of the few privileges enjoyed by the freemen of the city of Bath was their longstanding '**right of common**'. This was based on an agreement made in 1260 with the Prior that, in return for a small payment of a penny or halfpenny per beast, the freemen would be permitted to pasture their cattle at certain times of the year on Barton Farm (which was owned by the Priory). This right was exercised without interruption until 1617, when it was challenged by the new owner of Barton Farm, William Snigg. Consequently, a number of leading freemen (including William Sherston, mayor of Bath on eight occasions) appealed to the Court of Chancery - a suit which was eventually referred back to the Recorder of Bath (Nicholas Hyde) for arbitration.

In his judgment Hyde agreed that, on the evidence available, 'the citizens ought to have and enjoy the common as claimed'. However, he felt that it would make more sense if he were to allocate 'a certain portion' of Barton Farm (which was extensive) to the freemen for their exclusive use, leaving the residue for Snigg to enjoy without the inconvenience of any right of common. He therefore ruled that the West Field - an area of some 92 acres - should be set aside as '**Bath Common**' for the benefit of the freemen in general at an annual rent of forty shillings payable to Snigg. The mayor and corporation were to be responsible for drawing up regulations for the use of the common and supervising its operation. The new area of common land consisted in fact of five enclosed fields, all of which were being rented out at the time by Snigg. Hyde ruled that the leases should be honoured until their expiry, but that four of them should be placed immediately in the hands of the corporation. The rents from these (amounting to £323 19s 8d a year, plus two brace of capons) were to be enjoyed by the freemen, who would also have the right of common in all five fields from the outset. 'The common fields', ruled Hyde, 'were for the use and enjoyment of the free burgesses inhabiting the city and should remain for ever'.

At first the new arrangements worked extremely well. The corporation dutifully drew up its rules on a regular basis. In 1645, for instance, it resolved that no cattle should be put into the common 'till the hay be cut and carried'. Then, after the hay had been sold 'to the best advantage', the **overseers of the common** were authorised to take in cattle for the rest of the year. All profits from this operation, after the payment of Snigg's rent and other expenses, were to be 'divided equally among all the freemen'. The two overseers (increased to three in 1647 and four in 1662), who were appointed annually, were responsible for ensuring that the system was not abused. They were to check that the cattle were 'marked with a pitched mark' and to take careful note 'of such cattle as shall feed there and whose they are' (thus making certain

(below) A map by Mike Chapman to illustrate the field pattern around Bath and the five fields which made up the area known as Bath Common. The map is based on Thorpe's plan of the parish of Walcot in 1740 with the addition of some field names identified by Alan Keevil in a recent study.

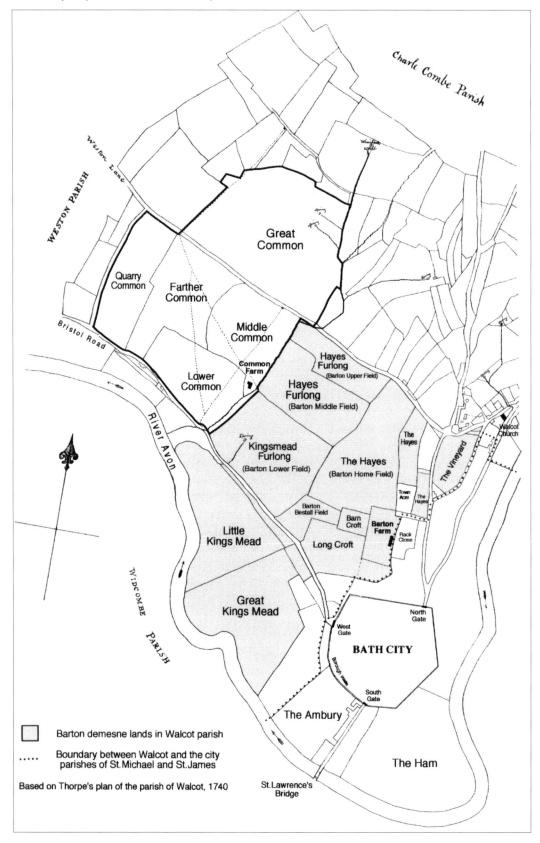

that the number of beasts allocated to each freeman was not exceeded).

The overseers worked in close association with the 'scavenger of the common', whose chief task was collect the 'night soil' or refuse from the city and suburbs and to spread it out over the common. Richard Ryall, who was appointed to that position in 1632, was paid an annual stipend of twenty shillings with the right to graze his three horses on the common. In 1647, however, Philip Holder held the post of **hayward of the common** (with the task of organising the cutting and sale of the hay) in addition to the post of scavenger - at a combined salary of fifteen pounds. The scavenger had use of the 'town plough', which by the seventeenth century was in reality a 'wagon'. This was kept on the common along with its team of four oxen which, from 1649, were housed in a purpose-built 'oxhouse'. The 'plough' was used for two purposes - to haul out the refuse from the city and to carry stones from the quarries at the far end of the common into the city for use in repairing the streets. Sometimes individuals were also permitted to quarry stones for their own use - including a Mr Hayward, who was authorised to do so in 1643 at a charge of three pence a load. From 1675, the corporation began to appoint a 'city ploughman', although in all probability this was simply a more refined name for scavenger.

The Bath Common - its Changing Function

In spite of the initial success of the new arrangements, there are clear indications that by the 1630s the system was being abused. The council therefore passed a series of resolutions aimed at re-tightening its control. Walter Symons and John Wood were censured, for instance, in 1631 for having taken sheep belonging to others to graze on the common in defiance of instructions. Furthermore, it threatened those who had 'wrongly taken cattle into the common' with the ejection of their beasts and the suspension of their rights. With a gradual decline in the involvement of some freemen in agricultural activity - as they turned increasingly to more attractive employment within the health resort - the rights of individual freemen to pasture a certain number of animals on the common were clearly being traded. The local butchers in particular were always interested in the chance to fatten up more of their sheep and cattle by extending their own rights of common. This could be achieved either by buying up the rights from other freemen or by paying a freeman to take their animals onto the common on their behalf. The council particularly disliked the ruthless way in which some freemen were becoming 'middle men' by systematically buying up other peoples' rights and then charging butchers for grazing additional animals. This practice was therefore strictly forbidden in 1631 with offenders being permanently banned from 'buying any other men's shares in the common'.

Similarly, the butchers themselves were attacked in 1634 for grazing far too many 'fat sheep', which caused distress by 'daily chasing over the commoners' cattle'. They were therefore forbidden to put any additional sheep onto the common as a result of buying up a freeman's share (only cattle were to be permitted). Furthermore, if a butcher bought a number of 'fat sheep' from a freeman, which had been legitimately grazed, he would need to remove them 'all at one time' or he would lose his own right of common for one year. This was designed to prevent the butchers, who preferred to take out sheep one-by-one for sale in the shop, from confusing the checking system devised by the overseers. To strengthen these checks, the council ruled in 1638 that any freeman who 'put in to feed any cattle or sheep' without first acquainting the overseers would lose his right of common for that year. There had clearly been many attempts to ride rough-shod over the regulations as commercial interests and attitudes gradually replaced old medieval traditions of trust and co-operation.

By 1650, it was becoming abundantly clear that the common was no longer working in the way that had originally been intended. It was perhaps no surprise, therefore, when the council decided on a totally **new policy for the use of the common** - sparked off by an urgent need to raise money for obtaining an Act of Parliament to make the river Avon navigable between Bath and Bristol. Consequently, on 3rd March 1652, eight councillors were appointed 'to be employed in obtaining the consent of freemen... to part with their interests in the common' in the cause of a navigable river (which would, of course, bring great economic benefit to the city). The eight selected representatives, working door-to-door in the streets that had been allocated to them, were so successful in the task of persuading their friends and neighbours to agree to this proposal that, just one week later, the council agreed to let the common for one year 'at a rack rent'. *[This was a high annual rent, which would equal the full value of the property - not just the minimal rent normally produced by the lifelong leases operating at the time in North Somerset (see below).]* Quite apart from any cash generated towards the cost of gaining the Act, the freemen were assured that each of them would receive out of the rent 'so much money' in lieu of the grazing rights they had surrendered.

Although John Masters, who had put forward a bid of £120 in rent for the common, was initially selected from among the applicants, he failed to raise the necessary money. It was therefore resolved that Henry Chapman should be granted the common for a rent of £110 - on condition that he permitted the four town oxen to graze freely and the town plough to have access for delivering in the night soil and carrying out the stones from the quarry. Although this scheme had been agreed for just one year in the first instance, it was in fact renewed indefinitely. From 1662, the four overseers of the common had responsibility for renting out the common 'at the best rate...for the advantage of the freemen'. They therefore established a competitive bidding process, which saw the rent rise from £110 in 1652 to a peak of £131 in 1677. By 1694, the figure had dropped to £112 10s 0d per annum, although the term of agreement had been increased from one year to five years. It is worth noting that normally the successful applicant was a member of the corporation (including the mayor himself, John Biggs, in 1659).

By the beginning of the eighteenth century, the common was being run entirely as a commercial operation for dairy farming with the freemen receiving an annual dividend from the profits on the rent. In 1708, the long chapter of traditional use of the common, dating back to medieval times, was finally brought to a close when it was agreed that 'the town oxen, plough and harness be sold with all convenient speed to the best purchaser that can be gotten'.

The Rural Landscape around Bath

By the seventeenth century, the old pattern of medieval England, based on a strip system of farming with a three-year rotation of crops in the open fields, had largely disappeared in the area around Bath. Furthermore, even by 1600, much of what had previously been arable land had been converted into pasture for sheep and dairy farming; while many of the old open fields and much common pasture had been parcelled up into small enclosed units. During the Civil War in 1644, Sir William

Waller complained that the local countryside was unsuitable for cavalry 'for there are so many rivers in every county and so much enclosure - and the lanes so deep in mud'. Maps of the period distinctly show a pattern of small fields, gardens and orchards in the area around Bath. Henry Chapman, writing in 1673, referred to 'the low meadows, in several small and great partitions, the pasture grounds above them, then the corn fields'.

As Ronald Neale has pointed out, the hilly land to the north of the city rising up to Lansdown was split into many small two or three-acre fields, whereas by 1639 the 329 acres in the Walcot lordship was divided into twenty-one separate units of between five and 140 acres. The 60 acres of Bathwick manor (which was in the possession of the Earl of Essex until 1726) was also let in small parcels of land. It was therefore only on the less steep slopes on the southern and western sides that a few larger, more open grounds were to be found - including Kingsmead Meadow (48 acres), Barton Farm (76 acres), Bath Common (92 acres), the Hayes (25 acres), Hayes Furlong (25 acres) and Kingsmead Farley (20 acres). Immediately beyond the South Gate of the city were the grazing grounds of the Ham (20 acres) and the Ambury (6 acres). There were, therefore, many small peasant farmers at work in the vicinity producing food for their own survival, as well as some more wealthy city dwellers, who farmed on a small scale in order to profit from a rising market. According to Neale, 'the division between town and country was not as great as the strength and durability of the town walls seemed to suggest'. The corporation itself held several areas of farming land outside the city, including Town Acre, Rack Close, Town Garden and Milsom's Garden - while various individual councillors and aldermen still rented farming land at the end of the century, including Messrs Axford, Atwood, Chapman, Howse and Saunders.

The process of enclosure had been quickened in England as a whole by the population explosion, the shortage of land, the shortage of food and the sharp rise in prices. The attraction of gaining high profits for food or high rents from tenants encouraged many wealthier gentlemen and yeomen farmers to enclose their land into much larger units. Unfortunately for the landowners in North Somerset, local land law was based on the tradition of leasing land in smaller units on long leases which were normally for three lives (i.e. the original leaseholder and his two immediate successors). These lifelong tenancies provided the landlord with income not so much from annual rents, which tended to be minimal, but from sizeable 'fines' which were paid when the lease was renewed or a new life was added to it. In view of the fact that these arrangements were normally protected by manor custom, the lifeholder was in a favourable position - whereas the landlord found it almost impossible to raise the rent to its true market value. This was particularly galling at a time when inflation was rampant.

William Snigg, lord of the manor of Walcot, was in many ways typical of the local would-be capitalist farmer, who was increasingly frustrated by his inability to consolidate his lands by amalgamation or to maximise his income by charging realistic rents. The annual survey he took of his property in the Walcot lordship and Barton Farm, which became something of an obsession between 1638 and 1641, revealed that the vast majority of the 610 acres in his possession was let out on lifehold tenancies, mostly in holdings of ten acres or less (each subdivided into fields of a mere two or three acres). In his somewhat frenzied jottings, he estimated that whereas the the real market value of the Walcot lordship (329 acres) was £343 per annum, it was actually producing a pitiful £10 3s 10d. He tried to draw up a scheme to buy out his tenants, but was ultimately thwarted in his ambition by the exactness of manor custom and the complexity of individual leases. He was not, therefore, able to create the type of large-scale commercial holding he desired, whereas his many small tenants continued to farm their plots on highly advantageous terms.

SOURCES USED IN CHAPTER 7

1. Printed material:

Chapman, Henry: *Thermae Redivivae: the City of Bath Described* (1673)

Chapman, Mike: *An Historical Guide to the Ham and Southgate Area of Bath* (1997)

Clark, Peter & Slack, Paul: *Towns in Transition, 1500-1700* (1976)

Collinson, John: *History of Somersetshire*, vol.1 (1791)

Keevil, A.J: 'The Barton of Bath' (in *Bath History*, vol. VI, 1996)

Neale, R.S: *Bath: A Social History, 1680-1850* (1981)

Warner, Richard: *The History of Bath* (1801)

Wroughton, John: *A Community at War: the Civil War in Bath and North Somerset* (1992)

Wroughton, John: *An Unhappy Civil War: the Experiences of Ordinary People* (1999)

2. Documentary material:

Bath Record Office:	Bath Chamberlain's Accounts, 1568-1734
	Bath Council Books, Nos. 1, 2 & 3 (1631-1715)
	The Survey of Bath, 1641
	Long v Fisher, 1656, Acc. No. 59, Bundle 2 (Crook, 1)
Somerset Record Office:	The Survey of Walcot Manor, 1638-41 (DD/BR/SB/N68.2)

CHAPTER 8

The Cloth Industry

The Traditional Broadcloth Industry

No industry suffered more from fluctuations of the economy than the cloth industry which had dominated the employment scene in North-East Somerset for many generations. During its golden period, in the first half of the sixteenth century, it had brought real prosperity to the area which was clearly evident to the traveller, John Leland. On the road between Bath and Frome, for instance, he had noticed 'certain good clothiers having fair houses and tucking mills'. The fine stone buildings in the city of Bath, depicted on Gilmore's map of 1694, bear further testimony to the affluence which had been generated by this trading activity.

The local industry specialised in the manufacture of broadcloth, each piece normally between fifty-four and sixty-three inches in width and requiring two weavers to handle it on the loom. It was made from short-staple English wool which had been carded (not combed) to provide, after fulling and finishing, a fine heavy cloth with a smooth surface. *[Leather 'cards' with metal teeth were used in carding to prepare the raw wool for spinning by teasing out the separate threads.]* Most of the cloths produced in this way in North East Somerset were exported as 'white' or undyed cloth to Holland and Germany where the final processes took place. The area was highly suited to the needs of the industry. The Avon and its tributaries provided both power for the fulling mills and clear water for scouring the cloths after fulling *[the fulling or tucking process cleaned and thickened the cloth]*; there was a plentiful supply of fuller's earth in the hillsides around Bath *[an absorbent clay used for degreasing the cloth during fulling];* the soil around Keynsham proved itself to be ideal for the growing of woad and that around Bath for the growing of teasels *[the dried, prickly flowers used for raising the nap on cloth]*; access to the markets was reasonable by road to both London and Bristol. By 1600, therefore, clothiers were already well established along the river valleys, which bordered the county, in such places as Frome, Beckington, Lullington, Rode, Freshford, Bath and Keynsham. They were a mixture of small independent weavers and large-scale capitalist clothiers who utilised the domestic or 'putting out' system, employing hundreds of local families in the work of carding, spinning, weaving and finishing.

(right) *Broadloom weavers at work in their cottage.*
(A drawing by Mark Withers)

John Ashe and the Revival of Fortune

Trade in this white broadcloth had already suffered a number of acute depressions during the second half of the sixteenth century. In 1586 the Privy Council had shown considerable concern for the way in which large clothiers were quick to lay off work 'the poorer sort of the people inhabiting about the city of Bath' when times were bad. The justices were therefore ordered to call before them all 'clothiers and other men of trade' and ensure that those with stocks of wool or with an 'ability to employ' immediately set to work as many of the poor as possible. However, in spite of a revival in the broadcloth industry during the first decade or so of the seventeenth century, the situation deteriorated rapidly from 1614 onwards and remained grave until the outbreak of the Civil War. By 1640 exports had been halved - but even as early as 1622 the mayor had informed the Privy Council that Bath had become 'a very little poor city, our clothmen much decayed and many of their workmen amongst us relieved by the city'. The privy council ordered merchants and dealers to help ordinary spinners and weavers by buying up surplus cloth and selling raw wool at fair prices. This did not, however, halt the decline which had been caused by a range of complex factors outside the control of local people - for instance, James I's ban on the export of undyed cloth in 1614; the disruption of markets caused by the outbreak of the Thirty Years' War in 1618; growing competition from Germany, France and Holland; and wars against both France and Spain in 1629, which blocked outlets to the Mediterranean.

The general decline of the cloth industry in North Somerset, however, was successfully reversed in the mid-1620s by the introduction of a new type of cloth known as Spanish medley. A mixture of previously-dyed fine Spanish wool and English yarn, it was lighter and smoother than the broadcloth - and therefore appealed to the more fashionable and expensive end of the market. One of the most successful exponents of this new technique from 1625 was John Ashe of Freshford, a man who was to forge strong links with the city of Bath (his son James, for instance, was elected MP for the city in 1646 and its recorder in 1652). A capitalist clothier, John Ashe used both his financial assets and his organising genius to establish a classic example of the 'putting out' or domestic system of production. His operatives supplied hundreds

of spinners and weavers (working in their own cottages in villages along the Avon valley) with the necessary raw materials before the cloth was eventually taken back to Freshford for dyeing and then for fulling in his own mill there. Each week he despatched this cloth in a convoy of wagons and packhorses to the family shop in London (run by his brothers Samuel and Edward). Then, by-passing the Merchant Venturers' Company and the factors at Blackwell Hall (where sales of cloth for export had traditionally taken place), the cloth was exported directly to Antwerp, where his son

John Ashe, 1597-1659, clothier of Freshford. Portrait attributed to William Dobson, 1610-1646. (By courtesy of the Methuen Collection, Corsham Court; photograph by the Photographic Survey, Courtauld Institute of Art)

(John, junior) acted as agent. Though this mammoth operation, he earned for himself a staggering fortune. Described by John Aubrey in 1686 as 'the greatest clothier in his time', Ashe was reputed to enjoy an annual income of £3,000 with personal assets of £60,000 (an enormous sum in the seventeenth century).

The Industry in Bath

In addition to the large-scale production in the villages outside, the cloth trade also continued quite vigorously within the city of Bath itself, even though the golden days of the sixteenth century had largely gone for ever. The main hub of activity was just outside the North Gate, as it had always been. There, in the large open space outside St Michael's Church, weekly markets were held flanked on the east side by two bustling inns, *The Horse Shoe* and *The Boat*. For James I's reign (1603-25), Elizabeth Holland has discovered the names of thirty-eight weavers, including eighteen who operated in their workshops in the area of Broad Street and Walcot Street - plus at least one cardmaker (Roger Field), who supplied 'cards' for the spinning process (see above); four tuckers or fullers (Peter Chapman, William Whitaker, William Teague and Thomas Commings); and twelve clothiers. The 1641 survey of corporation property gives confirmation of the fact that the industry was continuing to thrive on the eve of the Civil War, listing a number of important clothiers who held leases - William Sherston (a former mayor), Arthur Sherston, Councillor William Baker, Councillor Mark Dallemore, William Swallow, Henry Nor(ro)way and Alderman John Parker.

Although less affluent than John Ashe, these were men with capital to invest, who each organised a small, local operation in conjunction with market spinners (see below) and independent weavers. According to John Wood, even as late as 1660 'the clothing trade flourished so exceedingly that in the parish of St Michael's without the North Gate there were no less than sixty broad looms'. The clothiers were able to use the services of Bridget Cutt's tucking or fulling mill (known as Monks' Mill) outside the East Gate for the scouring and fulling of their white broadcloths. These were then stretched out to dry on large 'tenter' racks erected in the fields behind the houses in Broad Street - fields which had been appropriately named Over Rack Close and Rackham. Joseph Gilmore's map of 1694 clearly shows these large wooden frames on which the cloth was secured by stitching to prevent it from shrinking unevenly as it dried (a process known as 'tentering').

The independent clothiers and weavers of Bath operated on a much smaller scale than John Ashe. There is no evidence that they had abandoned the production of white broadcloth in favour of Spanish medleys, nor do their names appear as suppliers in the cloth books of the Ashe firm in London. It is also probable that, as comparatively small producers, they did not have the incentive to make regular journeys to the capital to take advantage of the trading facilities in Blackwell Hall. It is more likely that they were content to sell their cloth locally at the weekly markets in Bath and Bristol and at occasional fairs throughout the year. Most of them were too small and too lacking in capital to organise the sort of 'putting out' system favoured by large-scale businessmen such as Ashe. They relied instead on buying their spun yarn from market spinners, entrepreneurs who bought raw wool in bulk and then paid individual spinners in local villages to produce the yarn, before selling it on to independent weavers in Bath's weekly cloth market. These men could also supply the yarn ready-dyed if required.

In 1635, however, the local justices - anxious to support the livelihood of

(left) A woman spinning outside her cottage - part of a large work force which supplied spun thread for the independent weavers and capitalist clothiers. (By permission of the British Library: ref - Roxburghe Ballads, RAX.Rox. I, pt. 2.353)

impoverished workers while still maintaining control over quality - were concerned that certain abuses had been creeping into the system. In a letter to the Privy Council, they stated that the welfare 'the poor spinners of wool in these places' was entirely dependent on the successful trade of clothiers and market spinners in the area. They therefore drew up a set of rules for controlling the way wool was treated and used. To avoid confusion and later arguments, the poor spinners would in future only be allowed to handle wool from one customer at a time; clothiers and market spinners must only supply the spinner with one type of wool; and market spinners were to label each batch of yarn offered for sale in the market, stating the type of card used in carding and 'the name of him that made the same wool into yarn and the place of his dwelling'. Shoddy workmanship could then be traced back to the actual culprit. Anxious to protect the good name of their product, the clothiers and market spinners unanimously agreed to these rules at a meeting held in Bath and furthermore requested stiff punishments for any poor spinner who should damage the wool supplied. In the absence, therefore, of guild regulations to control their trade, local dealers showed a considerable degree of unity and co-operation.

Small clothiers and independent weavers could operate on a comparatively small amount of capital. Provided they had the resources or credit to purchase wool from the market spinner and survive until the cloth had been sold, they could maintain their business. The Bath clothiers were fortunate that the close proximity of both a fulling mill and weekly market enabled them to move their stock quickly. Nevertheless, their ultimate well-being often depended upon the possession of land or other assets to supplement their income and provide a greater degree of security. At least several of the people already mentioned had sufficient means to enable them to hold stock for a period when trade was bad or even to survive a major disruption. William and Arthur Sherston were members of a wealthy propertied family which had previously owned Barton Farm. John Parker, with substantial property in Northgate Street, not only ran a draper's shop but also rented 21 acres of land in Barton Farm just outside the north-west corner of the city. Mark Dallemore diversified in another way by owning two

A contemporary drawing to illustrate the dyeing of cloth (a dye-house operated in Bath outside the East Gate by the end of the century). Also note the cloths hanging out to dry on the large tenter racks. (Author's collection)

inns in Southgate Street, *The Cock* and *The Pied Bull*. William Marden, a silkweaver with a shop in Walcot Street, added to his income through his work as a button mould maker.

There is little doubt that the cloth trade continued in Bath and the surrounding area throughout the seventeenth century, although its importance to the local economy steadily declined with the rapid growth of the health spa. Gilmore's map, for instance, still displayed the tenter racks in the fields outside the city walls in 1694, while William Stevens took out a lease on a dye-house outside the East Gate in 1698. Furthermore, Marta Inskip has shown through her detailed study of the 1685 survey and related leases that - during the last quarter of the seventeenth century - there were at least eleven active clothiers, nineteen clothworkers, two fullers, seven feltmakers and ten weavers (most of whom were still based in the area of Broad Street, Walcot Street and Northgate Street). This significant decline in the number of weavers, however, is perhaps attributable to the fact that the production of cloth was gradually being transferred to the villages across the river - Twerton, Lyncombe, Widcombe and Bathwick - where operators were free from the tight controls which existed inside the city. Many tailors had already fled there from the restrictive practices of the Merchant Tailors' Company to set up their own workshops - including ambitious journeymen, who could not expect to gain full membership of the company; and disgruntled apprentices, who had run away from overbearing masters. John Bence, master tailor, lost two apprentices in this way - Thomas Stevens in 1673 and Joseph Holly in 1678.

SOURCES USED IN CHAPTER 8

1. Printed material:

Holland, Elizabeth: *Citizens of Bath: Occupations in Bath in the Reign of James I* (1988)
Mann, John de L: *The Cloth Industry in the West of England from 1640 to 1880* (1971)
Rutt, J.T. (ed.): *The Diary of Thomas Burton, 1656-59* (1828)
Smith, L.T. (ed.): *John Leland: The Itinerary of 1535-43*
Wilson, Charles: *England's Apprenticeship, 1603-1763* (1965)
Wood, John: *Essay Towards a Description of Bath*, 2 vol. (1765 edtn.)
Wroughton, John: *A Community at War: the Civil War in Bath and North Somerset* (1992)
Wroughton, John: *The Stuart Age, 1603-1714* (1997)

2. Documentary material:

Bath Record Office:	Bath Chamberlain's Accounts, 1568-1734
	Leonard Coward's Bundle, no. 5: Mark Dallemore's Will, 1647
	The Survey of Bath, 1641 - Furman Leases
Bodleian Library:	Aubrey 2, f62 (John Aubrey's *Worthies*)
Public Record Office:	Acts of the Privy Council, N.S. xiv 93, 1580
	Privy Council Records, 1639
	Calendar of State Papers Domestic, 1619-23, 1636-37
	Chancery Masters' Exhibit: The Cloth Books of James Ashe, C107/20
	SP16: State Papers Domestic, Charles I (16.345.5 - Ashe's petition)
Somerset Record Office:	The Popham Papers: Survey of Walcot, 1638-41, DD/BR/SB/N68 (2)
Wiltshire Record Office:	The Methuen Papers, 1742

Marta Inskip's unpublished card index of 17th-century leases

CHAPTER 9

The Baths

The Bathing Complex

The hot water baths, which had been under the control of Bath Priory until its dissolution in 1539, became the responsibility of Bath Corporation in 1554 after a legal wrangle. From that moment, councillors - realising the enormous potential of this natural asset for the local economy - worked vigorously to improve its facilities and market its medicinal powers.

By the start of the seventeenth century, there were five public baths, all of which owed something to the improving zeal of the corporation. **The Cross Bath**, which was cooler than the others, was - in the words of Dr Tobias Venner in 1628 - 'a dainty bath for young, weak and tender bodies' and was therefore recommended 'in contractions of any member, in obstructions of the breast, spleen, liver and kidneys'. It had originally boasted twelve stone seats round the edge (later increased in number) and a cross standing upright in the centre. During a major refurbishment in 1593-94 a sluice was installed to make possible the daily draining and cleansing of the bath, three dressing rooms constructed for the comfort of bathers and a new cross erected in a structure which incorporated four additional seats covered by a dome. This in turn was largely replaced in 1665. Then in 1674, with the rapid expansion of the health resort,

The Cross Bath by John Fayram (1739). This highlights the Melfort Cross, which was erected to celebrate the birth of a Catholic heir to the throne, following Queen Mary of Modena's treatment at the bath in 1687. (By courtesy of the Victoria Art Gallery, Bath & North East Somerset Council)

a covered stone gallery was erected for spectators at the north end of the bath by Lord Brooke in gratitude for his cure from diabetes - a gallery which also contained a pump to supply spring water for drinking directly from its source. A second spectator gallery was later added on the south side, although by 1687 this had largely been taken over by the musicians who provided entertainment for the bathers.

The King's Bath, which was the largest, was lavishly praised by Dr Venner: 'It is for beauty, largeness and efficacy of heat, a kingly bath indeed'. A century earlier, John Leland had noted the deep blue water which bubbled up from its spring 'like a seething pot'.

Venner commented that it was 'fitted with thirty-two seats of arched work, wherein men and women may sit apart'. The corporation had provided a further embellishment in 1578 through the erection of an elaborate stone structure over the central spring. This consisted of a pinnacled tower with recessed seats for bathers in an area nicknamed the 'Kitchen' (in view of the intense heat which rose from the spring). Later improvements included, from 1612, the provision by grateful former patients of brass rings set around the walls of the bath for the safety of bathers and, in 1624, a spectator balustrade (the gift of Sir Francis Stonor, who 'troubled with gout and aches in the limbs, received benefit by the baths'). Then in 1664, the Mayor of Bath (Henry Chapman) placed the city's first-ever advertisement in a national newspaper (*The Weekly Intelligencer*) announcing the construction of 'an enclosed bath in that famous bath called the King's Bath...wherein ten persons may in three several rooms sit private and secure from rain and wind...whereby this bath may be more useful at all seasons of the year' - a clear reflection of the city's desire to extend the bathing session in the interests of the local economy.

Its neighbour was the much smaller **Queen's Bath**, which had just eight seats. This had originally been called the New Bath following its opening in 1576, but had been renamed the Queen's Bath after Queen Anne of Denmark (wife of James I), who had visited the city in 1613 and 1615. The corporation, in commemoration of these visits, duly erected a central tower surmounted by a globe and a crown - with the inscription *Anna Regina Sacrum*. The bath, which was fed by the overflow from the King's Bath, was slightly cooler and had originally been used for the treatment of the

(below) The King's Bath, a drawing by Thomas Johnson in 1675 (showing also the Queen's Bath on the left). Note the fine lodging houses which overlooked the baths (including the Three Tuns Lodgings and the Hart Lodgings on the far left) and the vigorous social activity on the balconies surrounding them. (By permission of the British Library: ref - 1881-6-11-85)

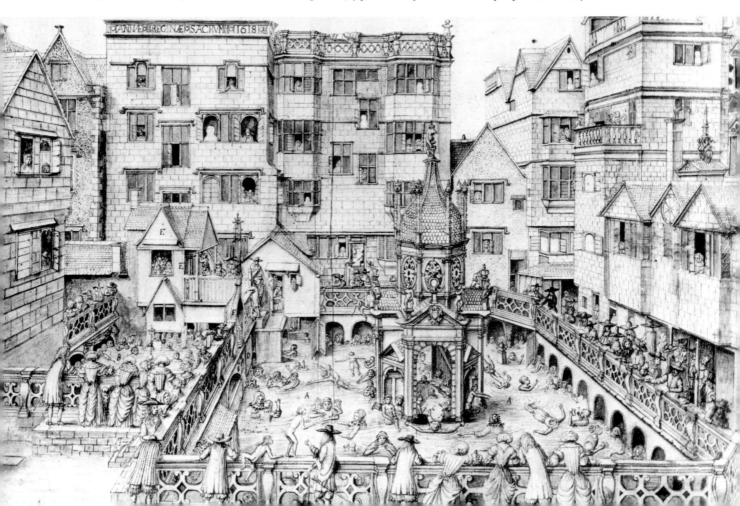

diseased poor who, from 1572, had had the right to travel to Bath under licence for
free treatment (see Chapter 11). According to Thomas Dingley in the 1680s, 'the
water that boils up in bubbles is of a bluish colour (or between that and sea green) and
thence fumeth a strong scent in a thin steam and vapour, occasioned by the veins of
sulphur and bitumen that it passeth through'.

John Leland in the sixteenth century had warned visitors to the city that **the
Hot Bath** - which, as its name implies, was the hottest of all - 'would scald the flesh
on first coming into it'. A century later, however, Dr Venner viewed the situation
much more positively by advising that the bath was 'convenient for cold and moist
diseases' (i.e. rheumatic complaints) which required a hot drying remedy. **The Lepers'
Bath**, which stood next to the Hot Bath, was fed by its overflow. Built in 1576 as part
of a generous initiative by Dr John de Feckenham, it had been specifically designed 'for
the benefit of people diseased with leprosy, pox, scabs and great aches' - thus heeding
the warning of Dr William Turner in 1562 of the need to segregate those with
infectious skin diseases from other bathers. The bath was closely linked with the
adjacent Lepers' Hospital, which accommodated some of the patients (see Chapter
11).

At the same time, Dr Turner had also suggested the importance of establishing a
bath for the many horses which clattered their way through the streets of Bath - a
move which, he believed, would benefit both the cleanliness of the city and the health
of the animals. In 1598, therefore, a '**Horse Bath**' (clearly visible on seventeenth-
century maps) was created just outside the South Gate fed by the overflow from the
King's Bath.

Attracting the Clients

Once the corporation had taken over control of the baths, a string of doctors and
other observers combined to give great publicity to the benefits to be derived from a
visit to the resort. In 1562, for instance, Dr William Turner (the Dean of Wells) wrote

(below) *The King's Bath in the mid -seventeenth century painted by Willem Schellinks.*
(By courtesy of Bildarchiv d.öNB, Wien)

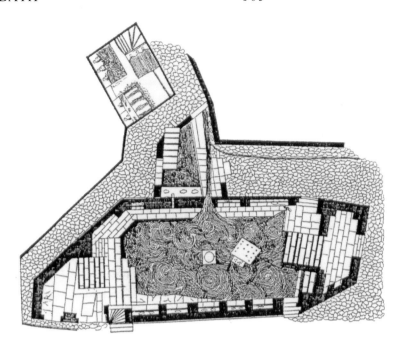

in praise of these 'baths of brimstone', which 'soften the sinews and scour and cleanse the skin'. He mentioned over sixty ailments which could be alleviated by treatments in the baths, including 'windiness', 'tingling in the ears', 'trembling of the heart' and 'worms in the belly'. Dr John Jones, writing ten years later, proclaimed that 'the baths of Bath aid wonderful most excellent *(sic)* against many sicknesses' - adding the catchy slogan that they were 'approved by authority, confirmed by reason and daily tried by experience'. Dr Tobias Venner, a physician at the baths, wrote with the authority of personal knowledge in 1628: 'They be of excellent efficacy against all diseases of the head and sinews, proceeding from a cold or moist cause, as rheums, palsies, epilepsies, lethargies, apoplexia, cramps, deafness, forgetfulness, weakness or trembling of any member, aches and swellings of the joints'. He also invited 'those that fear obesity, that is would not wax gross...to come to our baths'.

This seal of approval by the medical profession was further strengthened by an enthusiastic account of the baths portrayed in 1673 by Henry Chapman (former mayor of the city) in his book, *Thermae Redivivae: the City of Bath Described*. In all his travels, he claimed, he had never encountered 'any such waters as this city yields, in reference to the perpetual constancy of their quantity and quality' - hence his desire 'to publish this to the world, what continual and inexhaustible treasures are stored up in the bowels of the earth'. The waters, he said, contributed greatly to the national interest by 'conducing so much to the longevity and health of the nations, rendering them more numerous and hardy'. Furthermore, he concluded - as a bonus to all this - 'our air will make them valiant'.

These somewhat extravagant claims made chiefly by those with a vested interest in the success of the resort would, of course, have counted for little had they not been substantiated by the actual experience of those who came to the resort to sample the waters. Noblemen and courtiers not only set the trend by visiting the city for their own cures (often on the advice of their doctors in London), but also actively encouraged their friends to follow suit

(above) A 1676 plan of the Hot Bath, which fed the small Lepers' Bath next door. Also note the Poor Folks' Hospice at the top with space for eight people and its steps leading down into the bath. (Author's collection) (right) Dr Tobias Venner, 1577-1660. Venner, who wrote several works praising the healing qualities of Bath's waters, was appointed in 1652 as the first physician at Bellott's Hospital. (By courtesy of the National Portrait Gallery, London)

by writing letters detailing their successful treatment. In 1605, for instance, the Earl of Exeter wrote to the Earl of Salisbury from Bath partly to let him know that he had 'recovered that swelling in my leg, which I came for' and partly to urge Salisbury to try the Cross Bath ('so temperate a bath') for the good of his constitution. Meanwhile two other well-known figures had described to friends their successful visits to Bath - Sir Thomas Seymour for his lameness in 'leg and arm' and Lord Sheffield for 'a lameness' in one of his veins.

In 1682, no lesser figure than the Lord Chancellor (the Earl of Nottingham) wrote to the Secretary of State (Sir Leoline Jenkins) with the good news that 'the Bath agrees very well hitherto and I find myself in much better health than I was when I came down - and hope to return with better legs shortly'. Sometimes, however, treatment demanded a degree of patience from the ailing visitor, as Lord Clifford discovered in 1672. He wrote initially to a friend that 'the bath does not so well agree with me as the drinking of the water does - I am one day well and another ill'. A few days later, he confessed in another letter that he was 'in so much pain' that he was almost unable to write. Nevertheless, under a week later, one of his acquaintances was able to report back home that Clifford 'looks as well as ever I saw him, which makes me conclude that he has had very good effects by bathing and drinking the waters'. This was confirmed by Clifford himself just a fortnight after the treatment had started: 'I still grow better and better by the bath', he proclaimed. Word-of-mouth recommendations such as this did far more to spread the fame of the resort than any medical publication. The clear perception in the higher strata of society was that the treatment worked.

The excellent publicity gained through these unsolicited reports was, of course,

magnified to a much larger degree by widely heralded royal visits throughout the century - visits which were to make the resort highly fashionable as well as medically desirable. Anne of Denmark (wife of James I), who came to take the waters in 1613 (see above), was followed by Henrietta Maria (wife of Charles I) in 1634. Charles II and his wife (Catherine of Braganza) stayed for three weeks in 1663 in the hope that the waters would provide a cure for her infertility. 'The Queen will begin to bathe in a few days', reported a member of the royal retinue on 2nd September. Shortly afterwards, the king wrote to his Secretary of State (the Earl of Clarendon): 'My wife is well pleased with the baths and finds herself in very good temper after it; I hope the effect will be as she desires'. Sadly

(above) *Queen Anne (1665-1714). An engraving based on an original by Sir Godfrey Kneller. (Author's collection)*
(left) *Queen Mary of Modena by William Wissing, c.1685. (By courtesy of the National Portrait Gallery, London)*

the queen was disappointed. On the other hand, Mary of Modena (wife of the Catholic James II) gave birth to a son (Prince James Edward) after a visit to Bath in 1687 - a miracle which was attributed in part to the healing powers of the waters. This incident inevitably brought great national publicity to the city - as well as great political embarrassment (see Chapter 3).

After the Glorious Revolution, Princess Anne visited Bath and was given a royal welcome by the mayor and corporation - much to the displeasure of her sister, Queen Mary, with whom she was not on the best of terms. Nevertheless, after her own accession to the throne, Anne (who was probably suffering from gout at the time) visited the city again in both 1702 and 1703 with her husband, Prince George of Denmark. On the first occasion, according to Richard Warner: 'One hundred young men of the city, uniformly clad and armed, and two hundred of its female inhabitants dressed after the manner of Amazons, met the queen and her train on the borders of Somersetshire and accompanied them (by a road cut for the occasion from the summit of Lansdown) to the western gate of the city, where the corporation received the royal party and conducted them to their apartments'. Although the splendour of the occasion gave an enormous boost to the fame of the resort, a great deal of inconvenience was apparently suffered by regular visitors to the baths - 'for such a tribe of idlers crowded to it in the retinue of the queen, and in consequence of the novelty of her visit' that the cost of food rose by 'one hundred per cent' - and 'one guinea a night was paid by many for a bed'.

Managing the Facilities

Having taken control of the hot water baths in 1554, the corporation was quick to appoint a 'keeper of the baths' to be responsible for their management. As with most civic offices, the post was farmed out to individuals at a rent in the clear knowledge that the office holder would be able to make a handsome profit out of sizeable tips received from wealthy clientele. From the outset, it became normal practice to offer the post to **the sergeants-at-arms** (see Chapter 2 for their wider duties). Dr Thomas Guidott described the function of the sergeant in 1676: 'It is his business to allocate duties to the lesser officials, to regulate the rewards and to see that everything in the bath is done peaceably, quietly and modestly. He attends the bath daily, morning and evening; and every night during the bathing season, ringing a bell at ten o'clock, he sees to the shutting of the doors of the baths. He supervises the guides, who thoroughly cleanse the sides and the floors of the baths'. Celia Fiennes, writing a few years later, saw the sergeants from the bathers' point of view: 'There is a sergeant belonging to the baths that all the bathing time walks the galleries and takes notice order is observed, and punishes the rude; and most people of fashion send to him when they begin to bathe - then he takes particular care of them and compliments you every morning, which deserves its reward at the end of the season'. Tipping, therefore, was essential to ensure good and polite service. Samuel Pepys 'paid the sergeant at the bath' ten shillings after his short visit in 1668.

(right) Pepys, Samuel (1633-1703). An engraving based on an original by Sir Godfrey Kneller. (Author's collection)

As Guidott indicated, an important part of the sergeant's job was to supervise the cleaning of the baths. Although in John Leland's time (before the dissolution of Bath Priory), the baths were 'merely closed and left to purge themselves', a much more active process of cleaning was undertaken in the seventeenth century. By 1634, the baths were emptied and cleaned weekly (or twice-weekly in the case of the Cross Bath). Then, in 1645, the corporation resolved that all the baths should be drained daily 'at four o'clock in the afternoon and the doors shut ; and the baths to be stopped again at seven that they may be full in convenient time next morning'. With the rapid expansion of the resort after 1660, however, it became even more important to ensure that the baths were maintained in an immaculate state. Celia Fiennes was therefore able to report in the 1680s that the baths were first emptied each day 'as soon as the company goes out, which is about ten or eleven o'clock in the morning'. They were then refilled for use by the late afternoon bathers, before being emptied again at night. **The guides** were responsible in the meantime for cleaning the bottom (which was made of gravel) and the sides of the bath (which were tiled) - and for ensuring that any scum on the water was removed. 'There will be such a white scum on the bath', commented Fiennes, 'which the guides go and skim off clean before the company goes in' - otherwise it was likely to give the bathers 'the bath mantle', which made them 'break out into heat and pimples'. Thomas Dingley, in the 1680s, also noticed 'the sordid scum, not only exhaled from foul bodies paddling therein, but what by the heat and working of is cast off'.

The chief duties of the guides were to assist the bathers in and out of the water, to provide bathing costumes and to operate the pumps. During the latter part of the century, it became part of the treatment on offer to have water pumped vigorously over the afflicted part of the body (thus replacing the buckets of water which had previously been thrown over the patient). It was not an entirely relaxing experience, as Celia Fiennes explained: 'In it [the King's Bath] is the hot pump that persons are pumped at for lameness or on their heads for palsies; I saw one pumped - they put on a broad-rimmed hat with the crown cut out, so as the brims cast off the water from the face. They are pumped in the bath; one of the men guides pumps; they have two pence, I think, for one hundred pumps'. This treatment was sometimes taken to extremes. Alderman Benjamin Baber, for instance, was pumped for 20,000 strokes (over a period of some days, it has to be stressed) after an attack of sciatica in 1665. He not only survived his ordeal, but actually recovered!

As the century progressed the number of guides increased to eight males and six females for the King's Bath, plus a further four men and four women to cover both the Cross and the Hot Baths. Although Mary Ady and Eleanor Singers had each been paid £2 10s 0d a year in 1642 for their duties, during the latter half of the century the guides relied increasingly on tips. Samuel Pepys gave his female guide five shillings and his male guide two shillings and six pence during his visit in 1668. Such was the profit that they were able to generate that in 1694 the council resolved that the guides should each pay threepence weekly to help support a poor man in the city, Henry Wright. Similarly, **the clothlayer** at the Cross Bath (whose task it was to lay down a dry cloth for each bather in the slip or dressing area as he or she came out of the water) was ordered to pay five pounds a year 'out of her profits' to an unspecified poor person. A local resident actually made a note of the 'bath fees' expected in 1696 at the end of a stay - 5s 0d for the sergeant, 7s 6d for the guide and 2s 6d for the 'foot cloth woman'.

From 1661, the sergeants-at -arms were also responsible - at least initially - for controlling the new fashion for **drinking the waters**. It had long been believed that such an action could help to purge the body - although Dr John Jones was the first physician in Bath actually to advocate the drinking of water from the spa in a book published in 1572. As a consequence, a fountain was erected six years later in the King's Bath. Then in 1627, Dr Tobias Venner - one of the city's most eminent physicians - added weight to the practice by strongly recommending the internal use of the waters in his book, *The Baths of Bath.* Later in 1697, Dr Robert Peirce explained that it had indeed been an ancient custom 'to quench thirst'. It was also true that 'when, by spending the moistures in long and much sweating, the bowels were heated and dried and rendered constipate, a large draught of this water with a little common salt would

(above) *A drawing in 1739 by John Fayram of the first Pump Room, which had been opened in 1706. Note the sedan chairs, which had been used from the late 17th century to transport the visitors around the city. (By courtesy of the Victoria Art Gallery. Bath & North East Somerset Council)*

infallibly give a stool or two'. An important step in popularising the treatment was taken in 1661 with the installation of a drinking pump in the gallery of the King's Bath. This drew its supply directly from the spring, whereas water had previously been taken in a somewhat contaminated form from the bath itself.

So successful was this new craze for 'taking the waters' that by 1673 the water was being marketed commercially in bottles and casks both in London and throughout the western counties. At first the sergeants were permitted to handle the entire distribution and to enjoy the profits - but, from 1684, the council began the practice of appointing a '**Pumper**', who became solely responsible both for the consumption of water by patients locally and for external sales. In return for this privilege and the extensive profits he made from gratuities, he paid the corporation an annual rent, which amounted to £35 in 1695, but rose to £200 in 1706 with the opening of the first Pump Room. Not all people enjoyed drinking the water, however - Celia Fiennes, for instance, complained that 'it's very hot and tastes like the water that boils eggs - has such a smell'.

The Bathing Experience

Although by the end of the seventeenth century Bath had become an elegant and fashionable resort frequented by polite society, the scene had not always been quite as salubrious. In particular, there had been a long tradition of mixed nude bathing, which had its origins in the fifteenth century. According to Bishop Bekynton in 1449, local people apparently made sport by 'barbarously and shamelessly' pulling off the drawers and smocks, which visitors had put on, to reveal 'their privy parts to the gaze of bystanders'. There were frequent calls to segregate the bathers. Dr John Jones suggested in 1572, for instance, 'the dividing of the male from the female so that they may not see and embrace each other, it being a thing not only so undecent, but also a thing most uncivil and barbarous'. Under the influence of the Puritan revolution, the corporation tried to enforce some degree of order. In 1621, it proposed 'the decent severance of the men from the women in all the baths' - but to no avail.

Four years later, it received a stinging rebuke from the Privy Council complaining of 'the great disorders in the use of the baths' and the 'very unseemly and immodest' conduct of the bathers. Dr Edward Jordan was equally disgusted in 1631: 'The baths are bear gardens', he stated, 'where both sexes bathe promiscuously, while the passers-by pelt them with dead dogs, cats and pigs'. Three years later, William Harrison, while staying at the *Three Tuns Inn*, was even more forthright in his criticism as he witnessed a motley collection of bathers. To see them, he said, 'one with another...appear so nakedly and fearfully in their uncouth, naked postures would a little astonish and put one in mind of the Resurrection'. Although the situation improved greatly in the years following the Civil War, the corporation continued to show its concern by issuing periodic regulations about the whole question of mixed bathing and the wearing of proper attire - even as late as the 1730s.

A slightly more harmless tradition was also noted by a number of observers. In the early sixteenth century, Polydore Vergil commented: 'There are also now those baths where waters bubble and boil in a warm place, in which boys especially bathe themselves for pleasure's sake. I have seen those boys swimming in that pool and bring up with their teeth silver coins thrown in for fun by onlookers'. John Leland, too, noticed the same sort of activity. 'Here at the edge of the baths, a respectful throng of

(below) Detail from Thomas Johnson's drawing of the King's Bath (1675). Note the changing styles of dress, the bathing costumes with black ribbons used by women and the boys diving in for coins. (By permission of the British Library: ref - 1881-6-11-85)

diving boys waits for pence, thus repeating: *Throw now a few coins into the water that, being heavy, they may sink. We, leaping in, will search the depths. Do not wonder; we will restore your treasure'*. This practice, which continued throughout the seventeenth century, is clearly illustrated on Thomas Johnson's drawing of the baths in 1675. For his part, Samuel Pepys dutifully recorded in his diary for 1668 that 'before I took coach, I went to make a boy dive in the King's Bath'. It cost him one shilling.

Visitors to Bath, who came to experience the benefits of bathing at the spa, were first urged to seek medical advice from a local physician with detailed knowledge of the waters. In 1631, Dr Edward Jordan in his book *The Nature and Uses of our Baths in Somersetshire* stressed that some baths suited a patient's condition better than others. Patients, therefore, were 'ill-advised to venture without their physician upon any particular bath or to direct themselves in the use of it'. Those who failed to take advice were the very ones who went away from the city 'without benefit' and were then 'apt to complain of our baths'. Quack doctors were to be avoided at all costs. The genuine physician would recommend a period of two days rest before the course of bathing commenced, during which time various oils and ointments could be applied to the affected parts and medicines taken to 'purge' the body.

Once the first day of water treatment arrived, the more affluent patients would don their bathing attire in their lodgings very early in the morning - Samuel Pepys did so at four o'clock, but still found 'much company' had already assembled at the Cross Bath by the time he arrived. According to Celia Fiennes, the women wore 'garments made of fine yellow canvas, which is stiff and made large with great sleeves like a parson's gown; the water fills it up so that it is borne off [in such a way] that your shape is not seen - it does not cling close as other lining'. Their 'garments' in fact consisted of a 'shift' or bathing gown edged with black ribbons, 'drawers', slippers and linen caps. The gentlemen wore 'drawers and waistcoats' of similar material, the latter with 'pieces of lead affixed at the bottom to keep them down under the water'. These costumes are well-illustrated in Thomas Johnson's drawing of the King's Bath in 1675. Other bathers were able to change in the covered entrance passages or slips, which led down from the street or in the small, crowded dressing rooms alongside.

Many patients, however, were transported from their lodgings to the baths in small sedan chairs, which were enclosed, lined with red baize and sufficiently manoeuvrable to operate within the narrow confines of the staircase. They were taken straight into one of the slips, where they disembarked before being led down into the water by an official guide. The first-time bather instinctively felt insecure. As Celia Fiennes walked around the Cross Bath, she had a female guide to lead her 'for the water is so strong', she wrote later, 'it will quickly tumble you down'. There were also two male guides who walked in front of her 'to clear the way'. She was further comforted by the fact that on the side of the arches there were 'rings that you may hold and so walk a little way - but the spring bubbles up so fast and so strong and so hot against the bottoms of one's feet'. Celia was eventually led to a stone seat, alongside the other ladies, set in one of the arches around the side walls - with the gentlemen on seats around the cross in the middle of the bath. There she sat 'up to the neck in the water'. William Stukeley witnessed a similar scene at the King's Bath in 1724 and found it somewhat surprising that people should 'stand up to the chin and stew' in this way.

Dr Jordan advised his patients to spend up to an hour in one of the hotter baths and two hours in a more temperate one - with the treatment continuing for 'sometimes twenty days, sometimes thirty'. In any event, the first-time bather was urged 'to begin gently with the bath till his body be inured to it; and to be quiet from swimming or much motion, which may offend the head by sending up vapours thither'. More experienced bathers tended to pass their time by playing cards, although eating, swimming and sleeping were strictly forbidden. (Thomas Johnson does in fact show some people swimming in 1675.) Many of the ladies regularly brought small bowls, which floated in the water. In 1700, Ned Ward viewed with admiration 'the ladies with their floating Japan-Bowls, freighted with confectionery, knick-knacks, essences and perfumes' - ladies who waded about the bath 'like Neptune's courtiers suppling their industrious joints'. Samuel Gale also spotted these devices, which were 'tied to their arms with ribbons and swim upon the surface... to keep their handkerchiefs, nosegays, perfumes and spirits in case the exhalation of the water should be too prevalent'.

(below) A map showing the south west corner of the city (known as Binbury or Bimbery) as it was during the first half of the 17th century. This area, which was closely connected with the spa, was dominated by baths, hospitals, inns, lodging houses and homes of doctors. The map (based on a version of John Speed's map of 1610) has been re-drawn with added graphics by Mike Chapman. Attributions are taken from a revision of Elizabeth Holland's map of Stuart Bath (1970s).

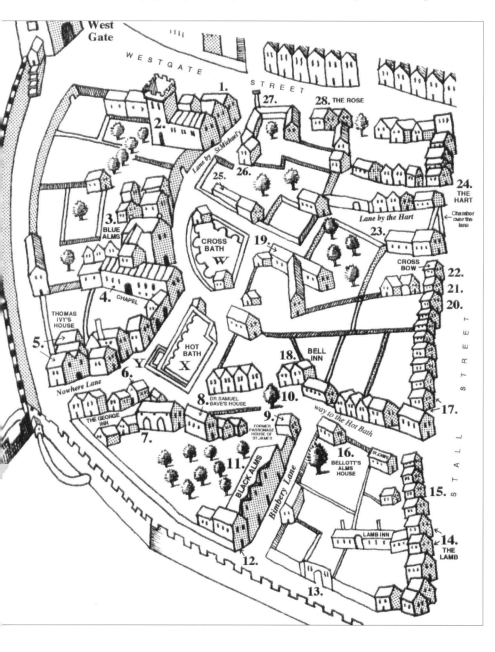

1. St. John's land, held by Richard Gay (lease of 1620). 2. The disused Church of St Michael's held by Richard Gay (lease of 1610). By 1641 assigned to Mr.Pratt. 3.St. John's Hospital House - the Blue Alms. 4. St.John's Chapel. 5. The property later known as Hetling House (now called Abbey Church House, plus no. 2 Hetling Court). Held in 1591 by Dr.Robert Baker, whose widow married Dr. Reuben Sherwood. In the reign of Charles 1, held by Thomas Ivy. 6. Site of hospice for poor folk (in later years dubbed a Lepers' Hospital). 7. The George Inn, on the site of the present Hot Bath Street. Held by Edith Smith in 1633. Later held by Samuel Wintle. 8. In 1641, Dr.Samuel Bave's house. Apparently previously held by Dr Thomas Venner. 9. Medieval Parsonage House of St.James, held in 1641 by John Dauntsey. Later became the Catholic centre known as Bell-Tree House. 10. The Bell Tree. 11. St Catherine's Hospital - the Black Alms. 12. By the later 17th century, called the Blue Anchor. 13. Entrance to the yard and stables of the Lamb Inn 14. Became known as the Lamb Inn. It seems to have been the early Christopher Inn. In mid-17th century, owned by Simon Sloper. 15. Became known as the Mermaid. 16. Bellott's Hospital. 17. Dr Jeremy Martin (cf. Survey of 1641). 18. The Bell Inn. 19. 'The New House" - once held by Dr.Lapworth (mentioned 1630). 20. Held by John Elmer or Hilmer, surgeon, in 1593. 21. Sir John Harington's lodgings, in 1597. 22. The Crossbow Inn. 23. Sites of the Cock and the Pied Bull Inns. 24. The Hart Inn. In 1616 held by Richard Chapman. By reign of Charles II, John Masters. 25. St. John's land. Once held by Dr. Edward Jordan. 26. By the 1660s held by Dr.Robert Chapman. 27. Became the Black Horse Inn. 28. The Rose Inn. Became the Rose and Crown. X. The Hot Bath. Y. The Lepers' Bath. Z. The Cross Bath.

Further amusement was provided by the activity in the galleries, which overlooked the baths. Celia Fiennes clearly felt that the social scene in the galleries of the Cross Bath was really quite civilised. 'The company that does not bathe that day', she recorded, 'walks and looks over into the bath on their acquaintance and company'. Indeed, Samuel Pepys made the point that the Cross Bath was used almost entirely by 'the gentry', whereas the King's and Queen's Baths were 'full of a mixed sort of good and bad'. In spite of these personal reflections, Ned Ward witnessed a far less genteel situation when he visited the Cross Bath in 1700: 'The spectators in the galleries please their fancies with the lady's face, another's eyes, a third's heavy breasts and profound air. In one corner stood an old lecher, whose years bespoke no less than three score years and ten, making love to a young lady not exceeding fourteen'. Entertainment of a more acceptable kind, however, had been provided by the corporation in one of the galleries from 1674, when 'a band of music' began to entertain bathers - although it quickly put a stop two years later to 'the progress of the vocal music' there after a number of complaints. Nevertheless, however great the attractions of the entertainment, the fact remained that there was little privacy for the bathers. They were overlooked not only by those who idled away their time in the galleries, but also by many prying eyes given a grandstand view from windows of the inns and lodging houses which stood alongside. This whole problem is vividly illustrated in Johnson's drawing.

When the time came to leave the bath, the bather went through a rather intricate routine of changing - a procedure described in detail by Celia Fiennes. First of all, she said, you went from the bath through a door into 'a private place' (i.e. one of the slips or entrance passages), where you climbed up the steps out of the water. There, with the door closed behind you, you 'let your canvas [bathing costume] drop by degrees into the water, which your woman guide takes off and the meantime your maid flings a garment of flannel, made like a nightgown with great sleeves, over your head'. You were then picked up again by the two men carrying the sedan chair, which was 'close and warm', and taken back to your lodgings where you were set down by your bedside. You then went straight to bed - as Dr Jordan advised - to 'lay and sweat' for at least an hour. The gentlemen were treated in a similar fashion. Samuel Pepys recorded that he was 'carried back, wrapped in a sheet and in a chair home - I stayed above two hours in the water, home to bed, sweating for an hour'.

The majority of visitors to the spa left the city at the end of their stay well contented. Some observers, however, expressed their doubts. In 1668, Pepys himself thought that it could not possibly be clean to have 'so many bodies together in the same water'. Furthermore, too much bathing, he said, was clearly bad for you. After all, 'those people who 'live all the season in these waters, cannot but be parboiled' - indeed, they 'look like creatures of the bath'. Ned Ward pursued a very similar theme in 1700, when he wrote: 'In this bath were at least fifty of both sexes...who by their scorbutick carcasses [i.e. bodies affected by scurvy] and lacquered hides, you would think had lay pickling a century of years in the Stygian Lake. Some had those infernal emissaries [the guides] to support their impotent limbs; others to scrub their putrefied carcasses'. He went on: 'The baths I compare to nothing but the boilers in Fleet Lane or Old Bedlam, for they have a reeking steam all the year'. This scene from hell was also described by John Macky a few years later during his journey through England: 'The smoke and slime of the waters, the promiscuous multitude of the people in the bath, with nothing but their heads and hands above the water, gave me a lively idea of several pictures I had seen of Angelo's in Italy of Purgatory, with heads and hands uplifted in the midst of smoke just as they are here'. Thomas Dingley was slightly less harsh in his criticism, although he was not at all impressed either by the guides or the general noise. 'Those clownish fellows and ugly old witches, who never knew how to govern themselves, are yet guides to others...The continued noise in the Queen's Bath is not unlike that at Billingsgate, London in the market time'.

Nevertheless, in spite of these harsh comments, the waters of Bath clearly satisfied the needs of two important groups of people. On the one hand, the majority of bathers went home feeling much better - as William Harrison observed after a visit in 1634: 'To such as stand in need of this place and the sulphurous waters, it brings exceeding ease and much content too'. On the other hand, the citizens of Bath rejoiced in the rapid expansion of their health resort - an expansion which provided much-needed employment after the gradual decline of the cloth industry. As Thomas Dingley aptly remarked in the 1682: 'The manufactures of the town are apothecaries' wares; the commodities are good mutton; but the people chiefly get their bread by their water - I mean the baths'.

SOURCES USED IN CHAPTER 9

1. Printed material:

Chapman, Henry: *Thermae Redivivae: the City of Bath Described* (1673)

Cunliffe, Barry: *The City of Bath* (1986)

Dingley, Thomas: *History from Marble*, vol. 1 (in Camden Society, vol. 94, 1867)

Fawcett, Trevor: *Bath Administer'd: Corporation Affairs at the Eighteenth-Century Spa* (2001)

Fawcett, Trevor & Bird, Stephen: *Bath: History and Guide (1994)*

Hamilton, Meg: *Bath before Beau Nash* (1978)

Harrison, William: *A Relation of a Short Survey of Twenty-Six Counties, 1634* (ed. Wickham, L.G, 1904)

Historical Manuscripts Commission: *The Salisbury Papers*, 9/16, 9/17 (1933)

James, P.R: *The Baths of Bath in the 16th and Early 17th Centuries* (1938)

Jordan, Edward: *The Nature and Uses of our Baths in Somersetshire* (1631)

Laurence, Godfrey F: *Robert Peirce, 1622-1710* (1993, unpublished, with a transcript of a local 1696 manuscript)

Leland, John: *The Itinerary of 1535-43* (ed. L.T. Smith, 1907)

Macky, John: *A Journey through History* (1724 edn.)

Manco, Jean: 'The Cross Bath' in *Bath History*, vol. 2 (1988)

Morris Chris (Ed.): *The Illustrated Journeys of Celia Fiennes, 1685-c1712* (1982)

Neale, Ronald: *Bath: A Social History, 1680-1850* (1981)

Rolls, Roger: *The Hospital of the Nation* (1988)

Rolls, Roger: 'Bath Cases - care and treatment of patients at the Bath General Hospital' in *Bath History*, vol.2 (1988)

Tunstall, James: *Rambles about Bath* (1889 edn.)

Venner, Tobias: *The Baths of Bath* (1628: in *Harleian Miscellany*, vol.2, ed. W. Oldys, 1809)

Ward, Ned: *A Step to the Bath* (1700)

Warner, Richard: *The History of Bath* (1801)

Wood, John: *Essay Towards a Description of Bath*, vol. 2 (1765 edtn.)

Wroughton, John: *A Community at War: the Civil War in Bath & North Somerset* (1992)

2. Documentary material:

Bath Record Office:	Bath Chamberlain's Accounts, 1568-1734
	Bath Council Books, Nos. 1, 2 & 3 (1631-1715)
Public Record Office:	Calendar of State Papers Domestic, 1603-10, 1663-4, 1668, 1672, 1682, 1685
British Library:	The Weekly Intelligencer, 28th March 1664

CHAPTER 10

Commercial Activity - and the Post

The Growth of Shops

It was once believed that proper retail shops, as opposed to street stalls, did not make their appearance in smaller towns until the late eighteenth century. In reality this was not true in the country at large - and it was certainly not true in Bath. As Peter Davenport has shown, shops were first described in leases as early as the thirteenth century and, by the fourteenth century, they had become permanent structures often with a kitchen behind, a cellar below and living accommodation above. The shop fronted the street with wooden shutters, hinged at the bottom so that they could be pulled down to form a display counter with the body of the shop behind. Examples of these are shown on Gilmore's map of 1694. Trestle tables were also used for the display of goods, although glazed shop windows (which were beginning to appear in London) were not seen in Bath until the end of the Stuart period.

Mr Ford's lodging house in Stall Street (taken from Joseph Gilmore's map of Bath in 1694) with a stall in front for the sale of goods. (Author's collection)

The number of shops increased noticeably as the century progressed with the rapid development of the health and leisure resort after 1660. However, even as early as the 1630s, the chamberlain's accounts frequently refer to fines or rents paid for the opening of new shops - Thomas Parker 'for setting up his shop window 1s 0d; Robert Sheppard 'for a shop standing on the city waste 8d'; and William Ball 'for an encroachment by setting out of a shop upon the city waste in Northgate Street 1s 0d'. The latter had clearly extended property which he was already leasing from the corporation onto spare or 'waste' ground. There was inevitably a limit to the amount of this type of expansion within the narrow confines of the city walls. Nevertheless, the demand for retail property continued unabated.

It was sometimes satisfied by subdividing existing premises. In 1680, for instance, Roger Cline's tenement was split into three with new leases granted to Cline himself for one half of his shop, a kitchen within the shop and a coal house in the cellar; Thomas Freeman the other half of the shop, a kitchen and a living room (all on the ground floor); and Robert Harford three rooms on the first floor above the shop. On other occasions, small existing properties were converted, especially in the area of the former churchyard of St Mary de Stall. In 1681, for instance, Benjamin Waters converted 'a low building' there into a shop, while in 1684 William White crammed a shop, a living room and a cock loft into another small space. Later still, from 1702, purpose-built shops with proper windows were erected on the Gravel Walks and

Terrace Walk (see Chapter 15). These were able to mount window displays of their goods, which were served from a counter inside the shop.

With increased opportunities to make profit out of the wealthy clientele visiting the resort, the corporation became resolute in its determination to keep out unauthorised traders ('foreigners' or 'strangers' as they were called). The new by-laws of 1650, therefore, reiterated the clauses in the charter of 1590, which strictly forbade the opening of a shop by anyone who was not a freeman of the city. The penalty in future for breaches of this regulation was to be a fine of five shillings for every week in which the shop was illegally in use. However, the corporation was soon to discover that it was fighting a losing battle as temptations to flout the ruling became irresistible (either through opening a proper shop or by trading illegally in the side streets or the courtyards of inns).

In 1689, for instance, it was reported that Joseph Cary, who had recently moved into the city, had opened up a haberdasher's shop, in spite of the fact that he was not a freeman. The council, having ordered its officers 'to shut down his shop window' by force if necessary, immediately agreed to indemnify them against any future action for compensation. When Cary appealed against the council's decision, it sent him for trial at the next County Assizes. However, even this strict stance did not serve as a permanent deterrent. Six years later, the corporation - alarmed that 'several strangers' had displayed goods for sale 'in open shop and private places' - decided to impose even harsher penalties, namely a twenty shillings fine for each offence (to be levied by the seizure of goods to that value) and automatic prosecution. It was all to no avail. In desperation, the corporation petitioned the House of Commons in 1714 for an Act to suppress 'unqualified persons from using trades in *any* city' - and paid forty shillings for an advertisement in the *London Gazette* to muster support for such a measure.

However, in spite of all these problems, the city quickly adapted to serve the needs of an increasingly affluent consumer society. The main shopping area was centred around Northgate Street, Cheap Street, Stall Street and the former churchyard of St Mary de Stalls. In addition, some smaller shops were to be found, alongside the workshops of masons, smiths and leather workers, in Southgate Street and the lanes running off Westgate Street. Between 1640 and 1660, a growing number of mercers (far more than the size of the city would warrant) ran businesses which sold a wide range of products, including cloth, clothing, sugar, gunpowder, musket bullets, belts, and metal goods - Richard Biggs, John Pearce, John Fisher and Richard Abbott in Cheap Street; Thomas Cole, George Collibee and Walter Chapman in Stall Street; Matthew Clift in Broad Street; John Bush in High Street; John Reed in Northgate Street and Robert Penney in Cox Lane.

The corporation, anxious to cater for its new clientele, issued a certificate in May 1632, authorising no fewer than sixteen shopkeepers to sell tobacco, including six mercers or grocers, four apothecaries, a bookseller, a buttonmaker and a shoemaker. For the period up to 1625, a total of sixteen shoemakers and twelve glovers has been identified by Elizabeth Holland. These were served by two tanners (who worked from tanneries, situated by the river) and two curriers (who dressed the

(left) *A contemporary drawing of a typical mercer's shop, which sold a wide range of goods. (Author's collection)*

skins). The popularity of cattle-grazing in the area created a ready supply of raw materials for the leather industry which, in turn, fulfilled the more fashionable requirements of the wealthier inhabitants and visitors.   Bath's consumer society was also served in the same period by three vintners, five bakers and ten butchers. As the century progressed, so an increasing number of individuals began to offer a range of luxury goods - including the Reeve family of silversmiths and goldsmiths from the 1620s; William Marsden, a silkweaver in the 1650s; and at least four bookshop owners - James Samford in the 1630s, Richard Pearce in the 1650s, Thomas Salmon in the 1660s and John Malden in the 1690s.

During the seventeenth century, shops and houses were not given numbers (indeed, it was not until the 1770s that this was done in London). Shops and workshops, therefore, relied heavily on clearly painted sign boards, which were hung nine feet from the ground (to enable a man on horseback to pass through without risk of injury) and indicated the type of goods sold. The location of ordinary houses was often indicated by reference to a nearby shop or inn (e.g. 'by the sign of...').

The Trade Companies

By the sixteenth century a number of trade companies or guilds existed in Bath, including the tailors, cordwainers or shoemakers, carpenters, plasterers, tilers, masons, joiners, mercers, barbers, grocers, upholsterers, butchers and bakers. The members of these companies claimed an exclusive right to exercise their respective trades, prohibiting others from doing so unless they had served a proper apprenticeship and had gained their freedom. However, as Richard Warner has pointed out, they were in reality self-created bodies with no legal rights based on either a royal grant or an Act of Parliament. Eventually, their restrictive practices   were   successfully

(top) *This typical shoemaker's shop catered in part for the rapidly expanding luxury end of the market in Bath with a fine array of leather shoes and riding boots. (Taken from J.A. Comenius,* Orbis Sensualiun Pictus, *1672 edtn.,* by permission of the British Library: ref - 1607.2351)   (bottom) *This contemporary drawing shows cutting out and sewing taking place in the tailor's workshop. Also note the flat pressing iron on the table. (Taken from J.A. Comenius,* Orbis Sensualiun Pictus, *1672 edtn.,* by permission of the British Library: ref - 1607.2351)

challenged in court in the eighteenth century, although in reality their strength had been greatly diminished many years earlier. Indeed, by the middle of the seventeenth century only the guilds of the merchant tailors, the shoemakers and the weavers had survived. Nevertheless, the corporation, anxious to keep out all types of illegal traders (see above), boosted their presence somewhat by approving constitutions and bylaws for two new (or revived) guilds - the bakers in 1681 and the haberdashers and feltmakers in 1687.

By far the most powerful of these trade companies was the **Guild of the Merchant Tailors**, the constitution of which had been fully ratified by Bath Corporation in 1593 before its eventual revision in 1628. At its head was the senior master (who held the company's funds), assisted by the junior master and two wardens, who acted as beadles to summon its members. Membership of the company consisted of the freemen (who had served their apprenticeship, gained their freedom and set up shop) and the journeymen (who were skilled workers, having served their apprenticeship, but who lacked the resources to operate a shop on their own account). Journeymen, who therefore became employees of a freeman and were paid by the day, were forbidden to undertake secretly any private work of their own on pain of a 13s 4d fine. Occasionally a journeyman managed to gain his freedom, but this was comparatively rare. Inevitably some of them became both frustrated and disgruntled, deciding in consequence to move across the river to Bathwick, Widcombe or Lyncombe where the power of the company did not operate. There they not only set up a trade of their own, but also managed on occasions to visit the city in secret to take orders from some of their old customers - later smuggling back the completed items under the cover of darkness. This of course was in serious breach of the company's regulations. In 1714, Samuel Alder and Nicholas Elkington were caught red-handed, prosecuted at the Court of Record and fined as illegal traders.

A religious foundation, whose patron saint was John the Baptist, the Merchant Tailors had originally held its services in the Church of St Mary de Stall. Each member was expected to pray daily for the other members of the fraternity, but in return could expect to be relieved from the company's funds if he fell sick or was impoverished - but not if his misfortune had been caused by 'his own fault in brawling, night-going or company-gathering'. A special collection was made on occasions to help those in distress - for James Stowell and John Webb in 1693, for instance, while Thomas Beacon was supplied with a pair of shoes in 1691 and Thomas Bigg with the sum of 2s 6d in 1682 to relieve their particular plight.

The company wore gowns for all major functions, including civic processions held to celebrate such anniversaries as the fifth of November, its own annual service, any burial services for deceased members and the traditional annual feast. A great stir was caused in 1679, however, when the senior master (Mr W. Tanner) objected to the feast on principle. The company was outraged, emphasising in its memoranda book that 'it hath been an ancient and laudable custom time out of memory that the senior master should on Midsummer Day make a feast for the freemen of this company and their wives'. For this task, it reminded everyone, he was given an allowance of forty shillings out of the company's funds to include also the cost of hospitality at its quarterly meetings held at the master's own house. Tanner was summarily dismissed.

The company exercised tight control over every aspect of its members' work and some aspects of its members' lives. It fixed the price of goods, regulated the wages of journeymen and imposed a fair degree of quality control. For instance, one of its articles ruled that if a member spoilt a garment during its making, compensation was to be paid to the purchaser - and all garments were to be subject to random inspections by the senior master. Nor were members free to dispose of their wares as they wished. In 1675, for instance, one of its quarterly meetings (which took place in March, June, September and December each year) ruled that if a member made a garment for another person to sell who was not a member of the company, he would forfeit a fine of five pounds for each garment.

Discipline was extremely strict. All members were in duty bound to attend the quarterly meetings, unless excused by the master, on pain of a 3s 4d fine. Suspension from the company (for serious cases) would mean that the member would also lose his freedom of the city. Before a newly-elected freeman could open a shop, he was required to swear an oath to obey the masters of the company and abide by its laws - including a promise not to open the shop on Sundays and Holy Days, not to entice away another tailor's servant and not to employ any journeyman before the expiry of his current contract. Furthermore, he was made to realise that any tailor who 'did much slander, reproach or abuse' another member or slander his workmanship would be heavily fined.

The senior master, who always enjoyed a close working relationship with the mayor, attended the Guildhall each Monday morning to discuss any applications for freedom from his members. The mayor seldom raised objections to those nominations made. Membership of the company remained buoyant throughout the century with 21 members in 1666, 39 in 1688 and 37 in 1700 - membership which was undoubtedly sustained by a successful **system of apprenticeship**. The father of the boy in question was expected to pay a premium to the master which, by the eighteenth century, varied according to the status of the job - £262 for a surgeon, £100 for an apothecary or draper, £70 for a plumber, £50 for a mercer, £20-25 for a cabinetmaker or saddler, £10-20 for a baker, £5-20 for a carpenter, £12-20 for a tailor and up to £20 for a cordwainer. The father would then make a legally binding contract for his son to serve a master of the trade for seven years at wages set (in the case of the tailors) by the company.

The indentures of apprenticeship were all very similar in content to those imposed on John Bryant, who was apprenticed to his father, a tallow chandler: 'Taverns, inns and alehouses, he shall not haunt. At cards, dice, tables and other unlawful games, he shall not play. Matrimony during the said term, he shall not contract'. In return, the master was to teach him the skills of the trade and provide 'meat, drink, washing, lodging and all other necessities'. The master (who was in *loco parentis* and was therefore responsible for the boy's moral guidance) was free to punish his apprentice in various ways, including - for severe offences - a whipping in front of the other members of the trade or a six-month extension to the boy's term of apprenticeship.

In the nine years from 1706 to 1714 inclusive, no fewer than 203 apprentices (who traditionally wore blue aprons) were bound to masters, averaging just over twenty-two a year. The forty-two

(right) *The growth of the leisure resort provided an impetus for the expansion and improvement of property - hence the importance of skilled carpenters. In this drawing, a timber-framed house is being erected with workmen busy using the axe and the saw to prepare the wood. (Taken from J.A. Comenius,* Orbis Sensualiun Pictus, *1672 edtn., by permission of the British Library: ref - 1607.2351)*

different trades filled by those apprentices clearly reflect the changing requirements of an expanding leisure resort at the end of the Stuart period. Inevitably the construction industry was well represented at a time when new developments were being undertaken in both public building and private housing. Six boys were therefore apprenticed to carpenters, five to plasterers, six to masons, four to joiners, two to locksmiths and one to a glazier. As Bath tried its best to mimic London as a centre of fashion, it was hardly surprising that no fewer than thirty boys worked for shoemakers, thirty-two for tailors, fourteen for barbers, three for periwig makers, four for feltmakers and one for a milliner. Furthermore, at this thriving health spa, fifteen boys chose to be apprenticed to apothecaries, while the tastes of the city's affluent clientele were catered for as one boy opted for a watchmaker, one for a brazier, eight for vintners, two for pastry cooks, two for cutlers and one for a chocolate manufacturer.

If apprentices had serious complaints about the treatment or training given by their masters, redress could be gained through an appeal to the borough court of Quarter Sessions, which had the power to transfer an aggrieved apprentice to another master. For instance, in 1687, differences had arisen between Thomas Sinnet and his apprentice, William Twinn. The court ruled that Twinn was to be discharged from his apprenticeship from Sinnet and, instead, serve his remaining term with Tobias Pearce - without prejudice to his right to be made a freeman at the end of the seven years. Between 1699 and 1715, the court dealt with no fewer than twenty-four such cases, including a complaint in 1704 that Samuel Lansdown (barber) had not provided food, lodging and training for his apprentice, Charles Walters. Sometimes masters complained about their apprentices - as in 1706 when Thomas Atwood (baker) claimed that John Collins often 'disobeyed and affronted' him. The court decided to reassign both Walters and Collins to other masters so that they could complete their training. Apprenticeship was therefore taken seriously by a community which saw part of its duty to care for the development of the young in a compassionate and understanding manner.

Inns and Lodging Houses

As a prime health resort, Bath could boast a fine array of inns and lodging houses. The survey of Bath, taken by the corporation of its property in 1641, recorded the following eighteen inns: *The Rose* and *The Black Horse* in Westgate Street; *The Bear*, *The White* or *Lower Swan* and *The Raven* in Cheap Street; *The Catherine Wheel*, *The Christopher*, *The Horse's Head* and *The Sun* in Northgate Street; *The Horse Shoe*, *The Boat* and *The Black* or *Upper Swan* in Broad Street; *The White Hart*, *The Three Tuns*, *The Golden Lion* and *The Cross Bow* in Stall Street; *The Bell* at the end of Binbury Lane; and *The George* in Lower Borough Walls.

(left) *Most visitors arrived at the health spa by either horse or coach - hence the need for an increased number of blacksmiths. The smithy and forge shown here are conveniently situated next to an alehouse or tavern. (By permission of the British Library: ref - Roxburghe Ballads, ROX.Rox, I, pt. 1.250)*

(right) *Visitors usually arrived at their inns or lodging houses in Bath by coach, often bringing with them a large amount of luggage. This sometimes even included bed curtains, tableware, furnishings and fuel for the fire. (A drawing by Stephen Beck)*

It has to be said, however, that visitors were not always unanimous in their praise of the standard of accommodation on offer. Some found the places inconvenient and uncomfortable with draughty rooms and spartan furnishings, although Celia Fiennes commented in 1687 that there were 'several good houses built for lodgings that were new and adorned with good furniture'. She was, however, concerned at their excessive cost, noting that the chief expense of a stay in Bath was in 'the lodgings and firing' - even though the servants 'give you very good attendance'. A report in 1683 concerning the suitability of the city as a regular centre for the County Assizes also concluded that one grave disadvantage was the cost of accommodation, which was a third dearer than anywhere else in Somerset. Samuel Pepys in 1668 was charged 3s 2d a day, which was about half the weekly wage of a labourer in Bath.

Lionel Cranfield, who stayed four nights at *The Bear* in 1608 paid £2 1s 0d 'for the reckoning' [i.e. the bill, which would include food], plus tips of twopence each for 'the maids' and 'the chamberlain' - and 1s 6d for 'the boy who brought the beer and washed the linen'. Stabling the horses cost him a further £1 11s 0d. While in Bath, he had clearly seized the chance to buy a few luxuries (including 'a great leather bag' for sixpence, a pair of leather boots for ten shillings and half a pound of sugar for tenpence) and to sort out a number of problems (including the repair 'of a new shoe' for four pence and the purchase of a stirrup for twopence). Visitors who came for a longer stay to be treated at the spa often brought with them a considerable amount of luggage to ensure maximum comfort. In 1604, for instance, Lord Cecil was advised by Dr John Sherwood to remember that it would be necessary to bring his own 'bed-hangings and plate' for use in the lodging house. Sometimes several carts were needed to carry a selection of bed curtains and other furnishings, pewter plates and mugs for the table, wood and coal for the fire. The Earl of Sussex had apparently required four carts for the purpose in 1578, while Anne of Denmark (wife of James I) had needed twenty - plus a supply of beer casks!

Quite apart from the inns, the city could also offer plenty of accommodation in **lodging houses**, where a room in 1714 could be rented for just ten shillings a week and a garret for five shillings. By 1694, there were twenty-nine large lodging houses, including the Hart Lodgings in Stall Street, the Three Tuns Lodgings overlooking the King's Bath, Walter Gibbs's Lodgings by the Cross Bath and John Bushell's Lodgings in Stall Street. Many of these were imposing three-storey buildings with decorated bays and a wide expanse of glass. Royalty and other distinguished visitors tended to stay at Abbey House (known also as the Royal Lodgings), which had been converted out of the former Prior's lodgings next to the Abbey. Some of the larger lodging houses contained

The Abby House or Royal Lodgings

The Hart Lodgings in Stauls Street

The three Tuns Lodgings by the Kings Bath

Three drawings from Joseph Gilmore's map of Bath, 1694. (top) *Abbey House where royalty and other famous visitors stayed during their visit to Bath. Situated conveniently near the King's Bath, it had formerly been the lodgings of the Prior of Bath Abbey.* (middle) *The Hart Lodgings in Stall Street overlooking the Queen's Bath.* (bottom) *The Three Tuns Lodgings overlooking the Queen's Bath. (Author's collection)*

up to forty rooms with a further seventeen garrets in the attic.

However, many visitors also found their accommodation with local professionals or businessmen who were willing to offer accommodation to the 'yearly concourse in the spring and fall, of people of all sorts and from all parts of this Kingdom'. Such hosts included in their number several doctors who, closely involved as they were in the hot water spa, tended to live near the baths in the area known as Binbury. Abbey Church House (as it is now called) was used for this purpose by Dr Reuben Sherwood in the first part of the century - a house well suited to the treatment of his patients in view of the fact that it boasted its own private bath with water drawn from the adjacent Hot Bath. Sir John Harington's house in Stall Street, opposite the Queen's Bath, was sublet in 1612 to Dr Ralph Bailey 'for the better entertainment and lodging of gentlemen and others who should resort to Bath'

Nevetheless, in the absence of any regulations governing lodging houses, a number of unscrupulous individuals organised something of a racket to exploit unsuspecting guests. According to Dr Tobias Venner, writing in 1637, the keepers of some houses sent out their agents 'in every corner of the streets' to locate the newly-arrived health visitors and persuade them 'to take their lodging at such and such a house, near to such and such a bath, extolling the baths near to which they dwell above the rest'. Then, having pressurised the visitors to stay in their own house, they would recommend a particular physician to treat them during their stay - usually 'a doctor of their own creating' or an 'upstart apothecary', whom they would praise as being 'the best physician in the town'. In reality the man had actually been chosen as someone who could be trusted not to double-cross them by removing the guests to another bath - even though the bath near to which they were accommodated was altogether unsuitable for their particular infirmities. In fact visitors were often warned to be careful about selecting their lodgings - 'be as near the bath which you will use that you be not long in the cold air', advised one local observer. It was therefore vital to consult first with a physician 'that knows the nature and use of the baths', so that he could advise on the most appropriate bath for the ailment in question. Only then should the lodgings be selected.

A War Office survey, which reviewed the extent of accommodation available throughout England in 1686, reported that the inns of Bath could between them provide 324 beds and stabling for 451 horses. Ronald Neale has calculated (on the basis of the expenses paid by Samuel Pepys for beds and resort entertainment) that, if all the beds were full for a season lasting 182 days, guests at inns would spend a total of almost £28,000. If to this amount is added the projected expenditure of guests staying at lodging houses, it is then realistic to suggest that something in the region of £60,000 a year was being injected into the local economy by the leisure resort at the end of the century. The citizens of Bath clearly benefited in terms of fuller employment for, by 1700, there were still only 335 households in the city (representing a population of about 2,000 people) to service all the inns and lodging houses - plus 58 alehouses, five baths and (within the next decade) the Assembly Rooms, the Pump Room and the theatre.

Traders' Tokens and City Farthings

By the end of the sixteenth century, the expansion of towns and the growth of retail shops had heightened the demand for coins of low face value. Although silver and gold currency had been minted over a long period, this was of little use for the payment of workers' wages, the purchase of small amounts of food or the relief of the poor. The old days of barter within the context of a small village community had largely disappeared. As a partial solution to this problem, James I granted a licence to Lord Harington in 1613 to mint a large issue of 'regal farthing tokens'. These were made up into bags containing twenty pounds' worth of farthings and despatched to the mayors of towns throughout the country. Each mayor was then encouraged to sell the tokens to local traders and employers - and was given the incentive of receiving a fee of two shillings for every pound weight of farthings sold within the first two months of the scheme. For their part, the traders were able - at least in theory - to change back the farthings into real money from time to time, when they had accumulated a surplus (receiving twenty shillings for every twenty-one shillings' worth of farthings returned).

In practice, however, they found it increasingly difficult to do so. By the 1630s, they had consequently become extremely reluctant to deal in them - and some had even started to issue their own **private tokens** for trade within the town. This practice was quickly suppressed by Charles I who, in 1636, issued a proclamation 'for putting down' illegal farthings. - a proclamation which was circulated to all towns, including Bath. Nevertheless, the general clamour against these 'regal' farthings' was so great that, once the king had fled his capital during the Civil War, they were abolished by parliament. The trial and execution of the king finally removed all constraint with the result that, from 1648, many traders and corporations up and down the country began to issue their own tokens in denominations of a penny, halfpenny and farthing. In Somerset, for instance, no fewer than sixty-eight towns and larger villages did so (as Sydney Sydenham has pointed out in his comprehensive survey of the subject).

In Bath itself, during a twenty-year period from 1652 to 1672, something in the

A selection of traders' tokens issued in Bath between 1652 and 1672. The name of the issuer usually appears on one side with a symbol of his trade on the other. Note the one issued by Henry Chapman innkeeper of The Sun (3rd row, right); and that issued by Bath Corporation (bottom row, left). From Richard Warner's History of Bath, 1801. *(Author's collection)*

region of thirty different tokens were minted. These were all farthings, struck in copper and bearing the name of the issuer on one side (often with an engraved emblem to represent the trade) with the place of issue on the other. The first wave took place between 1652 and 1656 when tokens were issued by Robert Fisher (mercer), John Pearce (mercer), John Clarke (mercer), Edward White (mercer), John Bush (mercer) and John Reed (mercer). Then, between 1664 and 1669, a second batch was issued by Richard Horler (chandler), Priscilla Hickes (innkeeper of *The Three Swans*), William Smith (clothier), Thomas Salmon (bookseller), George Reeve (goldsmith), Richard Collins (clothier), George Baker (clothier), William Landicke (innkeeper of *The Three Tuns*) and Ambrose Bishop (innkeeper in Broad Street). It is thought that - given such a variety of tokens - shopkeepers stored them in specially-made boxes with separate sections for each type. Then, when a sufficient number of one type had been collected, the tokens were taken back to the issuer for reimbursement in hard cash.

Meanwhile, Bath Corporation - seeing how successful the early issues had been - had also decided to take part in this profitable venture. In 1659, therefore, the council agreed to issue its own '**city farthing**', bearing the city arms on one side and the letters 'C.B.' on the other. The resolution was passed by 18 votes to 4, even though eight of the councillors present in the chamber were already issuing tokens of their own. When, however, the corporation struck a second issue in 1670, it firmly resolved that 'the public farthing' was to be that made by the corporation and that 'all other farthings were to be cried down'. A proclamation was therefore read out on market day announcing the 'new money' and the suppression of the other tokens, which then had to be redeemed by their issuers. The new farthings were minted by a Mr Garvill from

Birmingham, who travelled the country making tokens on behalf of individuals and corporations. Bath Corporation paid him a fee of £20 for doing so and for handling the sale of farthings to traders. For two glorious years, the corporation enjoyed an handsome return on its outlay - the chamberlain banking over £30 in profit in 1670, for instance, and some £32 in 1672. [Profit was gained, as before, when tokens were cashed in at the Guildhall with one shilling being retained as a handling fee for each twenty-one shillings returned in farthings.]

Unfortunately, in 1672, the scheme came to an abrupt end, when Charles II issued a proclamation suppressing all private tokens. He had decided instead on a general issue of official copper farthings to go alongside the new gold and silver currency which had become available from 1662. Traders and other individuals therefore hurried to the Guildhall in Bath to exchange their 'city farthings' for hard cash, the chamberlain paying out £33 14s 8d in 1672 alone. For its own part, the corporation - with thousands of useless tokens now in its hands - had no alternative but to sell them as scrap metal. In the event, John Axford, himself a councillor and a brazier by trade, bought 208 pounds of 'copper farthings' at ten pence a pound - raising £8 13s 11d for the city's coffers. This brought to an end a short-lived but highly successful venture in which, it is estimated, something in the region of 50,000 farthings were circulated in all.

The Post

Although the first postal service for general use was not established by royal proclamation until 1635, a system for the delivery of royal messages had been in operation from Tudor times. This was based on a network of 'postmasters' throughout the country, who were normally innkeepers based at appropriate distances along the main routes. Having paid a fee of £20 to gain the appointment, the postmasters had a monopoly of both providing royal messengers with fresh horses for the next stage of their journey and hiring out horses for independent travellers. The term 'riding post' therefore meant fast travel by means of a relay system of hired horses - whether or not letters were being carried. Royal correspondence was actually carried in a leather bag known as a 'maile' - from the French word *malle* - hence the expression royal mail.

By 1574, official communications from the queen or her ministers to the corporation of Bath travelled from London along 'the Bristol Road' via Marlborough, Chippenham and Marshfield, where letters for local delivery were unloaded. In view of the fact that Bath was not a 'stage' along the route, the postmaster in Marshfield was responsible for sending a messenger on foot (known as a 'foot post') with the delivery to Bath - a journey which could take up to three hours. By the early seventeenth century, the Marshfield postmaster was being granted periodic payments of 2s 6d for this additional work, although in 1613 the responsibility for collection and delivery between the two places was transferred to Bath Corporation. However, when James I's wife, Anne of Denmark visited Bath in 1613 to receive treatment in the hot water baths, her ministers decided to ensure a regular line of communication by establishing a series of new staging posts between London and Bath since there were no existing stages in place. Temporary stages (with fast horses at the ready) were therefore set up at Hounslow, Maidenhead, Reading, Newbury, Marlborough and Calne. It should be noted, however, that at this time both corporations and individuals were not permitted to use the royal mail for private purposes, but were forced to rely on paying

A postboy with his horn is shown in this drawing of 1647 - the year in which Bath first became a stage on the royal mail's official route between London and Bristol. (Author's collection)

messengers or general goods carriers to undertake the task for them.

The idea that Thomas Witherings presented to Charles I in 1635, however, was to cover the cost of conveying royal correspondence (for the cash-strapped king) through charges made for the carriage of private letters. A royal monopoly of the post would be established, banning all competition (although private individuals would still be able to send personal letters either by goods carrier or personal messenger). The new system envisaged five 'principal roads' to Chester, Yarmouth, Harwich, Dover and Falmouth (all of which became operational) - plus a sixth which ran via Maidenhead, where it would divide into two routes - one via Gloucester to St David's; and the other via Reading, Newbury, Marlborough and Bath to Bristol. According to the official orders setting out the scheme, this sixth route was not quite ready for use in 1635. This original scheme was extended later by an Act of Parliament in 1657, which established a General Post Office under a Postmaster-General.

It is not quite clear from existing records when exactly Bath became a staging post on Withering's new route (although it is likely that this happened in 1647 or 1648, when Bath's first postmaster was appointed). With the rapid growth in importance of Bath as a health resort attracting the wealthy and famous, it was clearly of the utmost importance that Bath should gain its own place on the royal mail's postal map. The change had certainly taken place by 1669, when Bath was actually named in a royal proclamation as a staging post in its own right on the route from London to Bristol via Marlborough and Chippenham. By this proclamation, the postmaster in Bath became responsible for ensuring that any items from London, addressed to Trowbridge, Bradford-on-Avon, Pensford and Norton St Philip, were taken there by his own postboys. By 1701, the London post was going out three times a week (on Mondays, Wednesdays and Saturdays) and returning with incoming mail on Sundays, Tuesdays and Saturdays. The Bristol and Exeter post also left three times a week - as did the Oxford post, while the Bristol and Chester post was limited to twice-weekly departures. However when the queen, Mary of Modena, visited Bath in August 1687 to bathe in the waters in the hope of curing her infertility, the *London Gazette* announced that 'the post will go to and return from Bath every day in the week during Her Majesty's abode there'.

The first known postmaster in Bath was John Boyse, who was a member of the council and a keen supporter of Matthew Clift's parliamentarian faction during the Civil War (see Chapter 2). An ardent Puritan in religion, he had fled to the safety of the Bristol garrison when Bath was first captured by the royalists, but had returned to play a leading part in civic affairs by undertaking at various times the offices of constable, bailiff, chamberlain, alderman, justice and (in 1656) mayor. He was, however, one of those members expelled from the council in 1662 under the terms of the Corporation Act (see Chapter 2) - and was arrested in 1663 on suspicion of treason, the corporation paying Henry Howell £1 4s 0d for arresting him and Robert Conicke 5s 0d for horses 'to carry witnesses against Boyse' to the County Assizes. A man of some considerable affluence (his property was assessed in the hearth tax of 1664 for ten hearths - far higher than the Bath average of 3.9), he leased a house in the old churchyard of St Mary de Stall built over the slip (or entrance passage) into the King's Bath. That house was therefore to become the first post office in Bath from 1647 or 1648. Like all postmasters, Boyse also hired out horses of his own (the corporation paying him in 1653, for instance, 'for horse hire to Keynsham') - and presumably used them himself for the conveyance of some letters within the local area.

From the chamberlain's accounts, it is evident that the corporation began to use the official postal system for important letters from 1648, always indicating this through the terms 'by the post' or 'post letters'. Thus, in 1648, sixpence was paid 'for sending a letter by the post to Mr Ashe in London', while in 1649 a further sum of 1s 6d was expended 'for two letters - one received, th'other sent to Mr Ashe per post'. [James Ashe was MP for Bath at the time.] Thereafter, a few letters were sent by the post each year - and, from 1652, 'Mr Boyse' was actually named as the agent (for example, 'to Mr Boyse for a letter to Mr Clift in London by the post - 1s 0d'). By 1660, with an increase in usage, he began the practice of submitting a periodic statement for his services - 'Mr Boyse for postage of letters for the corporation per bill - 8s 0d'.

From 1635, the bags of sorted letters from individual destinations along the route were packed into a portmanteau and carried on a second horse. **The postboy** was expected to maintain a speed of seven miles an hour in summer and five in winter, although this seldom happened in practice. To assist him in achieving this target, he was permitted to blow his horn in order to clear the road ahead - although this tactic had apparently been shamelessly adopted by others for their own selfish needs. An Act of 1575 had therefore made it illegal for 'a huntsman to blow his horn in order to cause others to give place, as many used to do for their pleasure'.

Quite apart from taking advantage of the royal mail, the corporation continued to rely on **private messengers** to carry letters on its behalf. Sometimes the messenger went on foot - 'Richard Wakely for carrying a letter to Camerton to Mr Carey - 6d'; 'Francis White for going to Batheaston - 6d'; 'a messenger going to Saltford for a minister - 6d'; 'John Robins for carrying letters to Littlecote several times - 10s 0d'; Brewer for bringing a letter from Gloucester - 2s 6d'. These footposts, which were frequently used in the seventeenth century, were often far more reliable than other methods of communication. A fit man, using a combination of walking and running

The slow wagon of a goods carrier, which would have been used on occasions to carry letters for Bath Corporation during the first half of the century. (Author's collection)

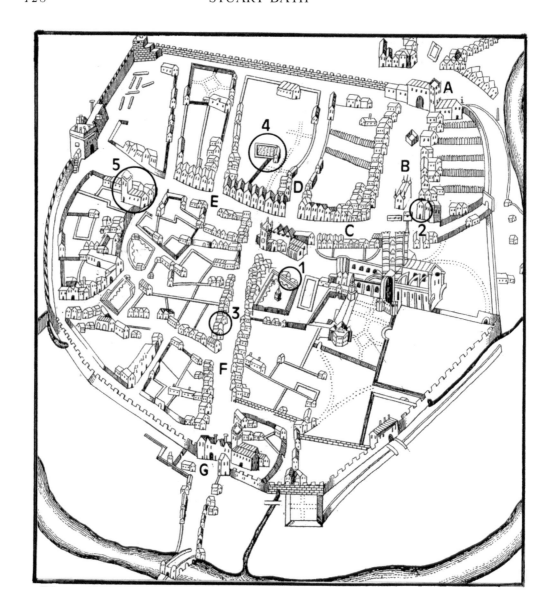

THE SITE OF THE BATH POST OFFICE, 1601-1714

(map by John Wroughton, based on research by Peter Basterfield and Marta Inskip)

1 1648-1662: John Boyses's house at the north-east corner of the King's Bath
2 1662-1672; 1681-1690: the Sun Inn in High Street, rented by Henry Chapman
3 1672-1676: two houses rented by David and Elizabeth Landicke in Stall Street
4 1676-1681: the Bear Inn off Cox Lane, leased by William Burford
5 1690-1727 : part of the disused Church of St Michael, occupied by Mary Collins and (from 1712) by Ralph Allen
A The North Gate **B** High Street **C** Cheap Street **D** Cox Lane **E** Westgate Street **F** Stall Street **G** The South Gate

over a long distance across rough ground, could often beat a horse, whose speed and stamina would badly flag as the miles increased. It is a fact that Thomas Lynne, the Bristol footpost in Elizabeth's reign, carried letters to London and back for fifteen shillings, averaging thirty miles a day - twice the speed of an ordinary goods carrier.

On other occasions a horse was clearly used to carry messages for the corporation. In 1647, for instance, it paid heavily for its town clerk to ride urgently up to London

id James Galley £6 16s 11d, his charges in riding
much more expensive than using the far slower
agon of a goods carrier - as the corporation
d just six pence for dispatching three letters to
in London 'by a porter'. Earlier still, in 1604,
letter 'by the carrier of Devon' (along with three
the carrier of Beckington' (along with 'a black

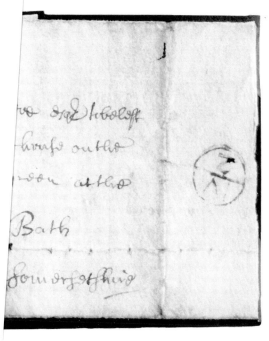

A letter posted in London in 1709 and addressed to Oliver Le Neve, Esq - 'to be left at the coffee house on the bowling green at the Bath Somersetshire'. (By courtesy of Peter Basterfield)

After his dismissal from the council, John Boyse was replaced as postmaster by his bitter rival Henry Chapman, who operated from his inn, *The Sun*, in Northgate Street. Chapman, a councillor who twice became mayor, held this office until 1672 when he was succeeded by David Landicke (1672-75) and then by Landicke's widow, Elizabeth (1675-76), who both worked from their house in Stall Street. As Peter Basterfield has shown, **later postmasters** in the Stuart period were William Burford (1675-81), who operated from *The Bear* in Cheap Street (of which he was proprietor); Henry Chapman, again based in *The Sun* (1680-84); Henry Townsend (1684-90), who continued the service from *The Sun*; Mary Collins (1690-1712), who moved the office to the disused Church of St Michael's by the West Gate, where she had rented a tenement for the previous fourteen years; and Ralph Allen (1712-48), who continued to use St Michael's as a base until 1727.

Allen, whose uncle and grandfather had both run post offices, took up the appointment at the age of eighteen. He was, of course, to become famous later for establishing a cross-post system, which linked up all parts of the country to provide a national postal service. The official salary paid to postmasters gradually increased with the volume of work. Whereas John Boyse had received forty shillings a year in 1659, Mary Collins was paid £25 from 1695 (as was Ralph Allen in 1712). Although she received a special bonus of £10 in 1702, when Queen Anne's visit to the city placed the post office under considerable strain, she had been forced to pay £3 out of her own money in 1696 to cover the loss of cash sent in her postbag.

SOURCES USED IN CHAPTER 10

1. Printed material:
Chapman, Mike: *An Historical Guide to the Ham and the Southgate Area of Bath* (1997)
Collinson, John : *The History of Somersetshire*, vol. 1 (1791)
Crofts, J: *Packhorse, Wagon and Post* (1967)
Davenport, Peter: *Medieval Bath Uncovered* (2002)
Eyles, William: *The Freemen of Bath and the Freemen's Estate* (1970, unpublished)
Fawcett, Trevor: *Bath Administer'd: Corporation Affairs at the Eighteenth-Century Spa* (2001)
Hamilton, Meg: *Bath before Beau Nash* (1978)
Hart, Roger: *English Life in the Seventeenth Century* (1970)
Hart-Davis, Adam: *What the Tudors and Stuarts did for Us* (2002)
Holland, Elizabeth: *Citizens of Bath* (1988)
Historical Manuscripts Commission, 80: *Sackville I, The Cranfield Papers* (1942)
Historical Manuscripts Commission, *Salisbury Papers*, 9/16 (1939)
James, P.R: *The Baths of Bath in the 16th and early 17th Centuries* (1938)
Manco, Jean: 'Bath and the Great Rebuilding' (in *Bath History*, vol. IV, 1997)
Marshall, C.D.F: *The British Post Office from its Beginnings to the end of 1925* (1926)
McInnes, Angus: *The English Town, 1660-1760* (1980)
Morris, Christopher (ed.): *The Illustrated Journeys of Celia Fiennes, 1685-c1712* (1982)
Murch, Jerome: 'Ralph Allen and the English Post Office' (in *Literary Essays*, 1880)
Neale, R.S: *Bath: A Social History, 1680-1850* (1981)
Picard, Lisa: *Restoration London* (1997)
Shickle, C.W: 'The Guild of Merchant Tailors in Bath' (in *Proceedings of the Bath
         Natural History and Antiquarian Field Club*, vol. ix, pt. 4, 1901)
Sydenham, Sydney: 'Bath City & Traders' Tokens during the 17 Century' (in *Proceedings of the Bath
         Natural History & Antiquarian Field Club*, vol x, pt. 4, 1905)
Waller, Maureen: *1700: Scenes from London Life* (2000)
Warner, Richard: *The History of Bath*, 1801
Wroughton, John: *A Community at War: the Civil War in Bath & North Somerset* (1992)

2. Documentary material:

Bath Record Office:	Bath Chamberlain's Accounts, 1568-1734
	Bath Council Books, Nos. 1, 2 & 3 (1631-1715)
	Furman Bundle 18, Item 10: Inventory of Thomas Chapman
	Freemen's Estate 118, Merchant Tailors' Quarterly Meetings, 1666-94
	Freemen's Estate, Freemen's Book - Apprenticeship Lists, 1697-1775
Public Record Office	State Papers 15.42 (34) - Withering's Scheme, 1635
	State Papers 29.263 (24) - royal proclamation re the post, 1669

The author is also indebted to John Boys (a descendant of Bath's first postmaster) for his helpful, unpublished notes on *Bath and the Post, 1584-1690;* and to Peter Basterfield for placing his considerable knowledge and research on the Bath postal service so willingly at his disposal.

CHAPTER 11

The Poor

Background to Poverty in the 17th Century

Even by the middle of the sixteenth century, Bath Corporation had been facing a major social and economic crisis with the steady influx of beggars on a daily basis. 'You cannot be without peril at Bath', wrote one visitor to Lord Burleigh in 1552, 'whither there is a daily resort from Bristol and specially of beggars and poor folks'. '**The Beggars of Bath**' gained such national notoriety that the very reputation of the health resort was placed in jeopardy. In desperation, the corporation decided to petition parliament for its urgent help in tackling this menace, which cast a heavy financial burden on the city's poor rates. The Poor Relief Act of 1572, therefore, gave recognition to Bath's unique problem (namely that 'a great number of poor and diseased people do resort to the City of Bath...for some ease and relief of their diseases', resulting in the inhabitants being 'greatly overcharged'); and then put forward a solution which forbade any 'diseased or impotent' person from visiting the city, unless he had been licensed to do so by two justices in his native county. The licence gave a guarantee that his own parish would eventually take him back and continue to support him financially. However, failure to produce this licence at the city gates would result in instant punishment as a vagabond - and, in 1572, this meant being branded on the chest with a 'V' and then being handed over to a farmer for two years of slavery.

Although this measure helped to control the influx of the diseased poor, it did little to solve **the general problem of poverty** which affected the entire nation. Many economic factors contributed to this situation. A population explosion saw the number of inhabitants in England and Wales rise from just over three million in 1550 to just over four million in 1601 and again to five-and-a-quarter million in 1650. Alongside this was a prolonged period of rampant inflation in Europe caused by inflationary pressures of war, debasement of the coinage in many countries, large-scale bullion imports from the New World and repeated harvest failure. Between 1500 and 1640, it is estimated that the price of food rose by 700% and that of industrial goods by over 300%. Meanwhile, the wages of agricultural workers had approximately halved in real terms during the same period. Furthermore, the country experienced three extended sequences of really bad harvests, which had a devastating effect on workers already living on the bread line - from 1594 to 1597; from 1646

Sturdy beggars and vagabonds were a familiar sight along roads leading into affluent cities such as Bath. (By permission of the British Library: ref - Roxburghe Ballads, ROX.Rox, I, pt. 1.42)

to 1650; and from 1657 to 1660 (all inclusive). The years of good harvest, which often followed, could never compensate for the suffering and starvation experienced by many of the working classes. With some 31% of the population under 14 years of age, the average expectation of life at birth in the seventeenth century was just under forty years.

Locally, in North Somerset, this whole situation was compounded by the **decline of the cloth industry** from the second half of the sixteenth century onwards - a situation which threw thousands of spinners, weavers and fullers out of work (see Chapter 8). Hundreds of these were already victims of the population explosion, which had turned many traditional agricultural families into landless labourers who were totally dependent on industrial employment. To make matters worse, these were the very same people who were also to lose their homes after the decision of Charles I in 1627 to sell off and enclose parts of the royal forest at Frome Selwood in Wiltshire - for it was there that many of the landless had settled in rough cottages on encroachments at the edge of the forest as they searched for work with local clothiers. Lack of legal title resulted in instant ejection. Their problem was aggravated even further in the 1620s and 1630s by severe food shortages in the locality coupled inevitably with the escalating price of wheat, which rose by 40% in Wiltshire in just four years. Thousands of people became destitute, particularly around Frome where, in the words of a petition for help, 'the cry of the poor had grown very great'.

It was desperation of this kind that provoked **food riots** in the locality in November 1630. For several years, Somerset magistrates had expressed fears that 'the multitude of poor spinners and weavers in the county, now without work, tend to mutiny'. Their worst fears were realised when three separate incidents involving attacks on licensed corn carriers were reported near Midford, just outside Bath. William Lansdown of Keynsham was travelling up Midford Hill on his way between Warminster and Bristol with five horseloads of wheat, when he was 'set upon by a great number of men and women to the number of 100 persons' who, making threats of violence, pulled down his sacks stealing four of them. On the same day, Thomas Wickham of Hinton Grange managed to rescue a man called Hawkins from Rode, whose horse was intercepted in Midford 'by a great number of people'. The ruffians withdrew after pulling down some of the sacks, urging others 'to follow their colours'. When various suspects were cross-examined at the subsequent investigation held in Bath, Agnes Hodson perhaps best typified the plight of local people. Denying her involvement in the raid, she admitted that she had carried away under half a peck of corn, which she had scraped up from the ground.

Meanwhile, successive governments from the middle of the sixteenth

SPECTATUM ADMISSI RI-SUM TENEATIS AMICI.

(left)   The Poor Law Act of 1601 made provision for unemployed vagabonds to be whipped and sent back to their home parishes. (By permission of the British Library: ref - Bagford's Ballads, vol. III, 51)

century had done their level best to tackle the growing problem of poverty. By the time of the **Poor Law Act of 1601** (which summarised the best features of previous legislation), a clear distinction was being made between the various types of pauper and the type of action needed in each category. Children from pauper homes were to be apprenticed; the aged and infirm were to be looked after in almshouses; the fit, but genuinely unemployed were to be set to work by the parish; and the wilfully idle rogues and vagabonds were to be whipped and sent back to their home parishes. It had also been established that the cost of maintaining the genuine poor was to be borne by the inhabitants of each parish through the raising of a poor rate.

The Treatment of Poverty in Bath

Bath Corporation tried hard to follow national policy on poverty throughout the seventeenth century. Nevertheless, its resources were often strained by the pressure to cater for the needs of its own resident poor, while at the same time dealing with the large number of beggars who flocked into the city from both the impoverished local neighbourhood and further afield. Bath, with its in-built affluence and its spa for well-heeled visitors, made it an obvious target for those in desperate need. As one visitor to the city commented in 1662 - 'where should beggars flock to in a hard frost, but to the barn door?' He went on to note that the local councillors had successfully combined a policy of toughness towards the undeserving with an attitude of compassion towards the genuine poor. Indeed, although laws, he said, 'are daily made to restrain beggars', they are 'daily broken by the connivance of those who make them; it being impossible, when the hungry belly barks and the bowels sound, to keep the tongue silent'. The result was that although the 'whip' was rightly used as 'the proper plaster for the cramp of laziness', local rulers were also quick to realise that 'some pity is due to impotent persons'.

The corporation therefore responded to the need to get as many unemployed people off the streets by providing them with work. The Poor Law Act of 1601, had enabled local authorities to establish **Houses of Correction** (or Bridewells) so that the fit, but jobless poor could be set to work in rather harsh surroundings. The magistrates in Somerset had decided as early as 1624, when poverty and unemployment were reaching a peak, to establish three Houses of Correction to serve the county at Taunton, Ilchester and Shepton Mallet, funded by rates charged on local residents. The one at Shepton Mallet provided for

(right)   Parishes became increasingly anxious that unmarried women with bastard children did not become chargeable on the local poor rates - hence their determination to ensure that the fathers were identified and made financially responsible. (By courtesy of the Museum of London)

people living in the five hundreds in the north-eastern sector. However, although Bath Corporation had the right to establish its own Bridewell, it did not take action until 1630 - the year of the Midford Hill riots - when the chamberlain received the first three voluntary subscriptions of £5 each 'towards the building of a House of Correction'. The city councillors had finally decided, in the face of such a threatening situation, to implement their work ethic and apply the 'whip' on 'the cramp of laziness'.

Two years later, as subscriptions continued to trickle in, they finally resolved 'to set the poor of this city to work'. Suitable premises were found in the north-western corner of the city (in what later became known as Bridewell Lane), when Mr Chambers was paid £5 to vacate his barn, stable and backyard for conversion into a House of Correction. A committee was formed to receive and list further contributions towards the vital task of transforming the existing fabric. The work was considered to be of such urgency that, as contributions began to dry up towards the end of 1634, the council resolved to charge a general rate on the whole town 'towards the finishing of the House of Correction'. Although little is known of its conditions, small clues appear in payments made for 'window bars' and 'wooden bars' (denoting its prison-like atmosphere); 'hooks and twists' (suggesting employment); and the loan of a rope by Goody Parker 'to dig the well at the House of Correction'. This centre continued in use for much of the century. Indeed, in 1664, the council showed its determination to check any slackness which had crept into the system by passing this resolution: 'The house called the Bridewell, being built intentionally to be a place wherein to set the poor of this city to work, shall be put to that use'.

Although the House of Correction was chiefly intended to cater for Bath's own resident poor, its prison-like qualities also made it suitable for the temporary detention of **rogues and vagabonds**. No records have survived to indicate the extent to which it was used for this purpose, although there are occasional glimpses of the tough line taken by the authorities towards such undesirable elements. In 1613, for instance, the council paid William Doulton, the metal smith, twelve pence 'for an iron to burn rogues with'. This indication of the sense of alarm felt by the authorities is nevertheless surprising in view of the fact that the 1601 Poor Law Act had dispensed with the earlier practice of branding vagabonds. In most places they were now severely whipped, before being returned to their home parish. It was of course crucial to ensure that visiting beggars did not become a long-term charge on local people. They were therefore removed, if necessary, by force - such as the impoverished soldier who was manhandled out of town by two paid workers on the mayor's orders in 1699; or the woman and two children who were carried away 'after the regiment' on the mayor's instructions (her soldier husband having dumped them on the city).

There is, however, no evidence to suggest that the behaviour of local councillors was normally characterised by undue harshness. Indeed, the picture we gain from the chamberlain's accounts and the minute books is one of a deeply compassionate society, strongly influenced by the growth of Puritanism in the years up to 1660. This is amply demonstrated by its attitude towards the **elderly and infirm** (i.e those who were no longer able to fend for themselves). The Act of 1601 had allowed parish officers to use the poor rate to provide assistance for people in this category either by supporting them in a poorhouse or by granting them doles of money, food or clothing. Bath provided this form of 'pity' to 'impotent persons' in two ways - through its maintenance of four almshouses for the elderly (see below) and through the regular supply of annual gifts to those in need: 'to the poor in bread at Lent', 'to the poor in

Bath Corporation adopted a compassionate policy towards the elderly or infirm by making regular gifts of bread, wood and coal and by helping individuals in distress. (Drawing by Stephen Beck)

coal at Michaelmas', 'to the poor in wood at Christmas'. Special additional payments were sometimes made to deal with particular circumstances: 'for provisions for the poor people out in the field', 'more for wood given to the poor of the city', 'for warm feed for the sick folks'. This gifts continued year-by-year throughout the whole century.

On occasions, during the first half of the century, the corporation showed considerable compassion towards **problem families** and bastard children - even though Puritanism at the time took a strong line against pre-marital sex. As Elizabeth Holland has shown, Julian (or Gyllian) Forest had four illegitimate children - Thomas (1597), Catherine (1599), Thomas (1608) and Anne (1612), all of whom were both baptised and buried in St James's Church by the age of four. Julian herself (who was possibly retarded) died in 1612 at the age of forty, after giving birth to Anne. For whatever reason, the corporation came to her assistance on a number of occasions - buying canvas to make her a coat in both 1598 and 1599; making her 'bastard's coat' in 1602; and paying for her own shroud at burial in 1612.

Similar compassion was shown in a regular sequence of small acts of kindness to **individuals in distress**. Thus, in the period to 1640, money was devoted to 'mending Joan Edmond's chimney' and 'Widow Tysock's window'; 'for a pair of shoes for Comings boy'; 'for 4 shirts for two boys of the Widow Uggins'; 'a shroud for Walter Werrett's child'; 'for making the grave and ringing the bell for Goody Uggins'; 'a shroud for a poor man that was drowned and for a grave'; to two-and-thirty poor widows - £1 12s 0d'; 'for 3 ells of hambrow and thread to make a blind man a shroud'. Apart from these gifts for clothing, funeral expenses and fabric repairs, the council sometimes provided money for the upkeep of pauper children who had been orphaned. Twelve shillings, for instance was paid to John Bush for 'the keeping of Goody Uggins youngest son'. Although this type of charitable giving was largely suspended during the years of civil war, it was certainly revived to a lesser extent after the Restoration. Sometimes the type of beneficiary was a little surprising - such as 'the coalworker given to drink' in 1664 - although most fitted into the more traditional category.

In 1670, for instance, twenty-four such gifts were made to impoverished or sick men, women and children (usually in the form of small sums of money) in addition to the cost of funeral expenses for a number of paupers. John Bailey not only benefited from the services of Robert Nash, who attended him 'during his sickness', but also after death from the cost of digging his grave, making his shroud and ringing the bell at his funeral. Shrouds for paupers were a frequent expense. Human dignity demanded that even the most humble being should be covered with something at burial (for only animals were buried unclothed). Many parishes placed the pauper in their 'parish coffin' during the service, but buried him in just a shroud. The result of Bath's twin policy of 'whip' and 'pity' was that poverty in the city never seriously got out of hand to disturb the enjoyment of visitors - 'for such care is taken', wrote Henry Chapman in 1673, 'that the wealthier sort eat their morsels free from such importunate clamours and outcries as are too frequently seen in other places'. The reason for this happy situation, he said, was that the magistrates ensured, at their quarterly distributions of aid, that 'the poorer sort' were not only generously treated but were also 'so tied up' that they were made to ration out the free supplies for their needy families rather than 'squander' them away quickly.

Nevertheless, by 1699 it is noticeable that very few casual payments were being offered to individuals in distress (although exceptions were made for a number of poor or maimed soldiers passing through, including money and fuel for 'the six soldiers in the hospital in the winter time'). This drying-up of support was probably caused partly by the fact that employment in the city had been given a major boost by the rapid growth of the health resort (so poverty was far less of a problem); and partly by the hardening of attitudes in the more materialistic and hedonistic society on which the spa was based. For in 1661 the Puritans had lost control of both the corporation and the Abbey (see Chapters 3 and 14) and their demise soon witnessed the demise of that more compassionate attitude, which had characterised the city during the first half of the century.

On the other hand, some people did care in every decade of the century. Among the hundreds of visitors who came to the health resort each year were a few individuals (as Jean Manco has shown) who were greatly moved by the sight of poverty and distress - individuals who subsequently decided to become benefactors by making a gift to the corporation for the relief of the poor. These included several contributions which were intended to stimulate the creation of work for the unemployed - such as the gift of £100 by the Marchioness of Northampton, which enabled the corporation to loan money to those employers willing to set to work a number of poor people. Bath (along with twenty-two other places on a rota system) also benefited from Sir Thomas White's Charity (established in 1566), which produced £100 per year. This proved an enormous boon to four selected freemen (or 'poor artificers', as they were styled), who each received a £25 interest-free loan for ten years to help them expand their businesses. In 1670 (when it was Bath's turn to qualify for the grant), two councillors rode over to Bristol to collect the money from the trustees.

Lady Elizabeth Booth subscribed £100 in all to relieve the city's own impoverished people; Nicholas Butcher donated a meadow in Wellow to the corporation, the income from which was to benefit the poor in the local hospitals; and capital given by Lady Booth and Edward Sturridge was invested to produce further income to assist poor children. Indeed, such was the extent of charitable giving by individuals that, as early as 1615, the corporation had decided to take an annual account 'of all the charitable gifts given to this city' and to do its best 'to see the same employed according to the wills of the givers thereof'. Henceforward, these gifts were 'to be recorded in the Book of Record for this purpose' - a book which was 'to be kept in the chest with the evidences of the city under four keys'.

The Hospitals

In addition to these spasmodic gifts and the building of the House of Correction, Bath Corporation was also heavily involved in the maintenance of the four almshouses (or hospitals), which catered for some of the city's aged and sick. [For a more detailed description see Jean Manco, *The Spirit of Care*.] **St John's Hospital**, situated near the Cross Bath, had originally been administered by Bath Priory, but had escaped closure at the time of the dissolution of the monasteries because a layman (and not a monk) had been in charge as Master. After briefly being annexed to St Michael's Church by the West Gate, it eventually became the responsibility of the corporation following a petition to Queen Elizabeth in 1572. This resulted not only in the Corporation being granted the right to appoint the Master of the Hospital, but also in the launch of a nationwide appeal for funds both to complete the building of Bath Abbey and to enlarge the hospital. By 1580, therefore, an additional floor had been created, thus making a total provision of twelve rooms plus the Master's own quarters. The extra space enabled an

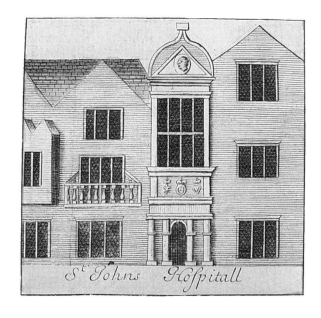

St John's Hospital, founded in 1180, maintained eight poor, elderly people. (Taken from Joseph Gilmore's map of Bath, 1694 - author's collection)

increase in the number of inmates, while at the same time allowing the hospital to raise income through the letting of accommodation to visitors. Founded originally in 1180 'for the succour of such sick poor as came hither for the benefit of the waters', by 1640 it maintained four poor men and four poor women each with a weekly allowance of 4s 2d, plus occasional treats such as a chicken at Christmas. Clothed in blue gowns with white cotton linings and clasps, the residents were under the care of three paid officials - the Master, the Reader (who took the services) and the Washer (who cleaned and took care of the laundry).

By the 1680s, the rules drawn up for the almsfolk stipulated that they were to be 'of a sober and civil conversation, and conformable to the present government'; married and over sixty years of age; and regular in their twice-daily attendance at the hospital's chapel in their livery gowns - and at the Abbey on Sundays. They were conduct themselves in a peaceable manner, refraining from 'tippling, swearing, cursing or any other scandalous crime'. Any money received as gifts from individuals was to be put 'into the common box within the chapel' for sharing out each quarter among the whole community. Individuals who broke the rules were to

(right) *Bath Corporation was responsible for the running of four hospitals or almshouses. It tightly controlled admissions and imposed strict standards of behaviour on all inmates. (Drawing by Stephen Beck)*

St Catherine's Hospital or the Black Alms House just prior to its demolition. By courtesy of Bath & North East Somerset Library and Archive Service (Bath Central Library)

lose one week's pay for the first offence and two for the second (fines which were also distributed between the other inmates). A third offence would result in expulsion. As an example of the standards it worked hard to maintain, the corporation imposed a ban on Sarah Dill who, it ruled would 'not be admitted into the almshouse' because she was 'a common beggar, swearer and curser'.

Not far away in Binbury Lane, near the South Gate, stood **St Catherine's Hospital** or the Black Alms House, which was originally endowed in about 1444. Rebuilt by the corporation in 1553, it was (according to John Wood in 1642) 'a mean structure, two stories high and containing fourteen tenements'. The intention was to support ten poor people of either sex (made possible by the further funding offered by Edward VI's substantial grant of property in 1552 for the founding of a grammar school and the maintenance of ten poor people). The residents received a weekly allowance of three shillings and sixpence each, plus a black coat with red lining once every two years. The council frequently concerned itself with repairs to the fabric and extra donations to the

Bellott's Hospital, founded in 1609, with the coat of arms of William Cecil, Lord Burghley displayed over the gate. (By courtesy of the Victoria Art Gallery, Bath & North East Somerset Council)

occupants, including wood or coal at Christmas and bread at Lent. In return they were expected to attend (in their gowns) two services in the Abbey each Sunday, including one communion a month - and to live a sober and respectable life. Failure to comply with these expectations resulted in expulsion from the hospital and loss of the gown - as Joan Sperring found to her cost in 1666 when she was found guilty of using 'very loud and scurrilous language' to the Mayor's wife.

Just round the corner from Binbury Lane was **Bellott's Hospital**, founded on the initiative of Thomas Bellott, Steward to William Cecil, Lord Burleigh. After witnessing the plight of sick and impoverished people on a visit to Bath in 1595, he invested in a suitable plot of land on which to build the hospital together with estates in Wiltshire for its endowment. By 1608 the Hospital, responsibility for which had been granted to the corporation, was ready for occupation by twelve poor strangers in need of medical treatment (but whose illnesses were not contagious). It was a small, single-storey building, containing fourteen apartments set around an inner courtyard. The Hospital was only open for two months in the spring and one in the autumn (the months when visitors normally arrived to make use of the baths) - and residents were only permitted to stay for a maximum of twenty-eight days. They were, however, not only given free use of the baths and four pence a day for maintenance, but were also cared for by a married couple (the keeper and his wife), who were paid £2 a year in salary in return for looking after the patients, cleaning the rooms and making the beds (which were supplied with decent sheets and bolster cases). However, the corporation paid a worker six pence from time to time to undertake the unpleasant task of emptying the 'jakes' or cess-pits.

What made Bellott's completely different from the other hospitals was the fact that the inmates also benefited from the services of a visiting doctor, who was initially paid an annual salary of one pound. An Act of Parliament in 1593, which had confirmed the right of the diseased and impotent poor from all parts of the country to

(below) A 19th-century watercolour by Henry Venn Lansdown of the courtyard of Bellott's Hospital, drawn shortly before its demolition in 1859. (By courtesy of the Board of Trustees of St John's Hospital)

enjoy the free use of the hot water baths in Bath for their recovery, empowered justices to license such people to travel there unimpeded. However, although the prospective patient would arrive at Bellott's clutching a licence indicating the genuine nature of his application, it was the task of the visiting doctor to examine the new arrival and make a recommendation to the mayor regarding his suitability. The situation was improved even further in 1652, when Dr Tobias Venner was appointed as the hospital's first-ever physician to give medical advice to patients in addition to their initial examination. This was made possible through a generous bequest of £200 by Lady Elizabeth Scudamore for this specific purpose, thus enabling the corporation to pay an annual stipend of eight pounds. Roger Rolls has pointed out that Bellott's was therefore Bath's 'first real hospital', providing both accommodation and treatment.

The admission records contained in the hospital's account books for 1616-1626 reveal fascinating glimpses of the patients and their problems, as Jean Manco has shown. They travelled to Bath in search of cure from all over the country - Somerset, Devon, Worcestershire, Leicestershire, Wiltshire, Surrey, Norfolk, Sussex, Dorset, London, Suffolk, Cambridgeshire, Gloucestershire, Staffordshire, Berkshire, Yorkshire, Oxford, Hampshire, Kent, Warwickshire and Bristol. Their ailments were generally described as pain in the back, thigh, neck, knees, shoulders or side; aches and numbness in the limbs; sciatica; or lameness. On the other hand, 'a poor man from Walcot' was admitted 'being bruised in his body'; while John Seward of Norfolk was in great pain on entry, 'his sinews and veins being knit up'; while John Evly was experiencing considerable discomfort after 'falling from a pigeon house'. Most patients stayed between 24 and 28 days, some of them finding 'great comfort' from the treatment, others 'small ease' and a few 'little or no ease'. Even the latter, however, were much better off than John Haynesford from Wells who, suffering from pain in his knees, 'died after twenty days'.

By the end of the century, however, the corporation was expressing great anxiety about the number of poor and sick people who were flocking into Bath each year. An urgent advertisement was therefore placed in the *London Gazette* throughout January and February 1696, giving notice to all parishes 'that shall think fit to send their poor cripples or lepers to the city of Bath for their cures' that they 'must take care, if they expect entertainment there, that they send with them certificates'. They were also to ensure that return travel costs were covered. The advertisement was repeated two years later, stressing that the hospital could only provide for twelve 'poor cripples' at a time and that those who arrived without testimonials would be sent back home. Dr Robert Peirce, who was the physician at Bellott's Hospital between 1666 and 1705, wrote to a friend in 1698 that 'the concourse of poor strangers', which had arrived even earlier than usual, was putting great strain on the funds normally set aside for the city's own poor. He was frustrated that some, who could not hope to gain any advantage from the waters, were abusing the system and simply arriving in the expectation of being maintained at the city's expense. A year earlier, he had commented that were the city 'to have a new name given it now, it might be called Cripple-Town'.

The other Hospital, which came under the control of the corporation, was **the Lepers' Hospital** (or Poor Folks' Hospice), situated in Nowhere Lane. Built through the generosity of Dr John de Feckenham in 1576, it provided accommodation for seven people with serious skin diseases. These were then able to use the Lepers' Bath, which had also been part of Feckenham's benevolence and designed 'for the benefit of people diseased with leprosy, pox, scabs and great aches'. Small in size, it was supplied with hot water from the adjacent Hot Bath. This initiative was largely in response to the plea made in 1562 by Dr William Turner for the segregation of those with infectious diseases from other bathers.

The Hospital of St Mary Magdalen (or **Magdalen's Hospital**, as it was known) on Holloway was not owned by the corporation, but was under the jurisdiction of the crown, which appointed the Master. By the seventeenth century, the original building had been rented out and the hospital itself transferred to an adjacent cottage. Anthony à Wood, who saw the place in 1678, described it as 'a little old decrepit hospital', which was then housing just 'two lunatics'. Bath Corporation limited its own involvement to an annual payment of £1 4s 0d 'to the poor at Magdalens at Christmas' and periodic casual gifts.

Areas of Poverty and Affluence inside the City

The hearth tax assessments for 1664-65 give a good indication of the levels of poverty experienced within the different sectors of the city and the areas in which poor people tended to congregate. Householders were taxed according to the number of hearths they possessed at the rate of two shillings per hearth, although the poorest families living in dilapidated property were exempt from payment. It is normally reckoned that houses with two hearths or fewer indicate a fair degree of poverty, whereas the possession of three to five hearths usually denotes comfortable homes occupied by craftsmen, smaller merchants and farmers. On the other hand, property with between six and nine hearths reflects the fairly high standard of prosperous living enjoyed by the larger merchants and farmers. In North East Somerset as a whole (including Keynsham, Frome, Kilmersdon and Wellow), there was an average of 2.5 hearths per household, indicating a standard of living just a little above the breadline. The city of Bath, however, enjoyed an average of 3.9 hearths per household throughout its three parishes, an indication of the prosperity that it still possessed in the middle of the seventeenth century. It denotes a far greater degree of affluence than was found in the cities of Newcastle (2.06 hearths), Exeter (2.59), Leicester (2.4) and York (3.2) - although Bath's average was certainly inflated by the large number of inns and lodging houses which dominated the city.

All the streets within the area of Bath's medieval walls contained comfortable stone houses with little sign of squalor (some of which are depicted on Gilmore's map of 1694). Binbury (i.e. the south-east corner, where many of the doctors lived in the vicinity of the baths) was the most affluent sector with an average of 7.3 hearths, followed by Westgate Street (4.8), Stall Street, where many of the councillors had property (4.5), Cheap Street (4.3) and Northgate Street (3.5). Poverty was most acute in the overspill areas outside the two main gates. It was worst in Southgate Street (1.9), while the available returns for Broad Street and Walcot Street indicate an average of 2.8. The poorest parish in the locality was Walcot, where no fewer than 89% of its population of about 190 people were distinctly poor, living in accommodation with only one or two hearths. Indeed, fifteen out of the thirty-seven houses were so dilapidated that they were exempt from paying the tax. 'The house is void and almost fallen down'; 'not rated to church nor poor by reason of his poverty'; 'very poor, no distress' are typical comments from the Walcot returns.

Even so, this figure of 40.5% tax exemption for the poorest parish on the outskirts of the city and just 11.4% exemption for people living in the city itself is distinctly favourable when compared with the returns from elsewhere. For example, 62% of the householders were exempt in Norwich, 52% in Colchester, 50% in Tonbridge, 41% in Newcastle, 39% in Exeter, 27% in Leicester and 20% in York. Indeed, it is generally reckoned that between 50% and 60% of inhabitants in the average provincial town would be living on the margin of subsistence - a clear reminder of the fact that, on the whole, the residents of Bath enjoyed a much more comfortable existence. As far as Walcot was concerned, the truth of the matter was that this run-down area had become something of a temporary refuge (just outside the tight restrictions of the city) for the unemployed, who swarmed on Bath like bees round a honeypot. The genuine inhabitants there had complained to the Quarter Sessions in 1638, for instance, that Robert Meslin had taken in three impoverished families to live in his small, dilapidated cottage - and that these had all become chargeable on the parish poor rates. To make matters worse, Meslin (who was fifty years of age) was already sharing the cottage with his wife and daughter.

Nevertheless, wherever they lived in the city, life was hard and luxuries rare for most of Bath's working population in the first half of the century. Wages for manual workers varied from one shilling a day for assistant plumbers and road repairers to 9d a day for 'Old Fry' whose job consisted of 'casting rubbish abroad'. The lowest paid worker would therefore average about five shillings a week and would always rely heavily on the supplementary earnings of the rest of the family. When it is realised that the poor people of St John's Hospital were allowed 4s 2d a week for maintenance, it soon becomes clear that ordinary workers outside - with rent to pay and families to support - would find five shillings scarcely adequate. More skilful workers, like the pump maker employed at the Bridewell could earn three shillings per day. Professional people were slightly better off and certainly more secure. Mr Mynn, the schoolmaster, for instance, was paid a salary of £20 per annum, plus board and lodging. By 1685 (when the county magistrates set maximum rates for wages) masons, carpenters and thatchers still had to settle for just 1s 2d a day in summer (when hours of work were longer) and 1s 0d a day in winter. Male servants, on the other hand, were to receive no more than £4 10s 0d a year (plus board and lodging), while their female counterparts earned just £2 10s 0d. Even by 1700 - in spite of steady inflation throughout the century - labourers were only earning one shilling a day for planting trees on the Old Bowling Green or working the plough on the common.

Although the exact **cost of living** is difficult to assess, prices of certain items are recorded in the Bath chamberlain's accounts. Small bread loaves and cakes cost a penny each; rabbits and chickens sixpence each; butter three pence-halfpenny a pound; a sack of coal eightpence; boys' shoes 2s 4d a pair; stockings 1s 4d a pair; and shirts 3s 1d each. It was extremely difficult, therefore, for most working families to provide more than the basic food, heat and rent. Clothes were made to last. William Barnard was therefore luckier than most in 1597 when a charitable donation paid for him to receive a new suit of clothes, consisting of a coat, doublet, breeches, stockings, shoes, shirt and cap. This cost £3 3s 0d - a princely sum, which would have taken most manual workers about thirteen weeks to earn. By 1700, the price of a bottle of sack had increased from eight pence in the 1630s to two shillings; while the cost of a pauper's shroud had risen from 3s 4d to between four and five shillings.

SOURCES USED IN CHAPTER 11

1. Printed material:

Bates-Harbin, E.H: *Quarter Sessions Records for the County of Somerset*, vol. 2 (1908)

Chapman, Henry: *Thermae Redivivae: the City of Bath Described* (1673)

Clark, Peter & Slack, Paul: *Towns in Transition, 1500-1700* (1976)

Collinson, John: *History of Somersetshire*, vol.1 (1791)

Coward, Barry: *The Stuart Age: England, 1603-1714* (1980)

Dingley, Thomas: *History from Marble*, vol. 1 (in Camden Society, vol. 94, 1897 - for rules relating to Bellot's Hospital)

Fuller, Thomas: *The History of the Worthies of England* (1662)

Holland, Elizabeth: *Citizens of Bath: Occupations in Bath in the Reign of James I* (1988)

Howell, R: *Newcastle Upon Tyne and the Puritan Revolution* (1967)

Hamilton, Meg: *Bath before Beau Nash* (1978)

James, P.R: *The Baths of Bath in the 16th and Early 17th Centuries* (1938)

Laurence, Godfrey F: *Robert Peirce, 1622-1710* (1993, unpublished; for details of the *London Gazette* advertisements etc)

Manco, Jean: *The Spirit of Care* (1998)

Outhwaite, R.B: *Inflation in Tudor and Early Stuart England* (1969)

Page, W. (ed.): *Victoria County History of Somerset*, vol. 2 (1911)

Rolls, Roger: *The Hospital of the Nation* (1988)

Sims, Alison: *Pleasure and Pastimes in Tudor England* (1999)

Smith, Alan: *The Emergence of a Nation State, 1529-1660* (1984)

Tate, W.E: *The Parish Chest* (1969)

Warner, Richard: *The History of Bath* (1801)

Wood, John: *Essay Towards a Description of Bath*, 2 vol. (1765 edtn.)

Wroughton, John: *A Community at War: the Civil War in Bath & North Somerset* (1992)

Wroughton, John: *An Unhappy Civil War: the Experiences of Ordinary People* (1999)

2. Documentary material:

Bath Record Office:	Bath Chamberlain's Accounts, 1568-1734
	Bath Council Books, Nos. 1, 2 & 3 (1631-1715)
Bath Municipal Charities:	Admission Register, Bellott's Hospital, 1616-26 (BH/5)
Public Record Office:	E179.256/16, Somerset Hearth Tax, 1664-5 (Bks 23-27)
Somerset Record Office:	The Survey of Walcot Manor, 1638-41 (DD/BR/SB/N68.2)

CHAPTER 12

Education

The Establishment of the School

One of the unforeseen consequences of the dissolution of Bath Priory by Henry VIII in 1539 had been the closure of the school which had been run by the monks for the teaching of Latin. Bath, however, was not alone in its loss, for throughout the country as a whole between three and four hundred such schools had suffered the same fate. It was not however until the reign of Edward VI that the problem was tackled, thanks in part to the influence of Bishop Latimer, who had awakened the young king's conscience to halt the 'devilish drowning of youth in ignorance'. In consequence, some thirty-three grammar schools were re-established with endowments drawn from old monastic lands after petitions received from local inhabitants.

It was as a result of a similar petition from the mayor and citizens of Bath to King Edward VI on 28th June 1552 that permission was granted for the establishment of a school to be funded by revenue drawn from 102 properties in the city previously owned by the Priory. The Letters Patent or 'Charter', which was sealed by the Great Seal on 12th July, granted 'that for the future there should be and will be one grammar school in the city of Bath, which will be called the free grammar school of King Edward VIth, which is for the teaching, education and instruction of boys and young men in grammar to continue for ever'. The mayor and corporation, as trustees of the endowment, were to be responsible for the running and maintenance of the school, including the appointment of the Master.

Life in the Seventeenth-Century Grammar School

A typical grammar school of the seventeenth century would have taken boys from all social backgrounds (unless they were Catholics) - the sons of lesser nobility, squires, clergy, traders, yeomen, lawyers, doctors or craftsmen. However, although King Edward's was styled a 'free' grammar school in the charter and although it was locally called 'The Free School' until the nineteenth century, education was not free of charge. Indeed, the first election of ten free scholars did not occur until 1822. The term 'free school' (based on the word *libera* in

An engraving by George Vertue depicting the presentation of a charter to the Mayor and Sheriffs of London in 1553 - a scene very similar to that experieced a year earlier by the Mayor and Corporation of Bath. (By courtesy of the Governors of King Edward's School, Bath)

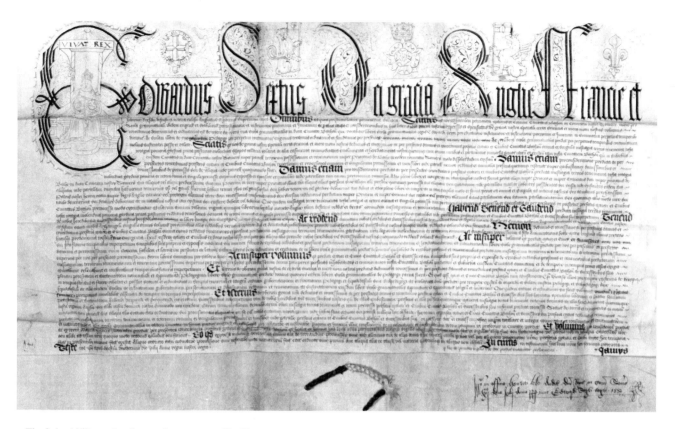

The School 'Charter' or Letters Patent granted by King Edward VI on 12th July 1552. (By courtesy of the Governors of King Edward's School, Bath)

Latin) meant in reality a school open to all boys and free from hampering restrictions from outside. Fees were therefore payable to the Master.

Boys normally entered the grammar school at the age of seven or eight, leaving at fifteen for university (or perhaps earlier if jobs or professions were to be followed immediately). Before attending the grammar school, the child would already have learnt to read and write in one of the 'petty' schools run by elderly dames. Instruction there was based on the 'horn-book', which consisted of a sheet of paper printed with the alphabet, the vowels and the Lord's Prayer. It was pasted on a simple board with a handle and covered with a piece of transparent horn for protection.

Once at the grammar school, however, boys were expected to concentrate on Latin (with perhaps a little Greek in the higher forms and a smattering of Hebrew). Latin was still very much the official language of the day used by diplomats, lawyers, doctors, civil servants and clerks. It was a basic requirement for entry to university and all the leading professions, including the church. No place would have been found at schools like King Edward's, therefore, for English or the increasing range of 'new' subjects, such as science, mathematics, history or modern languages. However, boys were taught the new greater catechism in Latin, which expounded the doctrines of the Reformation and was made compulsory in all schools from 1553 on strict instructions from Edward VI.

The school was divided into five forms, all housed in the same large schoolroom with one master presiding. As they progressed through the school, the boys were taught the basic rules of grammar, sentence construction and rules for the use of verbs, before proceeding to write Latin in both verse and prose - and to converse fluently in the language. Indeed, boys in the higher forms were forbidden to speak to one another in English. This somewhat unvaried programme of work was implemented through constant repetition, endless testing and constant memorising with tasks set to be undertaken at home.

Boys were expected to work hard for six days a week, reporting at six o'clock in the morning in summer and an hour later in winter. Morning school lasted until eleven o'clock with half an hour break at nine o'clock to enable boys to eat their packed breakfast. After returning home for midday dinner, they would return at one o'clock and work until five. The school bell, which summoned the boys to classes, was mended by the council in Bath in 1582 and provided with a new rope. Although Thursday afternoon was often a 'games afternoon', strict regulations were imposed on behaviour (judging by the rules issued at Ashby-de-la-Zouch Grammar School, which had been founded in 1567):

> In their play they shall use honest games; they shall keep themselves together; they that shall exercise shooting shall be in a place meet for that purpose; they shall not play in the streets, nor go to alehouses, nor play any unlawful games - or break into orchards or rob gardens.

Indeed, a very high standard of conduct was expected from pupils both inside and outside the premises. They were not to 'swear or fight with another or abuse or disturb one another or steal from any'. They were to show courtesy to both strangers and local people. 'When any stranger cometh into the school, the scholars shall arise, stand and salute them - and likewise civilly give the upper hand to those whom they do meet in the streets and courteously salute as it becometh scholars'.

Trustworthy senior boys (or monitors) were chosen to assist in the control and discipline of the school. Their task was to collect in written work, report older pupils who were spotted speaking in English, supervise behaviour in church, record absentees and teach first form boys both the church catechism and the basic rules in Latin. Discipline was strict. Two afternoons in the week were set aside for the punishment of offenders - punishment which could take the form of a stern rebuke, the loss of a place in the form, detention on the games afternoon or a beating. Rules for the conduct of the latter were clearly set out at Ashby-de-la-Zouch Grammar School:

When you are to correct any stubborn or unbroken boy, you make sure with him to hold him fast...appoint three or four of your scholars, whom you know to be honest and strong enough (or more if need be) to lay hands upon him together, to hold him fast over some form so that he cannot stir hand nor foot; or else, if no other remedy will serve, to hold him to some post (which is far the safest and free from inconvenience) so as he cannot hurt himself or others.

(left) *A woodcut showing the schoolroom in a typical grammar school of the 16th/17th century. Note that all the boys are being taught in the same room and that firm discipline is being applied by the Usher on the left. (Author's collection)*

Many of the schoolmasters of the period believed that God had 'sanctified the rod...to drive out that folly which is bound up in their hearts, to save their souls from hell and to give them wisdom'. It was therefore their duty to use it.

The First Schoolrooms

It was a school very similar to the one described above that started its life as the Free Grammar School of King Edward VI at Bath in 1552. Although it was originally thought that the schoolroom was first located in accommodation above the West Gate of the city, there now seems little evidence to substantiate this theory. Recent research by Elizabeth Holland and Marta Inskip has shown that King Edward's School was almost certainly based during this initial period in a house at the end of Frog Lane (see map). Situated on the site of the present New Bond Street, Frog Lane ran parallel to and just outside the city walls. Access to the lane was gained through a narrow passage beneath a house which fronted onto Broad Street. The school house itself was fairly spacious with a garden attached, looking out to the rear over a plot of ground known as the Rack Close.

Almost immediately after its foundation, the school benefited from the generosity and interest of one of the former monks, Dom Nicholas Bathe, who had been pensioned off from the Priory in 1539 to become the Vicar of St Mary de Stalls. It is more than likely that Sir Nicholas Jobbyn (as he now became known) helped to draft the petition for the establishment of the School in 1552. Just before he died a year later, Jobbyn made a will in which he bequeathed 'for the use of the Free Grammar

(below) *A section of Gilmore's map of 1694, showing the location of the grammar school's first two sites. 1 = a house at the end of Frog Lane (1552-1583); 2 = the nave of the disused church of St Mary by the North Gate (1583-1754)*

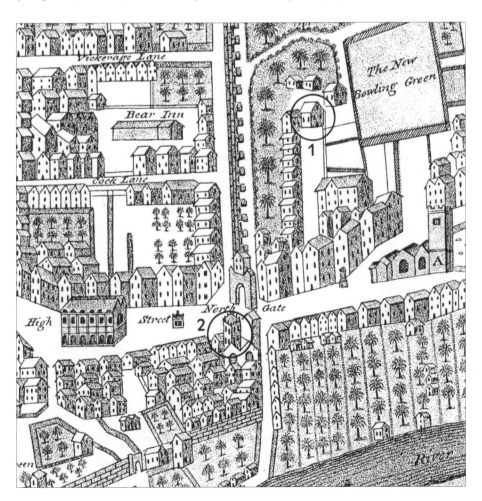

School, certain books of grammar and learning for the use of the schoolmaster and the scholars there'.

In 1583 the school moved to new premises - the nave of the disused Church of St. Mary's by the North Gate. The chamberlain's accounts for that year bear witness to the feverish activity undertaken to convert the church into a schoolroom. For instance, a thousand planks and boards were sawn up to make 'planking' for the school at a cost of fifteen shillings. The tower of the church was soon converted into the city gaol, from which apparently prisoners often shouted insults at travellers as they journeyed through the North Gate. History does not record what verbal contact was enjoyed between the prisoners and the boys of King Edward's! Evidence from the chamberlain's accounts suggests that the schoolroom, the school yard and the schoolmaster's house with its garden and stable were enclosed, partly by the city wall and partly by a wall built parallel to the street (see drawing). Access to the school premises was therefore gained through a door set in this wall. When Antony à Wood visited Bath he noted in his diary that, over the door leading into the school, was engraved this inscription on a stone tablet:

Schola Libera Grammaticalis et institutionem puerorum Bathon. in lingua Latina instructa ex institutione Edwardi Sexti quondam Regis Angliae anno regni sui sexto Anno Domini 1552.
[Free Grammar School provided for the education of Bath boys in the Latin language, by the foundation of Edward VI, formerly King of England, in the sixth year of his reign, A.D. 1552.]

Inside the enclosure there was, in addition to the school, at least one other dwelling place, the occupants of which paid an annual sum of six pence for the right to cross

(above)   *The disused church of St Mary by the North Gate in 1583. Boys gained access to the school yard and schoolroom through the gate, over which was a Latin inscription. (Drawing by Stephen Beck)*

the school yard. One subsequent tenant, Hester Horler, for easier access to her house, persuaded the corporation to allow her to knock a doorway through the city wall 'into the free school court' on payment of an annual rent of six pence. Presumably she had found crossing the school yard too hazardous a business! An earlier occupant of the house, George Matthews, had caused something of a stir in 1633 when he set up a workshop there overlooking the window at the east end of the schoolroom. The noise proved such a nuisance to the schoolmaster and his pupils that he lodged a formal complaint with the corporation. As a result George Matthews was forced to close his workshop. Beyond that house was a garden which was leased in 1682 by George Collibee for one shilling a year, plus the usual payment of six pence for the right to cross the school yard.

Further structural work on the school took place in 1585 as the school started to grow with payments being made for substantial repairs to the roof and major alterations to the schoolmaster's house - an indication that accommodation was now being offered for a few boarders. This was normal practice in grammar schools of this period and provided a welcome method of supplementing the salaries of schoolmasters. Another important development occurred in 1589 when the school was extended into the chancel of the old church. This entailed building a completely new roof and inserting a window into its gable end.

However, in spite of the new window, the schoolroom would undoubtedly have been dark and cold in winter, because it would appear that little provision had been made by the corporation for heating and lighting. Most schools at this time were heated by means of a fireplace and chimney built along one side of the room - indeed, the chimney at the schoolroom in Bath was repaired in 1628. Thus, in common with normal practice, the boys of King Edward's were probably expected to provide their own share of firewood and coal and to bring candles for their personal use in school. Nevertheless, conditions would certainly have been spartan. Elizabethan schoolrooms on average measured 50 feet long and 25 feet wide, catering for about fifty or sixty boys.

Improvements and repairs to the fabric continued throughout the seventeenth century. The problem of lighting was again raised in 1614 when 3s 10d. was paid 'for a glass light set up in the school loft window'. Any increase in the number of windows, however, was a mixed blessing to the master - and to the corporation which footed the bills. With curious regularity the glazier visited the school to repair broken windows (presumably those that faced out on to the school yard!). The roof was retiled in 1614 and again in 1640; the walls were plastered and painted white in 1640; the 'outer door' to the street, inevitably subjected to rough daily treatment, was constantly in need of repair; and in 1665 Goody Cole was paid one shilling 'for cleansing the Free School yard (where litter must have accumulated badly, since this was an irregular payment).

Inside the schoolroom, the master presided over the whole school from a large chair and desk set on a dais at the end of the room. The boys normally sat on benches or forms, working with the books on their knees. The forms were arranged in rows down the sides of the room with a writing table in a large space in the centre (see illustration). This is perhaps substantiated by payments made in 1628 'for a short table board for the schoolhouse'; and in 1633 'for a table frame at the schoolhouse'. Some schools, such as the grammar school at Stratford-upon-Avon, boasted desks for their pupils. King Edward's School, Bath certainly possessed one desk, for some of the earliest entries in 1583 included six pence spent on 'slitting of ii joists for posts for the School desk' and fifteen pence for 'a board for the desk'. This almost certainly was reserved for the exclusive use of the Master.

It is possible that desks were also used, as in other schools, for housing valuable books which were secured by chains. Some schools, such as Eton, gradually built up large 'chained libraries'. The books donated by Sir Nicholas Jobbyn (see above) would probably have fallen into this category. It is perhaps significant that when the corporation purchased two Latin dictionaries for the school in 1594, costing £ 1 3s 4d. and 19s 0d respectively, a directive against one of them read: 'to remain in the free school'. It is more than likely that these books were chained to a desk. In the same year a joiner was paid 4s 6d for 'a writing board for the school'. Blackboards like these were strongly recommended by educationalists of the day for teaching a pupil to write.

The seventeenth-century schoolroom. Details in this drawing by Stephen Beck have been based on expenses listed in the Bath Chamberlain's accounts - including the Master's desk and chair, the writing board and the writing table.

Even greater attention, however, was given to training a boy in the art of speaking Latin both fluently and stylishly. This was partly achieved through the performance of plays in Latin. Ben Jonson felt that this was being overdone in the country's grammar schools: 'They make all their scholars play-boys ... Do we pay our money for this? We send them to learn their grammar and their Terence, and they learn their play-books'. It is true that schoolmasters wrote plays for their pupils to perform for local citizens. In Bath, for example, John Long received payments of 6s 1d and 3s 4d from the corporation for two plays he wrote in 1583. The corporation also paid 6s 8d in 1602 to 'the young men of our city that played at Christmas' and 5s 0d to 'the children that played at Candlemas' - almost certainly the scholars of King Edward's School. Fluency was also achieved by composing and delivering orations in Latin. As early as 1600 the city gave a reward of five shillings to 'Doctor Sherwood's son for pronouncing an oration'. He was a scholar of King Edward's School and the first in a long succession of boys chosen to make a Latin oration to the mayor on Mayor-Making Day. By 1709 this had become an annual tradition, which continued until 1834 when the practice ceased.

Masters of the School

The men appointed by the corporation as Masters of the School during the seventeenth century were all ordained ministers of the Church of England - and most of them were young men of considerable scholarship, who tended to regard King Edward's as a stepping stone to more lucrative appointments elsewhere. Under the terms of the charter, the Bishop of Bath and Wells was empowered to oversee all regulations made for the running of the school; while government legislation stipulated that a licence from the bishop was required by all intending teachers. In 1615, for instance, John Walker of Twerton was severely censured at the Bishop's Visitation 'for keeping a school without a licence'. Governments of the day were determined to prevent the corruption of youngsters by heretical, subversive or immoral masters. Much legislation, like the Act of 1665, was concerned to ensure that teachers 'do themselves frequent the public prayers of the church and cause their scholars to do the same; and appear well affected to the government of His Majesty and the doctrine and discipline of the Church of England'. Catholics and dissenters were totally excluded. It is not surprising, therefore that the masters of King Edward's were almost all Anglican clergy until 1896.

Other legislation, like the ordinance of 1654 during Cromwell's Protectorate, gave power to eject schoolmasters who were 'ignorant, scandalous, insufficient or negligent'. Scandalous behaviour would include blasphemy, swearing, holding 'popish opinions', adultery, the haunting of taverns, the frequent playing of cards or dice and the countenancing of wakes, morris dancing and stage plays. There is no evidence to suggest that any of the seventeenth-century masters of the school were 'ignorant, scandalous or insufficient', although two of them were actually dismissed - one on grounds of religion and the other on grounds of negligence. On his visit to Bath in 1687, James II (a known Catholic) insisted that the corporation should replace the Reverend William Baker (who had been

In this contemporary drawing, the boys are working on benches or forms (although the two at the back seem to be chattering!); two boys are writing at the table; and the Master is inspecting the work of one pupil with his birch-rod at the ready! (Taken from J.A. Comenius, Orbis Sensualiun Pictus,1672 edtn., by permission of the British Library: ref - 1607.2351)

master for six years) with Mr Francis Carne, a member of a local Catholic family. An entry in the council minute book tells its own story: 'Mr Francis Carne elected schoolmaster of the Free School. By His Majesty's command'. His success, however, was short-lived. William Baker was quickly re-instated in the following year after the Glorious Revolution.

Francis Mynn, an Oxford graduate, had been appointed to the job in 1636 at the age of thirty-two. He had survived the turmoil of the Civil War and the disruption caused when 'the school was broke up" (see below). In 1662, however, he was dismissed after twenty-six years service because 'from time to time he neglected his duties therein; and his scholars by reason thereof have generally departed the said school, so that the same is now almost come to nought'. Mynn was given just one week's notice. Nevertheless, the corporation (on the intervention of the bishop) eventually gave him a pension, which amounted to one-third of his salary for the duration of his unemployment. It ceased a year later, when he was appointed Vicar of South Stoke.

This action by the corporation, however, was not as compassionate and generous as it might seem. Mynn's pension was actually taken out of the salary of his successor (the Reverend Richard Hoyle), who therefore did not receive his full entitlement until 1663. This characteristic meanness of the corporation towards salaries was indeed a feature of their trusteeship for some two hundred years after the school's foundation. In spite of the terms of the charter, which had stipulated that revenue from the endowment property was to be used solely for the benefit of the school and ten poor people, the corporation had systematically siphoned off the income for other purposes. Masters were therefore paid well below the average experienced in similar schools elsewhere.

Although the charter had indicated an initial salary of £10 a year and this had been increased to £12 by 1558, it was next raised seventy-three years later (in 1631) to a mere £20 - in spite of soaring inflation during the late sixteenth and early seventeenth centuries. It remained at that figure for the next 131 years - with one short-lived exception. By the end of his tenure in 1662, Mr Mynn was receiving £30 - a sum also paid to his two successors between 1663 and 1664. When, however, the corporation came to make yet another appointment in 1665, faced by mounting debts in their city accounts, they firmly resolved to make radical cuts in the new Master's salary. Events played into their hands. When one of the two candidates recommended by the bishop had the gall to ask £25 a year, he was quickly despatched in favour of the other man (the Reverend William Peake), who was content with a mere £20.

The salary, which was paid quarterly, was supplemented by fees charged to both day boys and boarders. Most masters seem to have taken a few boys from neighbouring towns and villages as lodgers in the school house. All scholars would be required to pay 'quarterages', which usually amounted to six pence a quarter for 'grammarians' and threepence or fourpence a quarter for 'petties' or juniors (some of which could still be polishing up their reading and writing and were under the instruction of senior pupils). In spite of these additional payments and rent-free occupation of the school house, the position was not at all attractive financially. Nevertheless, King Edward's did produce two Masters who went on to much greater things.

The Reverend John Long, educated at Eton and Cambridge, was appointed in 1576 and quickly made his mark as both a teacher and a preacher. He greatly assisted the corporation in drawing up plans for the consolidation of Bath's churches into one parish (see below) and was actually appointed as the first-ever Rector of Bath in 1583, before eventually becoming Primate of All Ireland. The Reverend Alexander Hume, who was Master between 1588 and 1591, was subsequently appointed Master of the High School, Edinburgh, and then Master of Dunbar Grammar School. He made a reputation for himself as an outstanding scholar, who published a Latin grammar book in 1612 (*Grammatica Nova*), which was ordered to be taught in all Scottish schools.

Distinguished Scholars

Entry to the Universities of Oxford and Cambridge was by no means easy for grammar school pupils in the seventeenth century. Most of the fully-fledged colleges were closed corporations, restricting their entry to founder's kin or those qualified to apply for their closed scholarships. Many young students, whose parents were able to afford fees, were therefore forced to gain entry at one of the unendowed halls of residence (such as Hart Hall or Broadgates Hall in Oxford) and wait for possible openings in one of the colleges. King Edward's School had, however, established close connections with two

Oxford Colleges - Corpus Christi College, which had two closed scholarships for candidates born in Somerset; and Oriel College, which not only had closed Somerset scholarships available, but also owned lands around Bath - particularly in Swainswick. Colleges frequently gave preference in the award of scholarships to the able sons of tenants living on their estates. Bright Swainswick boys like the Prynnes, the Webbes and the Clarkes, who learnt their Latin at King Edward's, found entry to Oxford easier than most.

One other Oxford college owned property near Bath. New College which, together with Winchester College, had been founded by William of Wykeham (Bishop of Winchester), owned the manor of Colerne. A priority was therefore often given in the education of scholars at both these institutions to residents of Colerne and its wider neighbourhood. Thus many boys from King Edward's throughout the century were able to proceed to Winchester College at the age of thirteen before transferring to the richly endowed New College for their degree courses two or three years later. The University records reveal that a continuous flow of boys from Bath reaching Oxford - boys who were almost certainly pupils of King Edward's - then the only grammar school in this part of the country (by contrast, very few attended Cambridge).

The school, therefore, was able to contribute handsomely to the revival of learning within the city and to the general enrichment of economic, social and intellectual life as boys returned from Oxford to take up positions of responsibility and leadership - doctors such as Thomas Bayly, who joined Oxford in 1631; barristers such as Thomas Harris (1660); educationalists such as John Rosewell (1663), who eventually became Headmaster of Eton; and clergy such as Richard Hadley (1600), who became Vicar of Twerton in 1623, Theophilus Webbe (1623), who became Rector of Bath in 1624, and James Masters (1627), who also became Rector of Bath in 1639. Others came back to play a full part in local government - such as William Prynne (1618), who became Recorder of Bath in 1647, and Walter Chapman, who eventually became an alderman and then

Boys were allowed time for games, some of which are illustrated in this contemporary drawing - including skittles, bowls and quoits together with the use of stilts, bows-and-arrows, whips-and-tops and swings. The scrumping of apples by the boy at the back was not an official sport. (Taken from J.A. Comenius, Orbis Sensualiun Pictus, 1672 edtn., by permission of the British Library: ref - 1607.2351)

mayor. Indeed, virtually the whole of the remarkable Chapman family, which made such a notable contribution to the professional and business life of the city, seem to have attended the school. The majority of parents, who educated their sons there, were drawn from the ranks of the middle class - clergy, lawyers, doctors and farmers - or from the ranks of the aldermen and freemen of the city.

Four pupils are worthy of more detailed attention in view of their national fame. Robert Peirce, son of the Rector of Combe Hay, attended King Edward's before going on to Winchester College and Lincoln College, Oxford. A student of medicine, he was elected Fellow of the College of Physicians and later entertained Charles II at the

Abbey House in Bath, attending him also as personal physician. Perhaps more than anyone, he firmly established the medicinal value and prestige of the city's hot springs.

The 'ever memorable' John Hales, son of the city's attorney, had perhaps the most distinguished academic career of all. A Scholar of Corpus Christi College, Oxford at the age of thirteen, he was subsequently elected fellow of Merton College and canon of Windsor before his appointment as Regius Professor of Greek at Oxford (1615-19). He later became Chaplain to Archbishop Laud. A friend of Milton and Ben Jonson, he was described by Lord Clarendon as 'one of the least men in the kingdom and one of the greatest scholars in Europe'.

William Prynne, son of a Swainswick farmer, became barrister-at-law at Lincoln's Inn in 1628 after graduating at Oriel College, Oxford. He became nationally famous in the 1630s for a series of pamphlets attacking both the court and the bishops. In consequence, he was twice tried in the Court of Star Chamber, being sentenced on each occasion to life imprisonment, a fine of £5,000, loss of his degrees and loss of his ears. On the second occasion he was also branded with the letter 'S.L.' (seditious libeller). Released from the Tower by the Long Parliament in 1641 just prior to the outbreak of civil war, he played a leading part in the trial of Archbishop Laud. After his return to Swainswick, he eventually became Recorder of Bath (1647), M.P. for Bath (1660-69) and collector of its records. He was also Keeper of the Records in the Tower of London from 1660 until his death in 1669.

Thomas Rosewell, the orphaned son of a gentleman from Dunkerton, was born in 1630. His own son wrote this about him later:

> Soon after his father's death, Mr Rosewell was by his guardian sent to school in Bath. There he was taken ill of the smallpox in the year 1641...Here he continued some time and made considerable progress in learning till the Civil Wars began to rage. And the king's army taking that garrison, their school was broke up and the youth were scattered...About this time, travelling a little from home, he accidentally saw King Charles the First sitting at dinner under a tree with some few persons about him. This made such a deep impression in his young and tender mind, as disposed in him the greater compassion and loyalty towards that unhappy monarch.

After gaining his degree at Pembroke College, Oxford, he later became Rector of Rode in Somerset. He was eventually ejected from his living under the terms of the Act of Uniformity in 1662 (see Chapter 14) and was forced to preach to non-conformist gatherings in private houses. It was, however, his arrest in 1684 on an absurd charge of treasonable preaching that made him nationally famous. He was tried and found guilty by the notorious Judge Jeffreys, only to be pardoned by the personal intervention of King Charles II. 'If your Majesty suffers this man to die', pleaded Sir John Talbot, 'we are none of us safe in our houses'.

Education for Girls

A young girl from a middle class family would either be taught at home or attend the petty school with her brother. There she would concentrate on learning to read (which was much easier than learning to write) and on gaining some numeracy (which would be useful later when shopping for food at the market). It has been shown that whereas 5-10% of women in London were able to write in 1640, about 48% of them could read in 1700. Nor was such a level of illiteracy confined to women. In 1675, of the nineteen members of the Guild of the Merchant Tailors of Bath who signed an order, eight of them (or 42%) were unable to write their names (using a mark instead) - including one of the two Masters of the Guild. In the seventeenth century, it was generally accepted that girls should not waste their time learning Latin at grammar school, but should rather learn from mother the skills of running a home. As Hannah Woolley commented in 1682, 'most in this depraved later age think a woman learned and wise enough if she can distinguish her husband's bed from another's'.

Children from the poorer homes had few opportunities to benefit from formal education, unless a charity school had been established in the town. This did not happen in Bath until 1711, when the Society for the Propagation of Christian Knowledge set up the Bluecoats School under a master (Henry Dixon) and a mistress (Mrs Bell). The school, which depended largely on charitable donations, was designed to take girls and boys from the deserving poor between the ages of seven and fourteen, before they moved into apprenticeships or domestic service. Great emphasis was placed on learning the elements of the Christian religion (they attended services in the Abbey), avoiding sloth, acquiring discipline (they were provided with uniforms) and grasping the fundamentals of reading, writing and arithmetic. By the 1720s, the school had moved into new premises in Upper Borough Walls.

SOURCES USED IN CHAPTER 12

1. Printed Material
Fawcett, Trevor: *Bath Administer'd: Corporation Affairs at the 18th-Century Spa* (2001)
Fox, Levi: *A Country Grammar School: a History of Ashby-da-la-Zouch Grammar School* (1967)
Picard, Lisa: *Restoration London* (1997)
Sim, Alison: *The Tudor Housewife* (1966)
Symonds, Katherine E: *The Grammar School of King Edward VI, Bath* (1934)
The Arraignment and Tryal of the late Reverend Mr Thomas Rosewell for High Treason (1718)
Waller, Maureen: *Scenes from London Life* (2000)
Wroughton, John: *King Edward's School at Bath, 1552-1982* (1982)
2. Documentary Material
Bath Record Office   Freemen's Estate 118 - Merchant Tailors' Quarterly Meetings, Memoranda and
                            Account Book, 1666-94

CHAPTER 13

The Daily Pressures of Civil War

Damage to the Fabric

In spite of the fact that Bath was a walled city, housing a garrison throughout the Civil War (1642-46), it escaped with surprisingly little damage to its defences and buildings. Other cities in the west country fared much worse. In Gloucester, for instance, the corporation ordered 241 houses outside the city walls to be destroyed in 1643 in an attempt to deny royalists cover for their assault; while in Bristol (for exactly the same reason), Prince Rupert sent out 'parties of horse with fireballs' in 1645 to burn the outlying villages of Bedminster, Clifton, Redland and Westbury-on-Trym as he prepared for attack by the New Model Army. Marlborough, with 53 houses burnt to the ground and 2,000 people made homeless during a royalist attack in 1642, actually did far better than either Taunton (which saw two-thirds of its houses destroyed during the 1645 siege) or Bridgwater (which suffered a great fire bombardment in the same year accounting for 120 houses out of a total of four hundred). The cost of the damage was colossal (£28,700 worth in Gloucester and £50,000 worth in Marlborough); the cost to human lives immeasurable with thousands destitute and homeless long after the war had ended.

   Bath, on the other hand, was never subjected to serious attack. Sir Ralph Hopton's royalist army, which had planned to take the city by force in 1643, was held at bay on Lansdown by Sir William Waller's parliamentarians - and when it returned a

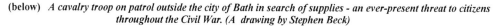

(below)   *A cavalry troop on patrol outside the city of Bath in search of supplies - an ever-present threat to citizens throughout the Civil War. (A drawing by Stephen Beck)*

week later, after routing Waller at Roundway Down, it entered the city unopposed. Furthermore, although there was a brief skirmish at the bridge in 1645, when a parliamentarian reconnaissance party clashed with the royalist garrison (which then surrendered in panic), at no time during the war was the city bombarded by heavy artillery. The fact, therefore that Bath was never besieged meant that it also escaped the on-going fear of starvation; the nightly terror experienced in Gloucester, where incendiaries and mortars rained down on the population; and the horror of post-siege plunder and atrocities which afflicted the inhabitants of Bristol in 1643 as victorious troops rampaged through the city. Charles Payman, who visited Bath in 1646 confirmed the lack of serious damage sustained during the war and attributed it to the fact the 'Mars made it not his house but his thoroughfare - and rather baited than dwelt therein'. Soldiers were indeed present throughout, but they caused no real damage and were 'pretty mannerly', according to Payman. Even the churches were spared the normal sort of vandalism inflicted by Puritan soldiers on statues, stained glass and other 'Popish' images (see Chapter 14).

The Intrusion of Troops

However, in spite of the lack of structural damage, the citizens of Bath did suffer greatly in human terms as the war progressed. For four whole years, the city was alive with troops - troops from the ever-present garrison force and troops from armies marching through. The garrison itself varied in size from one hundred for much of the war to one thousand in 1645, when the New Model Army arrived in Somerset to recapture the west. Just before the Battle of Lansdown in 1643, however, Sir William Waller had seven thousand troops camped on Claverton Down for the space of three weeks and there were major troop movements again in 1645 in preparation for the siege of Bristol by parliament. Not all these soldiers could have been accommodated inside the city, of course - some would have found billets in neighbouring villages - but Bath residents were always aware of the constant drift of soldiers wherever they looked.

Soldiers needed three things in particular from the local population - money for pay, beds for rest and food for both man and horse. By 1643, both sides in the war had introduced **a weekly tax** to be paid by all residents within their area of control. Parliament ordered Somerset to provide a total of £1,050 per week - to be divided out among all the parishes and collected by local officers. In 1643, the Bath chamberlain certainly recorded one payment of twelve shillings for a month's contribution to 'the weekly tax' - although normally this would have been collected on a house-to-house basis by the tax collectors and not paid for by the corporation. While people were very accustomed to the payment of taxes (such as the poll tax, ship money, subsidies, loans and the poor rate), there was general resistance to this weekly assessment in view of all the other demands made on them during the war (see below). In consequence, strong arm tactics were sometimes used with tax collectors accompanied by armed soldiers. This rather colourful piece of propaganda from a parliamentarian news sheet of 1644, relating to the methods used by the royalist governor of Bath, nevertheless contains a degree of truth concerning the use of force:

> He hath about 300 Irish under his command there, whom he sends out into the country
> to fetch in contributions at his pleasure. He daily offers many affronts and commits
> many insolences against the inhabitants, forcibly taking away their goods; and lately

offered to pistol the mayor of the town had not the women there, in the absence of most of his soldiers, threatened to pull him in pieces. On Saturday night last, he sent out a party, who fetched in about thirty of the countrymen thereabouts, and brought them in two by two for not paying the unreasonable taxes assessed upon them - most of them they imprisoned...

When special demands were made on the city over and above the weekly tax, the corporation collected a special rate from householders - as in 1643, when a rate was charged 'for provisions for His Majesty's army'; or, in 1644, when another one was gathered to satisfy an instant demand for £40 from Prince Maurice, the brother of Prince Rupert.

The billeting of soldiers in private houses on 'free quarter' was always costly in terms of the food provided, the damage inflicted and the property plundered. (A drawing by Stephen Beck)

But however much ordinary people disliked the regular demands of the tax collector, this was nothing compared with the horror, fear and disgust with which they greeted the arrival of troops in search of **free quarter**. The most unlucky householders could only submit to the demands of armed men for board and lodging, hoping that the ticket given in return would one day be exchanged for cash. It seldom was. At the same time, this 'free quarter', as it was called, was often accompanied by plunder, vandalism and drunken behaviour. John Turberville, a Somerset man, described his own experience to a friend in these words: 'My house is, and hath been, full of soldiers for a fortnight: such uncivil drinkers and thirsty souls that a barrel of good beer trembles at the sight of them; and the whole house nothing but a rendezvous of tobacco and spitting'. It should be remembered that many of the conscripts were the roughest and most uncouth of men. William Prynne, who later became Recorder and then Member of Parliament for Bath, recalled in a graphic account how he had been visited at his home in Swainswick in 1648 by thirty soldiers - quite the rudest and most boisterous he had ever quartered:

They climbed over my walls, forced my doors, beat my servants and workmen without any provocation, drew their swords upon me...brake some of my windows, forced my strong-beer cellar door...hollowed, roared, stamped, beat the tables with their swords and muskets like so many bedlams, swearing, cursing and blaspheming at every word; brake the tankards, bottles, cups, dishes wherein they fetched strong beer against the ground; abused my maid-servants, throwing beef and other good provisions against their heads, and casting it to the dogs as no fit meat for soldiers - and the heads and conquerors of the kingdom, as they called themselves...They continued drinking, roaring before, at and after supper, till most of them were mad-drunk and some of them dead-drunk under the table. Then they must have 14 beds provided for them (for they would lie but two in a bed) and all their linen washed...

Some villages on the edge of Bath suffered on numerous occasions during the war, particularly if they were on the main road to Bristol. This was certainly true of Twerton (a village of some twenty-eight houses and a population of about one hundred and fifty), which was forced to host in quick succession a company of Waller's own regiment, two hundred of Captain Abbot's cavalry 'when they marched against Bristol', forty-seven men of Sir Thomas Fairfax's own Lifeguards, thirty-one soldiers of the Bath garrison (who stayed for over six weeks), ten New Model Army troopers from Cromwell's regiment and finally eight hundred soldiers of Colonel Montague's regiment, thirty horses and eighteen oxen for one night when they marched from Bristol to Devizes. In between, they had accommodated thirty-one of Sir Thomas Fairfax's sick soldiers, some for a fortnight and some for a month. They were not paid for their efforts.

Combe Hay was another village nearby which had far more than its share of disturbance. In the three weeks prior to the Battle of Lansdown in 1643, they were forced not only to quarter a troop of sixty cavalry, but also to suffer the daily rendezvous of the whole parliamentarian army. This caused considerable damage to their crops as the troops trampled their way across fields 'ready for mowing' from their billets in other villages. Furthermore, much of their hay was requisitioned, eighty sheep stolen and Elizabeth Bailey's grey mare pressed into service to carry ammunition. In a later compensation claim, it was estimated that this episode cost the village £114. Two years later, the nightmare returned as troops gathered for the siege of Bristol. Indeed, the village had no fewer than eight visitations between July 1645 and January 1646. The first intruders seemed innocent enough (twenty-five officers and men from the New Model Army) until they demanded on departure beer, meat, bread and cheese for four hundred men at a rendezvous on Bathampton Down. But worse was to follow. After a regiment of eight hundred infantry had descended on the village on their way to Devizes, they were followed hard at heel next day by a total of thirteen hundred men 'which company', they later complained, 'spoiled and killed eighty sheep'. **Plunder** all too often was the bed-fellow of free quarter.

Such pressures were of course even more acute within the city of Bath itself, because troops were constantly in residence. By February 1646, the citizens were totally exhausted and were suffering from an extreme form of war weariness. Although the last of the garrison troops had left after parliamentarian forces had tightened their grip on the region, the western counties were still alive with the constant movement of troops. These soldiers, with no local loyalty and little human sympathy, descended on Bath with monotonous regularity for temporary shelter and sustenance - so much so that the inhabitants finally decided that they had had enough. The council, meeting in emergency session to discuss the situation, resolved as a first step to send a petition to parliament for release from all further demands for free quarter. Two of the councillors made the journey to London to deliver the petition by hand.

The Mayor of Bath, John Biggs, also took the precaution of writing to John Harington of Kelston, a good friend to the locality, imploring him to persuade his son, Captain Harington, to use his influence in the army on behalf of the city. In particular,

(left) *The plundering soldier of 1642 caricatured with an artichoke for a sword, a cooking pot with duck for a helmet, a dripping pan for a shield, a spit with goose for a musket and wine bottles for powder cartridges. (By permission of the British Library: ref - 669F (12) - 'The English Irish Soldier')*

he was asked to ensure that no further demands for money were issued in view of the city's evident distress. Visits by previous troops had caused terrible devastation in private houses, as soldiers on the rampage had indulged themselves in looting and wanton destruction. 'Our houses are emptied of all useful furniture, and much broken and disfigured; our poor suffer for want of victuals', complained Biggs. 'We have now 400 troops in the town and many more coming; God protect us from pillage'. Captain Harington responded by bringing his own company to Bath so that he could keep an eye on their behaviour and protect local people.

The move clearly worked. The mayor's subsequent letter of gratitude to Captain Harington gives a graphic picture of the horrors of free quarter and its associated terror of plunder, even though Harington's presence had prevented the worst sort of excesses, which often characterised soldiers on free quarter. On the arrival of the troops, a demand for money had indeed been made (in spite of the mayor's plea), backed by the threat of pillage to those individuals who 'had not monies ready'. Although the city was spared the normal request for new conscripts to be provided from amongst the inhabitants, it was nevertheless required to produce eighteen horses for the army's use. There was little plunder as such, 'excepting in liquors and bedding', but food set aside by families for the day's meal was taken at will by a troop from Marlborough (though 'they restored it again to many of the poorer sort' when pressurised by Harington). The discomfort endured by local people in a tightly-confined city seething with disreputable humanity cannot be overstated.

Family life was disrupted ('our beds they occupied entirely'); city administration was interrupted ('the Town House was filled with troops'); and religious worship was thrown into turmoil ('the churches are full of troops, furniture and bedding'). And this was a friendly troop! People lived continuously in a state of fear and suspicion. Even the mayor was obliged to find a poor man to smuggle his letter to Harington: 'I dare not send a man on horseback', he wrote, 'as the horse would be taken. God preserve our kingdom from these sad troubles much longer'. Fortunately, the petition to parliament had some effect. By May, 1646 permission had been granted for the council to demolish the city's fortifications (i.e. the earthworks that had been dug outside the walls, the barricades erected in front of the gates and the temporary drawbridge over the ditch) - a month after the last army had made its way across the county. The war at last was over.

Even so, the army itself had not been disbanded and was still on manoeuvres. In December, therefore, the corporation was again forced to impose a rate on householders to pay for the quartering of thirty-two soldiers and horses for six days in the first instance, but with the threat that the stay might well be extended. The total cost for the city was calculated at £4 per day (or £24 for the first six days). Although the two appointed assessors would calculate exactly how much each of the three hundred and twenty households would contribute, the average charge per household would be 1s 6d (or a quarter of a labourer's weekly pay).

Loss of the Quality of Life

Quite apart from the personal impact of soldiers on the lives of ordinary families, the normal flow of everyday activity was badly disrupted during the war. In spite of the fact that the council itself was spilt politically (with two-thirds supporting parliament and one-third supporting the king), the council continued to meet regularly with members of both persuasions sitting side-by-side throughout the war in an attempt to maintain essential services. That, above all, was their immediate priority. Of vital importance was the need to retain an healthy balance-in-hand in the annual accounts - no easy task in the middle of a war with the city permanently occupied. It was to their enormous credit that this goal was achieved in each successive year (£229, for instance, in 1646 - compared with a heavy deficit of £606 and near bankruptcy in Worcester in 1645). Equal success was gained in maintaining the city's water supply by checking the pipes and repairing them regularly; in securing the community from disease by ensuring that the scavenger safely disposed of the 'night soil' well outside on the common; in continuing to support the deserving poor through the city's four hospitals and the seasonal gifts of bread, wood and coal; and in keeping open the market, the very lifeblood of the community. The council therefore never failed in its duty to appoint market officials (the ale tasters and the supervisors of leather, fish and meat) or to control the use of the common, ensuring that hay was cropped and cattle grazed as before.

Nevertheless, in other less vital areas, there was a noticeable **breakdown in basic administration**, particularly during the years of royalist occupation (1643-45), when relationships were badly strained with the garrison. Very few freemen, for instance, were elected during this period; the collection of rents fell badly behind

(below) *Extract from the Bath Chamberlain's Accounts, 1643, detailing expenditure for the defence of the city. (By courtesy of Bath Record Office, Bath and N.E. Somerset Council). The lines read as follows:*

Imprimis payd for placinge the barrells of match in the hall * Item paid for mendinge a locke
Item paid for paper to make upp powder in * Item paid for hoopinge the markett pecke and two old
barrells to hold bulletts in * Item paid to sev(er)all men for timber for posts at the chaines
Item paid for carriinge a letter to Honad Streete * Item paid to Joseph Holder for cleansinge the way by the Burrowalls
Item paid to labourers for settinge upp and takinge downe the barricadoes at East and West gate
Item paid for mendinge the lanthorne * Item paid for the criers coate and makeinge
Item paid for bread and beare for them that brought the greate guns

schedule; and it became extremely difficult to transfer leases on property. Furthermore, two major areas of normal expenditure suffered badly. Whereas previously the council had been noticeably generous in making random gifts to people in distress outside the hospitals (such as clothing to destitute children, repairs to a widow's chimney or a shroud for a pauper), these acts of kindness almost ceased.

Secondly, whereas the Council had taken great pride in maintaining and improving its public buildings before the war (i.e. the Guildhall, the market house, the school, the baths, the prison, the House of Correction and the public drinking fountains - not to mention the roads and the bridge), **the fabric of the city** was now badly neglected. From an average annual expenditure of over £26 during the 1630s, the total spent on repairs slumped to just 13s 4d in 1644. The reason for this decline was partly the feeling that repairs were pointless in time of war, but chiefly the need to spend heavily on defence (i.e. building up stocks in the armoury, repairing the walls and the gates, erecting earthworks and barricades or employing special 'courts of guards' at night). Before the war in 1637, for instance, the defence budget had only accounted for 2.4% of the annual expenditure; by 1645, it had risen to almost 40%.

A 'Court of Guard' on nightly duty by the West Gate of the city during the Civil War. (A drawing by Stephen Beck)

Citizens of Bath, therefore, found that their environment became increasingly grubby as the war progressed and their life, in many small ways, became far less certain and far more worrying. They suffered from a **restriction in movement**. The curfew was strictly enforced with three 'courts of guards' patrolling various sectors of the city at night. These were often intrusive - as Mr Ernley of Westgate House found to his cost. After six years of campaigning, he finally gained a rent rebate from the council in 1652 as recompense for 'the loss and damage suffered by reason of the court of guards kept there' when the city was garrisoned. Other citizens suddenly found that they had lost their own private doors through the city walls, which had been granted in peace-time for convenience of access. These were now all blocked up.

A general concern over growing restrictions to the free movement of local people was voiced in the council in 1645, highlighting the fact that travel through the city gates had been badly hampered by the large earthworks that had been erected outside. It was therefore decided to build a drawbridge over these earthworks at the West Gate 'to the end that the gate may be opened and left open for the general ease and use of the city'.

Everyday life was also affected in unexpected ways by the consequences of military action. The inhabitants of Widcombe, for instance, were deeply concerned about war damage of a different kind - damage to the three main roads which ran through their village. 'Since these unhappy wars', they stated in a petition to the County Assizes in 1647, 'by reason of the often passage of armies and carriages through those ways and the lack of timely repair, the ways are grown so ruinous that the inhabitants, being for the most part very poor and eaten out with free quarter, taxes, contributions and billeting of soldiers... are not able to sufficiently repair them without some competent contribution from the city of Bath'. Such **damage to roads and bridges** (some of it deliberate, of course, to slow down the movement of enemy forces) was one of the costly and lingering effects of the war. Farming activity was often seriously hampered in consequence with access blocked to both fields and markets. The citizens of Bath itself suffered revulsion from the terrible mess which the soldiers had left on their own narrow streets after the Battle of Lansdown. The council paid a number of men to remove what filth they could, including a dead horse which had to be dragged out of the water course - and another which had fallen in a street corner.

Threats to the Local Economy

The livelihood of Bath's inhabitants was highly dependent upon its status as a health resort, which provided major employment for many local people - not only in the hot water baths, but also in the inns, lodging houses, shops and workshops; and on its tradition as a centre for the cloth-making industry. Once war started in 1642, prospects looked bleak for the local economy.

Indeed, business in **the health trade** was badly hit once hostilities had commenced, partly because many of the city's regular clients had already joined the king in York. A newspaper reporter commented: 'The inhabitants of Bath express great griefs that they have had little company this summer...The poor guides are now necessitate to guide one another to the ale-house, lest they should lose their practice. The ladies that are there are fallen into a lethargy for want of stirring cavaliers to keep them awake...The poor fiddlers are ready to hang themselves in their strings for a pastime for want of other employments'.

However, in spite of this initial setback (which had seriously threatened the employment of hundreds of people), business quickly revived as the city adjusted to changing circumstances by catering for a different type of clientele. Those who now flocked into Bath included wounded soldiers looking for a cure for their mutilated limbs. Lord George Goring, for instance, arrived in 1645 in the hope of curing his lameness; while, in 1644, the king himself arranged for a hostage to take the place in custody of his old friend, Sir Gervase Scroop (who then lay wounded in enemy hands) so that Scroop could take the waters of Bath - believing this to be his only hope for survival.

Bath also gained heavily as a health resort from the large number of political and military leaders who chose to be based there, rather than in Bristol (the official military headquarters for the West). Bristol was regarded with good reason as an unpleasant and unhealthy place : 'The city itself is now so nasty and filthy', wrote one observer, 'that a traveller that comes out of the fresh air can scarce endure it'. Both King Charles and his son, therefore, much preferred the purer air of Bath, where the water was uncontaminated. Sir Thomas Fairfax, Major-General Skippon and General Cromwell were all to follow in their footsteps in 1645 and were duly honoured on arrival by the council with gifts of wine and sugar. Bath therefore remained a bustling and vigorous centre throughout the war, attracting large numbers of distinguished guests and maimed soldiers alike into its inns and lodging houses.

The major problem facing those involved in **the cloth-making industry** around Bath was that goods on their way to market were always liable to be intercepted by soldiers. This was certainly the experience of John Ashe of Freshford, who employed an enormous workforce of two thousand spinners and weavers working in their own cottages in local villages. Ashe sent a weekly convoy of cloths up to the family firm in London for later export to the continent - cloths collected not only from his own workshops, but also from those of his friends and family nearby. One of these convoys, in March 1643 - consisting of eight cartloads and twenty-four horse loads (amounting to three hundred and eighty cloths in all) - was seized and confiscated by the royalist governor of Reading. Judging by evidence contained in the Ashe firm's account book, trade from North Somerset had been badly disrupted during the previous autumn, when the Thames Valley was alive with military activity as the king made an abortive attempt to regain his capital. Not one of Ashe's normal convoys managed to reach London in the November and only one in the December. Circumstances did improve later in the war and production certainly continued in Freshford and its satellite villages.

Quite apart from those inhabitants in Bath and its immediate locality who worked for Ashe, there were also a number of independent clothiers who operated chiefly in Broad Street and Walcot Street (see Chapter 8). Their operation, of course, was on a much smaller scale and they therefore traditionally traded in the local markets of Bath and Bristol. In view of the fact that these remained open and were largely accessible for much of the war, it is more than likely that these men were able to secure their own livelihood and that of their dependent workforce of spinners and weavers. Furthermore, many of them had interests in agriculture, which made them less dependent on the uncertainties of trade.

The goods of traders on the way to market were always likely to be intercepted by troops in search of supplies - as is the case with this convoy sent by local clothiers. (A drawing by Stephen Beck)

On the other hand, some people experienced **commercial benefits from the war**. It should be remembered that producers and craftsmen of all kinds often gained considerably from army officers and garrison commanders in search of supplies for their troops. Although, as we have seen, armies on the march often plundered their way around the land, living off the countryside at the expense of ordinary people - it is also true that army quartermasters seldom relied totally on requisitions. They were always ready to spend money raised from taxes in local markets on food, shoes, stockings, cloth for uniforms, bullets and weapons - just as ordinary soldiers (with pay sometimes in their pockets) were keen to supplement their meagre diet in local shops and taverns. Indeed, it was customary for organised markets to exploit this demand by following in the wake of armies on the march. Established markets within the stable conditions provided by a garrisoned town were therefore always likely to do equally well.

Details of such local transactions are seldom recorded, except where disputes later arose over unpaid bills. As late as 1662, John Russell, a Bath butcher, was still petitioning the corporation for reimbursement. His complaint was that 'in the last late wars, upon the coming of the king's army into this city, he delivered by the order of the then mayor and justices so much beef unto the constables of this city for the provision of the said army, as came to the value of three pounds and fifteen shillings'. Happily, the corporation agreed to pay him in full. Thomas Gibbs was not so lucky in 1669, however, when the corporation turned down his request for 'the money due for beer and other things by his father delivered in the time of the war'. The presence of a garrison in Bath greatly increased the number of consumers and therefore benefited those with goods to sell.

****

How badly, then, was the community of Bath affected by the war? There is no doubt that the hostilities caused temporary disruption to daily routine and economic activity. There is also no doubt that the war seriously reduced the quality of life for inhabitants, all of whom were forced to endure discomfort, humiliation, anxiety and deprivation at the hands of soldiers. Local people looked on with disgust as their homes were turned into barracks; citizens watched with horror as their health resort was transformed into a garrison. Fabric was neglected, privacy lost and morale lowered. But more than anything, the hostilities induced a state of war weariness and a deep loathing of military intrusion.

Even after the ending of the war in 1646, local citizens were obliged to face up to the cost of its lingering effects. All parishes, for instance, were expected to contribute to the 'maimed soldiers' rate', which helped to provide modest pensions to those permanently disabled or widowed by the war. Forty-six years later, Bath Corporation was still contributing to this fund, although the annual contribution had been reduced from £2 19s 0d to £1 5s 8d.

Nevertheless, in spite of it all, the markets continued to function, the health trade was revived, the cloth industry survived and the people were fed. Even Bath's fortifications escaped largely unscathed. Existing records give no hint of large-scale unemployment or food shortages within the war period. In some ways, of course, army recruiting officers helped to solve the problem of unemployment and poverty by mopping up surplus labour. Furthermore, the people themselves were resilient. After all, to a community accustomed to natural disasters, regular harvest failure and widespread unemployment in the previous two decades, the Civil War was just one further setback to normal life. The city's in-built affluence, epitomised by the council's constant balance-in-hand, enabled it to survive with comparative ease this latest crisis in the series.

SOURCES USED IN CHAPTER 13

1. Printed material

Harington, H: *Nugae Antiquae*, vol. 2 (1779)

Oldmixon, John: *History of England during the Reigns of the Royal House of Stuart* (1730)

Wroughton, John: *A Community at War:the Civil War in Bath & North Somerset* (1992)

Wroughton, John: *An Unhappy Civil War: the Experiences of Ordinary People in Gloucestershire, Somerset and Wiltshire, 1642-1646* (1999)

2. Documentary material

Bath Record Office:	Bath Chamberlain's Accounts, 1642-1646
	Bath Council Minute Books, No. 1, 1631-1649
Bodleian Library:	Rawlinson MSS, D.945 (34) Charles Paman's Letter Book
British Library:	Thomason Tracts - *Special Passages, 9th-16th May 1643*
	Mercurius Aulicus, 21st-28th March 1643
Public Record Office:	Calendar of State Papers Domestic, 1667, 1683, 1693
	C107/20, The Cloth Books of James Ashe

CHAPTER 14

Religious Life

The Completion of Bath Abbey, 1600-1616

By 1617, the city was in proud possession of a fine new parish church. This had been resurrected from the shell of the old church, which had been started in 1499 by Bishop Oliver King as a church for Bath Priory in response to God's challenge to him in a dream.

(below) *Jacob Spornberg's drawing of the Abbey's west front, which appeared in Richard Warner's* History of Bath *in 1801. The fine west door, donated by Sir Henry Montague in 1617, is clearly visible - as are the stone carvings, still largely undamaged by the passage of time. (Author's collection)*

Work on the project, however, had been totally halted by the dissolution of the monasteries in 1539, after which the site had been badly plundered. However, forty-five years after a nationwide appeal for money by Queen Elizabeth I in 1572, the splendid church (dedicated to St Peter and St Paul) was completed at last. Inside the building, the choir, which was partitioned off from the nave, had been fitted out for divine service with an organ, stone pulpit, pews and galleries. A vestry had been built with a fine Jacobean ceiling, thanks to the beneficence of John Hall of Bradford and Sir Nicholas Salterne of London, whose arms were displayed inside - together with those of King James I. The nave, at last, had been given a handsome timber roof with the arms of Bishop James Montague, its chief benefactor, set in the ceiling. This complemented the original stone fan vaulting over the choir, constructed by the master masons of Henry VII's Chapel at Westminster and St George's Chapel at Windsor, which had survived from the Priory church. The new west door, which greatly enhanced the west façade, had been donated by the bishop's brother, Sir Henry Montague, Lord Chief Justice. Not everyone was to admire that façade, however, with its representation of Bishop Oliver King's dream carved in stone. Daniel Defoe later condemned it as 'almost blasphemously decorated...the work of superstition', whereas John Wood remonstrated that the flock of angels on each ladder looked like 'so many bats clung against the wall'.

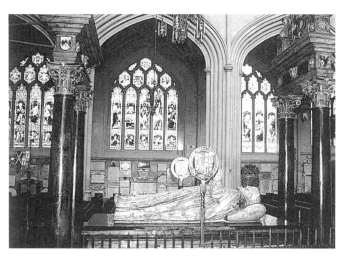

The tomb and effigy of Bishop James Montague (Bishop of Bath & Wells, 1608-13), built in 1618-1619. (Author's collection - by courtesy of the Rector of Bath Abbey)

Almost before the church's completion, striking monuments had started to appear inside. It was most appropriate that a splendid altar-tomb should have been erected in 1618 for Bishop Montague, showing the recumbent figure of the prelate at prayer,.Although he was, by the time of his death, Bishop of Winchester, his will had emphasised his wish to be buried 'in the Great Church of Bath...to stir up some more benefactors to that place'. In some ways it seems strange that the most prestigious place of all in the sanctuary should have been granted to Bartholomew Barnes, a Puritan merchant not from Bath, but from London. Although it is true that he had left a small legacy to the Abbey (but a much smaller sum in fact than those donated by others), he had given the project an enormous boost, at a time when it was flagging. In one great act of optimism, he had decided to commission his own funeral monument for that very spot in 1608 long before the building showed any sign of completion. This proved a great inspiration to all involved. The other striking monument of this period, situated in the south transept, is that of Lady Jane Waller (who died in 1637), seen in effigy with that of her husband, Sir William Waller, a keen Puritan who fought for parliament in the Battle of Lansdown in 1643. The dead, like Lady Waller, are always shown in horizontal posture, whereas the living, like Sir William, are depicted either upright or in semi-recumbent pose.

While all this building work had been taking place at the Abbey, serious thought had been given to the future use of all the other churches. In 1572, the corporation had bought up the advowsons [i.e. the right to appoint clergy to livings within the

(right) *The tomb of Lady Jane Waller, Sir William's first wife. Built in 1633 by the sculptor, Epiphanius Evesham, it displays alabaster effigies of the couple, which were later damaged by royalist soldiers. (Author's collection - by courtesy of the Rector of Bath Abbey)*

church] of all the city churches and had then proceeded (by gaining an Act of Parliament in 1583) to consolidate these into one rectory [i.e to make one rector responsible for all the churches with the help of assistant clergy]. As a result, the Abbey became the parish church under a newly-appointed Rector, John Long, and three of the existing churches fell into disuse - St Michael's by the West Gate (known locally as St Michael's *within* the walls), which was later used as a chandler's shop and then as a post office; St Mary's by the North Gate, which was soon converted to house both a school in the nave (until 1762) and a prison in the tower (until 1765); and St Mary de Stall at the top of Stall Street. This had previously been both the parish church, where the corporation held its formal services, and the church of the city guild, where the freemen of Bath met to admit new members. It quickly fell into a state of disrepair, its buildings plundered for their stone and its churchyard built over with shops and houses. By the seventeenth century, therefore, just two other churches had survived apart from the Abbey - St Michael's outside the North Gate (or St Michael's *without*) and St James's by the South Gate.

The Puritan Revolution, 1600-1660

By the time of the Abbey's completion in 1616, the city was tightly in the grip of a Puritan revolution. The Reformation in England, launched by Henry VIII in the 1530s, had been slow to take root at parish level, where Catholic teaching and ceremony continued largely unchecked until the reign of

The medieval church of St Michael, which was demolished in 1731, as depicted in a lithograph of 1835 by Joseph Holloway. (Author's collection)

Edward VI. Altars were then suddenly swept away as the service of high mass was replaced by that of holy communion; many outward symbols of Catholicism removed and a new prayer book introduced, which was written in English rather than Latin. The churchwardens' accounts of St Michael's Church clearly indicate that **sweeping reforms** of this nature took place in the churches of Bath between 1547 and 1552.

For instance, payments were made for 'pulling down the high altar', for 'making the communion table', for purchasing 'the service book in English' and for simplifying internal decoration by 'white liming the church'. The churchwardens' accounts, which had previously been written in Latin, were compiled in English for the first time in 1547; while Archbishop Cranmer's English Bible (which had been sanctioned for use in churches in 1643) was adopted - to be replaced in 1572, at a cost of twenty shillings, by Archbishop Parker's new translation.

Nevertheless, although Protestantism had now been established in England, the more extreme Protestants were bitterly disappointed by Elizabeth I's church settlement of 1559, which sought to accommodate both Catholics and Protestants within the same church by means of a typical English compromise. The extreme Protestants (increasingly known as Puritans) were not impressed. They therefore launched a vigorous campaign for the total purification of church interiors *and* church teaching from all remaining traces of Rome. This growth of Puritanism was to have a major impact on Bath Abbey, the religious life of the city and the involvement of local people in the Civil War. Even by 1620, the Puritans had seized control of North Somerset, placing ardent Puritan clergy in many local churches. This revolution, with widespread popular support, was backed by leading gentry and powerful city councillors, most of whom attended the Abbey or its two dependent churches. Their desire was to establish a godly community - 'a city set on a hill' - like those being so successfully developed by Puritan corporations at Salisbury and Dorchester. The evidence for the moral reformation which followed in this area is strikingly clear.

Unsatisfactory clergy, for instance, had been disciplined or removed for lax behaviour - such as William Powell, the Rector of Bathwick, who had been presented several times between 1606 and 1610 for the bishop's censure on charges of disorderly behaviour, calling the constable of Bath 'a knave', 'being a haunter unto many vain and profane sports', 'for suspicion of incontinent life' with various women, 'for omitting to say morning prayer on Wednesdays and Fridays' and 'for attempting the chastity of Elizabeth Noble'. Bath Corporation, too, had expressed severe dissatisfaction in 1641 with George Webb, Rector of the Abbey (for which they were responsible as patrons), because he was a pluralist who drew income from several churches and failed to give the Abbey his undivided attention. They resisted the temptation to sack him, however, preferring instead to issue a new contract which would tie him solely to the Abbey at a slight increase in salary.

Another indication of Puritan activity was discontent about the lack of sermons in churches, because Puritanism demanded a much greater emphasis on **scripture-based preaching** at the expense of the communion service. The heartfelt cry uttered by the villagers of Bathwick - 'we have not our sermons as we ought to have according to the canons' - was echoed by complaints in Bathampton (five or six within the year...and no more'); and Langridge ('they have not their monthly sermon...but six every year'). There were signs in Bath by 1639 that some people had begun to boycott churches that failed to offer a sufficient number of sermons. Such

The Orthodox true Minister,

(left) *Under the influence of the Puritan revolution, the preaching of sermons became much more important in Bath Abbey and other local churches. (Author's collection)*

absences were, of course, against the law. Consequently, Jacob Burton and four others from St Michael's Church were censured by the Bishop 'for coming only to hear preaching and not the prayers of the church'; Thomas Dyer and eight others were similarly censured for non-attendance; while both Francis Minn and William Hay were reported for marrying their respective wives 'without banns or licence at an unlawful house' (presumably at a conventicle).

To counter this growing drift, Bath Corporation had not only built up an endowment fund to sponsor sermons in the Abbey on special occasions throughout the year, but had also taken the initiative in setting up a system of regular **mid-week lectures**. From the 1620s, each Wednesday, a godly Puritan minister was invited to visit the city to deliver a lengthy exposition of the scriptures in the Abbey. This was funded out of the local rates, although aldermen and common councillors were expected, on a rota basis, to accommodate the minister for the night and entertain him to dinner on the lecture day. Thus the city council with its Puritan majority became totally involved in the religious life of the city.

Part of this involvement was to ensure that **the sabbath** was given much greater protection. At the Bishop's visitation of 1615, therefore, Markham Bennet of St James's Church was punished for 'keeping ill order in his house by entertaining divers persons drinking there in time of divine service'; Eleanor Gibbins of Widcombe for causing her mill to grind on Sunday mornings; and John Tucker of Bath for opening his alehouse for 'tippling and drinking...at the time of divine service on Sunday'. The offence was compounded, of course, by those caught idling away their time on the sabbath by playing unlawful games - such as John Pinckin, censured for causing his bull to be baited on Whit Sunday 'to the profanation of the sabbath'; and William Powell (Rector of Bathwick) 'for bowling on the sabbath'.

A contemporary drawing to illustrate a 17th-century family under the tight control and discipline of the father - the puritan ideal. (Author's collection)

Furthermore, nine people from the locality - together with Robert Corbett, a minstrel - were censured in 1606 because they 'maintained dancing to the evil example of others' during the time of divine service on Midsummer's Day. The Puritan's insistence on order, discipline and respect also demanded that any unseemly behaviour in or near the church should not go unpunished. Evidence was therefore given against John Bigg of Midford 'for beating William Beacon, an old man, in the Abbey churchyard at Bath'; and, from the Abbey congregation, both Peter Perman 'for not coming orderly to church' and John Murford 'for quarrelling with Francis Kingston in the churchyard'.

Ale-houses were also targeted by local Puritans, because of their tendency to corrupt the young and undermine family discipline. Somerset justices had demonstrated their anxiety over the growing number of alehouses within the county by issuing a series of orders from 1594 aimed at their control. In 1618, local justices were instructed to. carry out a survey of all alehouses within their district, listing those that were disorderly and needed to be suppressed. Five years later, the mayor of Bath reported to the Privy Council in London that he had suppressed all unnecessary alehouses and, furthermore, had regulated the strength of all beer brewed within the city. At the same time, many traditional activities (including revels, certain games, festivals, fairs, animal baitings and performances by travelling players) were banned largely because of the disorderly and drunken crowds they attracted (see Chapter 15).

Breaches of sexual morality were also dealt with in a firm manner. Unruly women who became involved in brawls or were unfaithful in marriage were shamed by giving them a drenching in the river via the ducking stool - a device constantly in use in Bath during this period (see Chapter 4). Women who offended sexual or social standards could arouse the anger of the whole community, especially if their actions were likely to prove a costly burden to the poor rate. During the 1630s, several members of the congregations in Bath were severely censured for immoral conduct - Alice Spurrier 'for having had a base child about half a year'; Henry Driall for being 'the reputed father of the child of Alice Garland, who is now great'; and Elizabeth Broome, who was pregnant, for failing to perform a public penance (which the reputed father had already undertaken). Concern with sexual morality within the city's hot water baths had already led the corporation to separate the sexes for bathing in 1621. Even so, in response to local pressure, the Privy Council in London later ordered the corporation 'to remedy the great disorders committed in the common use of the baths by men and women together' - a practice which not only drew together 'a great concourse of wicked persons', but compelled 'grave and sober persons to forbear the place'.

By 1620, therefore, the Puritan revolution had been firmly rooted locally. But the strength of this godly reformation was to be sorely tested during the 1630s by **a vigorous counter-attack** staged by William Laud, Archbishop of Canterbury, who tried to revive High Church practices within the church. His objectives included an end to the system of lectures; a revival of parish festivities; and an insistence that all communion tables were to be taken out of the nave (where the Puritans had put them) and railed off as altars in the chancel. To many, this smacked of a return to

Catholicism. It was hardly surprising, therefore, that local people also developed a strong dislike of William Piers, Bishop of Bath and Wells, who had introduced many of Laud's reforms into Somerset with unseemly relish. His attack on the lecture system brought him into headlong collision with the churchwardens of all three Bath parishes, who were presented to the Bishop in 1638 'for permitting their minister to appoint strange preachers to preach'. So fierce was the opposition to his policy on the creation of altars that the churchwardens of Beckington, backed by the local gentry and one thousand local people, defied the Bishop's ruling by

(left) William Piers, Bishop of Bath & Wells, 1580-1670. (By courtesy of the Lord Bishop of Bath & Wells from a photograph supplied by the Paul Mellon Centre for Studies in British Art)

refusing to move the communion table out of the nave and were imprisoned in consequence. They were only released after they had made a humiliating apology from the pulpit of Bath Abbey.

A War of Religion, 1642-1646

Given all this background, it is perhaps not surprising that the people of Bath and North Somerset were to become deeply involved when Civil War broke out in 1642. Indeed, their passion and commitment were almost unmatched in the country at large - because - for them - the war was above all a war of religion. Indeed, three weeks before the king had signified the start of hostilities by raising his standard at Nottingham on 22nd August, some 12,000 local inhabitants had staged **a spontaneous uprising** at Chewton Mendip in favour of parliament. Although no more than an enthusiastic rabble, they had assembled in this remarkable gathering to oppose the efforts of the Marquis of Hertford, who had been sent by the king to raise Somerset for the royalist cause. Local people had a deep suspicion that the marquis (who had established his headquarters in Wells) carried with him a hidden agenda - namely, to suppress their Puritan culture and reimpose Catholicism.

The scene on the Mendips was therefore far more reminiscent of a religious convention than the rendezvous of an army. Indeed the men, who spent the night sleeping rough on the hill overlooking Wells, passed the time in fasting, prayer and singing psalms. In a great upsurge of feeling, they were given massive support by the local community. According to one eyewitness, the country people for miles around showed their love by sending in 'cartloads of provisions, enough for breakfast and dinner'. Then, after the marquis (who had only attracted a mere nine hundred supporters) had wisely decided to flee from the city, the mob rushed down the hill and into Wells - led by Alexander Popham's Bath Regiment of trained bands. There they cried out how they had vanquished the Papists; tore down all the stained glass in the cathedral and sacked the Bishop's Palace, destroying the organs and pictures. According to another eyewitness, a portrait of the Virgin Mary 'was put on a spear and

A contemporary print, which depicts puritan soldiers (such as those in Popham's Bath Regiment) ransacking a church to destroy altars and other 'popish' symbols. (By courtesy of the Ashmolean Museum, University of Oxford).

carried about in contempt and derision'. A newspaper correspondent also noted that many villagers had joined the throng, 'bringing pitchforks, dung picks and suchlike weapons, not knowing who they were to fight, but supposing they were Papists'.

Nor was this attack an isolated example. The Wells Chapter Library Book records that, in the following year, Popham's Bath Regiment returned to the city and 'broke down divers pictures and crucifixes in the church and Our Lady chapels. Likewise they did plunder the Bishop's Palace and broke all such monuments and pictures they espied'. A month later, they were back again - 'Mr Alexander Popham's soldiers...after dinner rushed into the church, broke down the windows, organs, fonts, seats in the choir, and the Bishop's seat, besides many other villanies'. Throughout these three incidents, it is clear that Popham's men (many of whom were members of the churches in Bath) targeted everything that was perceived to be a symbol of the Catholic religion.

With the outbreak of civil war in 1642, many communities quickly found themselves bitterly divided in the way depicted in this contemporary cartoon. (Author's collection)

Bath Corporation - although largely parliamentarian in sympathy - did contain a sizeable minority of royalist supporters (see Chapter 3). Political and religious controversy, therefore, always bubbled away just below the surface as the city found itself divided, in the way depicted by a contemporary cartoon, between roundhead curs and cavalier dogs. The new Rector of the Abbey, James Masters (appointed in 1639), turned out to be a close ally of Bishop Piers and Archbishop Laud. When, therefore, after a period of occupation by royalist forces, Bath finally fell to the New Model Army in 1645, Masters fled from the city and joined Prince Rupert's garrison in Bristol, 'preaching much against parliament' during the ensuing siege. He was in consequence ejected from his position as Rector of Bath in September 1645 on parliament's instructions. When, however, Bath Corporation appointed two Puritan ministers (Messrs Cothrington and Oliver) to succeed Masters, his wife caused a local sensation by barricading the rectory to keep them out! The poor divines were clearly not up to the demands of sustaining a prolonged siege against so formidable a foe and they disappeared without trace. It was not, therefore, until 1648 that parliament, concerned that the city had been 'for a long time destitute of a faithful pastor', confirmed the appointment of George Long as the new minister.

Inevitably, the Civil War was **a period of great turmoil** for worship within the city. The churches in Bath were frequently used as barracks by armies on the march from both sides - and also as hospitals during the days following the Battle of Lansdown in July 1643. In the Abbey, the large open space of the pew-less nave offered an ideal resting place for wounded and dying soldiers, as they lay on straw provided by the generosity of Bath Corporation. Many of them were also prisoners of war, waiting to be interrogated. Services were therefore badly disrupted during this period.

However, in spite of the presence of troops, the Abbey miraculously suffered very little damage during the war and there were few deliberate acts of vandalism. The

worst **vandalism** occurred when royalist troops, garrisoned here between 1643 and 1645, noticed the effigy of Sir William Waller, victorious commander of parliament's army at the Battle of Lansdown. In vengeful spite, they hacked off both his nose and his sword hand. Samuel Pepys, writing twenty-five years later, recorded that he had seen Waller's monument, 'he lying with his face broken'. This rather dispels the old tradition that the damage was caused by King James II on a visit to the Abbey later in the century, when glancing across at the effigy, in a moment of malice, he drew his sword and hacked off the nose.

Perhaps surprisingly, the stained glass windows and the organ, which had been installed earlier in the century, survived the hostility of Puritan soldiers (unlike those at Wells). Samuel Pepys recorded the fact in his diary that the organ was still in use on his visit in 1668. It is possible, of course, that it had been carefully dismantled and safely stored until the return of better times, as at Salisbury; or that the organ pipes had been hidden under the floor of the tower, as at Warminster. In all reality, the Abbey (unlike most cathedrals) had very little stained glass - a visitor to Bath noting in 1634 that the windows were 'large and fair, though plain without painting'.

It is perhaps more probable that, from the outset, Bath Abbey had never been tarnished with a reputation for Popish symbols or idolatry. For the Abbey, unlike most cathedrals, was itself the product of the Puritan revolution and the direct result of a petition submitted to Queen Elizabeth by the Puritan-dominated council. This petition specifically stressed the need for a larger place in which 'to hear sermons', lamenting the fact that the lack of space in existing churches meant that sermons could only be preached in the open market place. Bath Abbey, therefore, was completed and refurbished at the instigation of the Puritans as a preaching centre and it remained in operation as a preaching centre throughout the turbulent post-war years.

Other cathedrals were less fortunate. Some, like Hereford, were dismantled; others, like Durham, were used as prisons; and others, like St Paul's, served a dual role with the nave used as stables for the cavalry and the cloisters converted into a shopping arcade. There is little doubt that Bath Abbey received a great deal of protection from local people, whose families had contributed so generously to its construction - including families of benefactors who supported parliament in the Civil War (the Prynnes, the Haringtons, the Pophams, the Hungerfords) and families who supported the king (the Bassetts, the Hoptons, the Hydes, the Smythes). Perhaps even more dramatic is the realisation that the two main opponents in the Battle of Lansdown - Sir William Waller and Sir Ralph Hopton - had each contributed to the Abbey building appeal. The chief threat to its fabric during the war, therefore, came not from local participants, but from marauding armies from outside the county marching through.

Mention must be made of one member of the Abbey congregation who firmly committed himself to the cause of parliament during the war. This was **Richard Druce**, a man of great moral courage, a baker whose shop was situated in Northgate Street and whose headstone is to be found in the north transept. In 1643, he willingly supplied bread for wounded soldiers in the Abbey on instructions from the corporation. But one year later, he refused to bake bread for the royalist garrison and was, in consequence, imprisoned on charges of attempting to starve the king's army. After the war, following his election as Mayor in 1649, he was encountered by the 'Water Poet', John Taylor, who has left us this description: 'I went to his stall or shop window. Mr Mayor was pleased to welcome me most kindly (with his hands in his pockets) and like a man of few words, forebode to say welcome to town; so, we parting, I left him in his shop, Lord Baron of the Brown Loaves and Master of the Rolls'.

By the end of the Civil War in 1646, a revolution had taken place in the religious life of the nation. Archbishop Laud had been executed; the offices of archbishop and bishop had been abolished; royalist clergy had been ejected from their posts; the Prayer Book had been replaced by a new Directory of Worship and **a new Presbyterian Church** had been approved to replace the Church of England. Disagreement, however, was already in the air among the victors of the Civil War. The body of puritans in the country at large consisted of two main groups - the Presbyterians (who had a majority in the Commons and wanted a national system of religion with little toleration outside); and the Independents (who had a majority in the army and wanted freedom for each congregation to decide its own form of service). As the army quickly gained control of events in London, so the drive to establish a national Presbyterian Church gradually failed.

Nevertheless, such was the force of Presbyterianism locally, that Somerset was one of only nine counties in England actually to establish the system which parliament had ordered. It was William Prynne (barrister from Swainswick and Old Boy of King Edward's School, Bath) who was the inspiration behind the scheme, in alliance with John Harington of Kelston, son of the fund-raiser. The parishes of North Somerset were joined together into what was called the Bath and Wrington Classis under the control of a group of local ministers (including Joseph Bowden from the Abbey) and a group of elders drawn from local congregations (including William Prynne, John Ashe and John Harington - the very same men who had inspired the rising of 1642). Nevertheless, one problem faced in making the scheme a success was the difficulty in recruiting able puritan ministers for the low stipends available in many local parishes (just £10 a year in Bathford, for instance). There was no such problem in Bath itself, however, where the minister received £100 and his assistant £50.

There is little doubt that the new Directory of Worship replaced the Prayer Book in both the Abbey and the other Bath churches (although this happened in less than 25% of parish churches nationally) - for, during the brief episode in 1648, known as the Second Civil War, local royalist sympathisers staged a major demonstration in the streets of Bath in favour of restoring the Prayer Book. According to a newspaper report, 'One Henry Chapman of the city of Bath [and baptised member of Bath Abbey]...had not only openly affronted Mr Long, the minister there lately settled by the parliament, but likewise called on Dr Jones,...a late chaplain in the king's army, to read the Book of Common Prayer and preach publicly against the parliament's proceedings in St James's Church'. The mayor apparently sent his officers to the church twice to try and prevent the use of the Prayer Book (which was now a criminal

(right) *A contemporay cartoon to illustrate the way in which, at the end of the Civil War, the bible was pulled in different directions by conflicting factions within the Puritan movement. (Author's collection)*

offence in England), but to no avail. Another Prayer Book service was held again in the evening, Chapman being 'guarded from the church by about 100 malignants, some of them armed with swords'.

The Presbyterian system of religion, however, was short-lived as gradually the army, with its Independent majority, seized political control in London. Their policy of toleration fostered the growth of many radical sects, with army chaplains seizing the opportunity to preach from the pulpits of parish churches as they marched across the country. A contemporary cartoon showed the bible being torn in different directions by conflicting factions within the puritan movement. A hint of the confusion that slowly developed in religious life - and the open clash between Presbyterians and Independents - is given by Charles Paman, writing to a friend in 1646 after a visit to Bath: 'The most remarkable things in town', he said, 'are the church and the baths; and the latter are the most zealously frequented, though I think the pulpit to be the hottest bath in town; for it one day sweats independency and presbytery the next, and that so violently...How sad are these contests'. So great became the division between these two groups that, in Exeter Cathedral (which, like Bath Abbey, remained in use as a preaching centre), a central partition was built to keep the Presbyterians and Independents apart.

Religious Life after the Restoration, 1660-1700

(i) Anglicans

Eventually, with Cromwell dead, the monarchy was restored in 1660 in the form of Charles II. The bellringers at the three Bath churches were paid handsomely for ringing the church bells to celebrate his landing, his proclamation as king and his coronation. However, much as the members of the Abbey congregation welcomed back the monarchy, many of them had hoped to retain their Puritan brand of religion for which they had fought the war. Nevertheless, by 1662, the bishops were back (including Bishop Piers who conducted a visitation to Bath that year); ejected royalist clergy were back (including James Masters, who had regained the Abbey at the expense of George Long); and the Prayer Book was back (albeit in a revised form). But, worst of all, the fundamental changes, which the Puritans had introduced, were largely undone. For instance, under the Puritans there had been a total ban on the celebration of Easter, Whitsuntide, Saints' Days and Christmas ('on which', stated the ordinance of 1644, 'men took liberty to carnal and sensual delights, contrary to the life which Christ himself led on earth') - a ban which had not been universally popular. To replace the traditional parish communions on the three great feasts of Christmas, Easter and Whitsuntide, the second Tuesday of each month had been set aside as a day of thanksgiving on which communion might be taken. Access to communion under the Puritan regime, however, had been restricted to those who, after prior examination by the minister, had received a formal docket stating that they were spiritually prepared. Admission to these 'closed communions' had therefore been by ticket only!

There is little doubt that many of these changes had been adopted in Bath during the turbulent post-war years. For it was only after the Restoration in 1660 that old, familiar items started to reappear on the churchwardens' shopping lists at St James's Church - bread and wine for the Easter communion; and rosemary and bay for decking out the church at Christmas. Furthermore, Thomas Bulman was paid expenses for two journeys to Wells in 1662, during which he purchased a 'Book of Order'. This of course was in dutiful response to the Act of Uniformity which compelled churches to use the new Anglican Prayer Book at all services (thus finally replacing the Presbyterian Directory of Worship). In the following year, a sum of £2 14s 0d was spent on the making of a new surplice - a clear sign that formality had returned to worship; while the council spent ten shillings on work on the organ gallery - an indication that music was back in fashion.

Meanwhile, the restored Rector of Bath (James Masters) had already been rebuked at the Bishop's visitation for 'not instructing the youth of the parish in the church catechism'; and for neglecting and not observing the yearly perambulation in Rogation Week, according as it was commanded in the Common Prayer Book'. The latter was a signal that special celebrations and festivals in the church's year were again to be enjoyed (many of which, including Rogationtide, had been abolished by the Puritans out of a fear that such occasions would encourage unruly and drunken behaviour). Although life in the church had in most respects largely returned to normal, there was nevertheless one great legacy of the Puritan revolution. The system of mid-week lectures by Puritan divines, attended by the mayor and corporation, had given a great boost to the importance of the sermon. Therefore, in spite of the local demise of the mid-week lecture by 1663, the principle of having two sermons each Sunday was gradually adopted as the norm in Anglican worship. For his part, the Rector of Bath quickly revived the practice of preaching special sermons on Trinity Sunday, Ascension Day, Good Friday, All Hallows, New Year's Day etc, while at the same time doing his best to find 'lecturers' to preach on Sundays.

The Abbey next hit the national headlines in a sensational manner in 1687 when James II, an avowed Catholic, visited the church in the company of his chaplain, Father John Huddleston. He was greeted there by the Bishop of Bath and Wells, Thomas Ken - but Ken had no idea of what was in store. Without any warning to the bishop, Huddleston arranged for a special ceremony to take place between the two normal Prayer Book services. He decked the altar, ordered the ritual along Catholic lines and preached a sermon to the crowds, urging them to return to the Church of Rome. However, what horrified many people even more than that was the decision by James II, as part of

(left) Thomas Ken, Bishop of Bath & Wells, 1685-90.
(Author's collection)

that service, to 'touch for the King's Evil' (a ceremony dating from medieval times, which claimed supernatural cures through the divine nature of monarchy - especially for scrofula, a disease with glandular swellings). Those to be cured were brought forward by the surgeon; they then knelt before the king for the touch of his hand across their cheeks and the gift of a gold coin strung on a white ribbon. According to cynics at the time, the promise of the latter always ensured a large attendance with many returning for repeat prescriptions! It is estimated that Charles II had treated four thousand such patients each year. Protestants of the period, however, simply regarded this ceremony a silly superstition, which smacked of both popery and the divine right of kings - against which they had fought in the Civil War.

(below) *King Charles II at court 'Touching for the King's Evil'.*
(By courtesy of the Pepys Library, Magdalene College, Cambridge)

(left) An engraving of King James II from an original by Sir Godfrey Kneller. (Author's collection)

During the last forty years of the 17th century, therefore, the churches in Bath and its surrounding area largely conformed to legislation imposed on them by parliament, reverting to a moderate form of Anglicanism which avoided the extremes of both High Church Laudism and radical Puritanism. It has to be said, however, that in the process they lost many of their former Presbyterian ministers, who were ejected for their refusal to accept the Prayer Book; and many ordinary parishioners, who left to set up their own non-conformist conventicles (see below). The removal of these able preachers and committed individuals from the congregations of the three city churches was to have a decisive impact on the direction of religion in Bath over the next century. Samuel Pepys, who visited the Abbey in 1668, was clearly angered by the 'vain, pragmatical fellow' who preached 'a ridiculous, affected sermon'.

Faced with a rising tide of commercialism as the city was transformed into a centre for health tourism, the churches temporarily lost their sense of mission as they entered an age of respectability and compromise. Pews were now available for rent and, by the end of the century, attendance at Abbey services had become part of the social round. As early as 1700, Ned Ward, on a visit to Bath, had recalled in his diary the admonition rendered to the congregation by a preacher in the Abbey: 'He was afraid most of them came more out of custom and formality than in devotion to the sacred deity'. Ward then went on to relate just how many *billets-doux* he had seen passed to the ladies in the crowded congregation - including one conveyed in a candied orange to a lady in the gallery, which he was able to read when it was dropped by accident. The note to her concluded thus: 'At six this evening, I shall be in the meadows. Pity your poor slave and grant me some relief'. By 1700, there was no one left to protest at such conduct. The Puritan revolutionaries, with their crusading zeal to establish that 'city set on a hill', had long since been driven out of the established church to set up their own dissenting chapels.

(ii) Presbyterians

After the Civil War had ended, Bath and its immediate locality remained largely in the grip of Presbyterian ministers. It is true that the continued presence of regiments of the New Model Army, which were dominated by Independents and other Puritan sects, ensured that religious debate was by no means silenced as army chaplains mounted local pulpits. In 1646, one observer remarked: 'We have numerous sectaries, Anabaptists, Antinomians, Seekers and I know not what: all shows our dissolution to be near'. Furthermore, with the occupation of London by the army in August 1647 and the subsequent introduction of religious toleration, it became largely impossible to operate a nationally-organised Presbyterian system of the kind which had been envisaged by parliament in 1643 (see above).

Nevertheless, many individual churches in North Somerset (including those at Bath, Combe Hay, Charlcombe, Mells, Frome, Beckington, Kilmersdon and Norton St Philip) continued to support Presbyterian ministers until 1660. In Bath, for instance, the minister appointed in 1646 to be responsible for the city's churches was Joseph Bowden with Thomas Creese as his assistant. By 1648, Bowden had been replaced by George Long and Creese by Matthew Randall. Although Long was to continue in office until 1660, William Green and William Baker took over as his assistants in 1657. The restoration of the monarchy in 1660, however, quickly threatened the security of their position. Although Charles II had expressed himself in favour of a degree of toleration, the Savoy Conference in 1661 failed to work out a church settlement which would be acceptable to both Anglicans and Presbyterians. Many Presbyterians were therefore ejected from their churches. Indeed, an Act of Parliament in 1660 had already restored those Anglican clergy (including James Masters at Bath Abbey) who had been ejected during the revolution, thus displacing some 695 ministers nationwide from their positions (including twenty-eight in Somerset). Furthermore, the Act of Uniformity in 1662 restored the use of the revised Prayer Book and restricted the holding of church livings to those clergy who had been ordained by bishops. [Many Presbyterian ministers - including the minister at Frome - had been ordained by 'presbyters' after the abolition of bishops in 1646]. Some nine hundred clergy (including thirty in Somerset) refused to comply with these regulations and were therefore ejected from their livings.

The Restoration therefore heralded a period of persecution for all dissenters, which was to last until 1688. Many of the most ardent Puritans found this return to the old ways of the Church of England totally unacceptable and proceeded in consequence to set up their own nonconformist conventicles. Around the city of Bath, for instance, conventicles of Presbyterians up to three hundred strong met in houses, barns or inns to listen to sermons given by ministers who had been ejected from their churches. Indeed, according to one observer in 1661, local dissenters had boasted that they were planning to hold 'a meeting of a thousand near Bath'. These were dangerous times for religious dissent, however, as the government gradually tightened its grip.

The Conventicle Act of 1664 forbade meetings of more than five people for worship, unless the Prayer Book was being used; the Five Mile Act of 1665 banned ejected ministers from coming within five miles of their own parish or of any city or town; and the Elizabethan Act, which had made church attendance compulsory, was rigorously enforced. Punishments for the breach of these laws ranged from increasingly severe fines to imprisonment or even transportation. A measure of relief was briefly offered in 1672 when Charles II's Declaration of Indulgence suspended the penal laws against nonconformists and permitted them to license their

(right)   *A group of anxious Presbyterians hold an illegal open-air conventicle. (By courtesy of the Mary Evans Picture Library)*

worship by registering their ministers and meeting houses. In the following year, however, parliament forced the king to repeal the Declaration - and the registers, which had been compiled, were simply used by the authorities to quicken the process of persecution.

There is little doubt that the situation described above was more than familiar to Presbyterians living in the Bath area. Nevertheless, they continued to find strong support throughout the 1660s both inside the city and throughout the surrounding neighbourhood. One observer commented in a letter of 1667 that the Rector of Bath (Joseph Glanville) found himself 'environed with manifold dangers by the crowds of fanatics about Bath' and that the local justices, far from protecting him, had 'exposed him to the rabble'. Indeed, he said, people of all classes continued to stir up a hatred of Popery in a manner reminiscent of '1642' (i.e. when the Civil War had broken out).

A few days later, Glanville himself wrote to a friend confessing that he was so troubled 'to see the uncontrolled madness and disorders of the people in these parts' that he was 'almost weary of living'. The fanatics (i.e. the Presbyterians), he continued, grew daily 'in numbers and insolence', insisting on total freedom of worship and smashing their way into churches 'to vent their sedition and rebellion'. Having tried hard to win over his own congregation by preaching twice a day - without notes - in the plainest language possible, he had reluctantly concluded that 'he that will be a minister must be content to be a martyr'. At least he was slightly better off than the minister at Marshfield, who was often forced to abandon his services for the lack of a congregation in the galling knowledge that 'five hundred' were meeting 'in a barn in the town' fully equipped with seating.

However, as opposition increased and the new legislation began to bite, meetings were increasingly held in secret, while some individuals sought to cover their tracks by attending their local parish church as well as the local conventicle. The danger, of course, was always that of being betrayed by one's neighbours, because opposition to nonconformity was often strong in towns which came increasingly under the control of former royalists. John Taylor (the 'Water Poet'), who visited Bath in 1649, typified the attitude of many towards dissenters in these rather disparaging words:

> These kind of vermin swarm like caterpillars
> And hold conventicles in barns and cellars
> Some preach (or prate) in woods, in fields, in stables,
> In hollow trees, in tubes, on tops of tables.

George Long, the Presbyterian minister in Bath for twelve years from 1648, was to experience personally the power of a hostile mob. Ejected from the Abbey in 1660 to make way for James Masters (the former minister, who was now restored), he soon found himself in prison with others as a result of a petition from local citizens. He had clearly continued to minister to a local conventicle after his ejection and was therefore accused of organising 'a seditious meeting'. Although he was released some months later, he died in 1665. Joseph Bowden, who had been minister in Bath between 1646 and 1648, continued his ministry until his death in 1672, in spite of much persecution. An ardent Presbyterian, he had launched a powerful attack on Independents in Bath Abbey in 1646. He later became Vicar of Wotton-Under-Edge in Gloucestershire until his ejection in 1662. Thereafter, he maintained the letter of the law by attending the parish church on Sunday mornings before preaching to a conventicle in his own house on Sunday evenings. By 1669, he was additionally preaching to groups in Batheaston,

(right) *Presbyterian and Baptist ministers in the Bath area, actively persecuted by the authorites, were often forced to preach in barns or in the open air.*
(Author's collection)

Dunkerton and Bath, where the congregation met in an inn.

Perhaps the minister who best displayed the stamina shown by many Presbyterian ministers in defying persecution was Thomas Creese. After serving as assistant minister in Bath (1646-47), he worked as Rector of Combe Hay from 1647 until ejection from his living in 1661. He nevertheless continued to preach at various conventicles in the area - including, in 1669, those at Monkton Combe, Batheaston, Dunkerton, Cameley and Glastonbury (meeting at the latter in 'in a barn where a pulpit and seats are built'); and was licensed briefly as a Presbyterian minister at Dunkerton in 1672 under the terms of the Declaration of Indulgence. By the early 1680s, however, he and other Presbyterian ministers suffered personally as opposition began to mount. In 1683, John Bushell (the Bath town clerk) wrote to a friend telling him of a campaign to halt local conventicles. 'Mr Langton disturbed a meeting at Englishcombe', he reported, 'and intends to bind over most of the meeters to the County Sessions. He has granted a warrant to levy £20 [fine] on the owner of the house'. Among those bound over, he said, were Francis Fuller (preacher at Combe Hay) and Thomas Creese (Englishcombe), both of whom had not only preached since 1666 'in unlawful assemblies or conventicles', but had also illegally taken up residence in Bath contrary to the terms of the Five Mile Act.

By 1690, once the second Declaration of Indulgence (1687) and the Toleration Act (1689) had made possible the establishment of registered meeting houses, Creese was preaching fortnightly at Bath, Englishcombe and Monkton Combe. When Matthew Calamy visited Bath in 1692, he wrote: 'There I conversed with good old Mr Creez, who then lived in that city, a worthy man, though of a melancholy disposition'. His own house in Bath was certified in 1694 as a place of worship. Meanwhile, in the more tolerant atmosphere, the first official meeting house for Presbyterians in Bath had been registered at the Quarter Sessions in 1688, when Christopher Taylor had been appointed as its first minister (1688-99). At first situated in a 'shearing shop', it was later moved in 1692 to newly-built premises in Frog Lane just outside the northern gate of the city [on the site of the present New Bond Street]. Clearly marked as 'The Meeting House' on Joseph Gilmore's map of Bath dated 1694, it continued in use until its demolition in 1805. At first Taylor met with considerable opposition in the city, but he gradually won respect 'by his solid teaching and prudent conduct'. Then in 1692 he was joined by an assistant, Benjamin Coleman (1692-1700), who was a profound scholar, an impressive preacher and a committed philanthropist. By the time that these two man had been replaced as ministers by Henry Chandler (1700-19), the congregation - made up largely of farmers, tradesmen and labourers - had increased considerably.

(iii) Quakers

The Quaker movement, which gradually emerged under the guidance of George Fox, had extended its influence from Bristol to North Somerset by 1654. Believing that God revealed Himself to individuals through an 'inner light', the Quakers were therefore opposed to formal church services and the mediation between God and man by priests in their 'steeple-houses' (i.e. parish churches). In consequence, they refused to pay tithes to the church or fees for the registration of births, marriages and burials. Believing also that all men were equal before God, they refused to acknowledge their social superiors by raising their hats or speaking in respectful language (i.e. by using such customary terms as 'My Lord', 'Your servant' or 'Master'). Unwilling also to take the name of God in vain, they shunned the swearing of oaths - a fact which meant that their testimony was never accepted in court, while their refusal to take the oath of allegiance (particularly after 1661) resulted in automatic imprisonment. The Quakers, drawn as they largely were from the lower middle and lower classes, were therefore perceived as something of a radical threat to a society based on deference.

Nor did they help their cause by disrupting church services or aggressively proclaiming their faith in the streets. There were disturbances, for instance, in Bath Abbey in 1655 when Thomas Murford of Englishcombe, 'being under a religious concern to publish the testimony of truth, went into the steeple-house in Bath', was beaten up by the congregation and subsequently imprisoned for two years. George Fox himself wrote to the 'magistrates and teachers of Bath' pleading for Murford's release. Nor was it any more acceptable to seek converts in the street. Katharine Evans of Englishcombe, for instance, was not only 'abused by the rude people at the instigation of the priest at Warminster and had her clothes torn off her back', but was also 'tied to a whipping post in the market' at Salisbury and whipped on the mayor's instructions. Local Presbyterian leaders did not hesitate to excite public opinion against this minority sect. According to Joseph Besse, three Quakers - Nicholas Jordan, Jane Murford and John Evans - were 'assaulted and abused by the rabble' in the streets of Bath in 1658, as they 'passed to and re-passed the gaol' (presumably in some sort of demonstration against the arrest of other Quakers inside); and John Slade was 'grievously abused as he was travelling quietly on the highway'. Local people had allegedly been instructed by the mayor 'to use them so, because they were Quakers'.

Members of the sect were increasingly targeted as marked men. John Evans of Englishcombe had been arrested earlier in 1658 as a vagrant in Wells, because he was travelling eleven miles from home - even though he was a man 'of considerable estate'. He was taken before a magistrate and imprisoned for four months, chiefly because he appeared before the court 'with his hat on'. Quakers also fell foul of the local clergy because of their refusal to pay tithes. Thomas Murford, John Evans and Julian Evans (a widow of almost 100 years), all of Englishcombe, were imprisoned in 1660 after a charge

(left) *James Naylor, a leading Quaker, was found guilty of blasphemy after his supporters had worshipped him as he rode into Bristol on a donkey. He was ordered to be pilloried, his forehead to be branded and his tongue to be bored with a hot iron. He was then whipped through the streets of Bristol as he rode backwards on a horse. (By courtesy of the Mary Evans Picture Library)*

had been laid by their parish priest. On the other hand, William Sergeant of Bathford, who had refused to pay the £5 demanded in tithes in 1657, had £15 worth of his goods confiscated in consequence. Then, later in the year, he was again arrested on a similar charge and imprisoned at Ilchester. His wife and two servants were also arrested shortly afterwards, in spite of the fact that they were busy harvesting the corn. All this was at the behest of the vicar of Box, who allegedly was 'endeavouring to complete the ruin of the whole family'. Sergeant eventually died in prison after being held for twenty months. During a three-month period in 1660-1661, two hundred and twelve Somerset Quakers in all were imprisoned at Ilminster.

After the Restoration in 1660, the movement gradually became more organised with the establishment in 1668 of general meetings for all Quaker groups in Somerset on a quarterly basis and local divisional meetings at monthly intervals in between. In that year a Bath and Bathford group was registered with just three members, although there were clearly several other individuals on the edge. This group met weekly for worship, alternating the venue between Bath and Bathford (although, by 1698, there was a move to make the Bath meetings more frequent in order to accommodate the many Friends from outside who resorted to the baths). The group was attached to the Northern Division of the county, the monthly meetings of which sought to regulate the marriages of members, impose discipline on their behaviour and distribute aid to those in need from its 'public stock' fund.

In 1693, therefore, the meeting ruled on the proposed marriage of Henry Canning of Batheaston and Jane Morley of Bathford (who was a Quaker) by refusing to sanction it. Uncertain of Canning's faith, members decided to wait in the hope 'that a sense of Truth might be borne upon the young man'. In 1687, the monthly meeting ordered a local investigation of 'the unclean and immodest behaviour' of one member (Richard Collins of Bath), who had indulged in 'too much familiarity with a strange woman', whereby 'a public reproach was brought on the Truth'. He was duly expelled until he repented. Four years later, Walter King, who was found guilty of 'unseemly behaviour and disorderly walking', was declared 'an enemy of the Truth' having expressed his enmity towards the movement publicly in Bath.

Several individuals, who emerged as leaders of the Bath and Bathford group, played a noticeably dominant role in the

(right)   *A meeting of the General Quaker Synod at which the Somerset Assembly was represented by its deputies. Seated on the right of the chairman (George Whitehead) is William Penn, the founder of the Quaker colony of Pennsylvania. (By courtesy of Ashmolean Museum, University of Oxford)*

organisation - including John Cowlings, junior (a clothier from Bath), Richard Marchant (a tailor from Bath) and John Tylee (a pipemaker from Widcombe). Marchant, for instance, collected contributions from the Bath group for the public stock fund; distributed aid to local Quakers in need (5s 0d each to Hannah Colling and Rebecca Skreen); spoke to Daniel Holbrook of Chew Magna about 'his unruly practice of speaking in meetings'; warned John Hill of Beckington about 'having a servant in his house who is not a Friend' and 'showing too much familiarity to her'; and recorded 'the sufferings' of members for the non-payment of their tithes. Although Tylee, as overseer of the local group, had investigated the behaviour of local members and had generously taken on two impoverished youngsters (Charles Ismead and Rachael Rowland) as apprentices, he himself was the subject of an investigation in 1702. The monthly meeting expressed concern that he had run into debt 'beyond his stock' and that he had absconded 'to the great scandal and reproach of the Truth'. Nevertheless, after expressing his sorrow and repentance, he was supported by the charity of the Society until he was able to recover his position.

Both Tylee and Marchant had occasionally offered their own houses in Widcombe and Bath for monthly meetings of the Northern Division - a reminder that meetings for both business and worship were at first held in private houses, in barns or simply in the open air. These meetings, however, were always liable to be raided by the militia or by constables and magistrates accompanied by the local crowd - for the Conventicles Act of 1664 had forbade meetings for worship of five or more people who were not of the same household. The Quakers frequently suffered imprisonment (some 15,000 were fined, imprisoned or transported for offences between 1660 and 1685) for, unlike other sects which often worshipped in secret, they insisted on meeting openly in the usual places. Toleration, they believed, was their inalienable right and imprisonment was in fact a means of testifying to their faith. As the situation eased, William Penn, a prominent Quaker, preached in Bath in 1687 on the old tennis court by the King's Bath. However, it was not until ten years later that a permanent meeting house was established in Bath, following the easing of restrictions on non-conformist worship in the Toleration Act of 1689 - one of several built in Somerset at that time, including those at Glastonbury (1690), Chard (1692), Taunton (1693), Shepton Mallet (1695) and Calne (1696). In the meantime, local Quakers had continued to suffer. In 1660 for instance, the Bath chamberlain had paid 'for carrying two Quakers' to the prison at Ilchester on the Mayor's instructions, while two years later, a church court had censured Edward Power of St Michael's parish in Bath, 'for being a professed Quaker'.

(iv) Baptists

During the period 1642-1660, two puritan sects - the Presbyterians and the Independents - had been most dominant in the religious life of the country. However, after the restoration of the monarchy in 1660, which was accompanied by the restoration of the Anglican Prayer Book and the bishops, both groups struggled for survival. Whereas locally the Presbyterians managed to meet in secret conventicles to keep their movement alive, the Independents (who had never been as strong in North Somerset) vanished almost without trace. In the period 1660-1700, therefore, active local non-conformity consisted largely of groups of Presbyterians, Quakers and Baptists - all of which, after suffering persecution in the twenty-seven years immediately following the Restoration, established official meeting houses in the aftermath of the Declaration of Indulgence (1687) and the Toleration Act (1689). By 1715, out of a population in England of 5.25 million, it is estimated that in the nation at large there were 179,350 Presbyterians; 59,940 Independents; 39,510 Quakers; 40,350 Particular Baptists; and 18,800 General Baptists - together amounting to just 6.5% of the population.

Although most groups of Baptists believed that membership should be confined to those who had undergone a believer's baptism, they were divided on doctrine. Whereas the General Baptists believed in the ideas of the Dutch theologian, Jacob Arminius, that salvation was open to all through good works, the Particular Baptists followed the teaching of John Calvin on the salvation of those who have been preordained by God (i.e. predestination). It was the Particular Baptists who had first made their appearance in the west country by the 1650s. Initially they were to suffer both misunderstanding and persecution because most people confused them wrongly with the Anabaptists of Germany, who preached anarchy and communism. At the Archdeacon's Visitation of 1662, for instance, William Russell of Bath Abbey was presented by the churchwardens for censure and punishment 'for leaving their church and being a reputed Anabaptist'. His wife was also presented 'for not baptising two of her children', as was Robert Mingins (three children) and several others. This provides some evidence of the presence of individual Baptists within the city, but not for the establishment of a Baptist congregation there. William Russell was in fact a member of the city council, who refused to swear the oath of allegiance in 1662 and was therefore ejected from that body according to the terms of the Act of Uniformity a year earlier.

The first recorded meeting of the Western Baptist Association was at Wells in 1653, when eighteen churches were represented (including one from Bristol, but not one from Bath). Indeed, the first Baptist congregation locally was formed not inside the city, but in Haycombe and was clearly operational by the 1660s (as Kerry Birch has shown). By 1669, according to Episcopal Returns, it had a congregation of fifty people meeting 'at the house of Richard Gay', who was their preacher. The Gay family had held land in Haycombe since the sixteenth century and it is clear that Richard Gay set aside one of his properties for use by the local church. His great-granddaugter later described the room 'where the meeting was held. It had 'a chimney and a fireplace, where stood up a high settle where our family used to sit. It must be the good minister Richard Gay that built the house (for that was built in 1665), who was so cruelly persecuted'.

Indeed, the Haycombe church of Particular Baptists came into being at a time of great difficulty for non-conformist conventicles. The Conventicle Act of 1664, for instance, had forbade meetings for worship of more than five people with heavy fines imposed on transgressors - punishments which were soon experienced by the congregation at Haycombe. According to another family descendant, the local clergyman (Mr Morris) joined forces with two hostile neighbouring families (the Langtons and the Cobbs) to hound the Baptists. As a result, Gay was fined £5 and his members fifty shillings each, when they were first charged with holding an illegal meeting. This failed to deter the congregation, which continued to meet in defiance of the authorities - and was therefore repeatedly fined. The rapidly deteriorating situation at Haycombe was later described by his great-granddaughter: 'He lived in the troublesome times...He and his hearers were much persecuted for religion. He paid the fine for himself and his hearers as long as they would take any money. They then refused to take money any longer, [and] said they would have his person...Accordingly they had him to Ilchester Castle, where they confined him for three years'. His wife was left with several young children in her care. Tradition has it that, while he was in prison (possibly in Newgate), he met another inmate, John Bunyan. According to family sources, Bunyan apparently 'greatly respected him and dedicated a book to Mr Gay'.

Richard Gay was also much respected within the ranks of the Western Baptist Association, occasionally representing them as a 'Messenger' on special business. Although many of the churches struggled on during an increased period of persecution during the 1670s, it was not until the easing of restrictions from 1689 that non-conformists groups were able to worship freely in their own registered meeting houses. The Western Baptist Association was therefore re-formed in 1689, consisting of thirty-five churches - including those at Haycombe, Frome, Warminster, Melksham, Calne, Bradford-on-Avon, Southwick and Malmesbury. The Haycombe congregation continued to meet in the latter years of the seventeenth century, in spite of growing problems which had reduced it to 'a small number'. Apart from anxieties about 'the national state', they were also experiencing disputes about the place of singing in worship and the importance of education. Nevertheless, Richard Gay remained as committed as ever, frequently representing Haycombe in the years following 1689 at meetings of both the General Assembly of Baptists and the Western Assembly.

(v) Catholics

There were in fact very few resident Catholics in Bath throughout the whole of the seventeenth century - and, indeed, very few in the area of North-East Somerset. Increased pressure had been steadily applied on all subjects to comply with the Elizabethan church settlement. The Act of Uniformity of 1559, for instance, had imposed a weekly fine of twelve pence on those guilty of 'recusancy' (i.e. failing to attend services of the established Anglican Church) - increased to £20 in 1581 as the threat of a Spanish invasion mounted. Furthermore, an Act of 1593 stipulated that all avowed Catholics (or 'recusants') were to return to their home parishes, where they were to register and undertake not to make journeys of more than five miles in distance from home. However, if they had a good reason to travel beyond this point on matters of vital business, they could seek to secure a special licence from two justices with the backing of the bishop or a deputy lieutenant.

This stipulation therefore enabled many Catholics to visit the waters of Bath under licence on health grounds. The Jesuit priest, John Clare, was granted permission to attend, having been 'taken in a dead palsy' in 1624; in the same year, Sir Francis Stonor, an Oxfordshire Catholic, helped to pay for improvements to the King's Bath in personal gratitude for its healing waters; Father Richard Timelby, a Jesuit, arrived in 1678; and many others journeyed great distances from such places as Yorkshire and Durham. This inevitably meant that there was always the fear that the crowded streets of Bath could provide effective cover for the rendezvous of conspirators. In 1605, for instance, several of those involved in the Gunpowder Plot apparently assembled for meetings in the city. Thomas Winter, one of the group, admitted 'that he hath had many meetings at Bath about this hellish design' - including discussions with Robert Catesby and Lord Monteagle.

Very few local individuals, however, were named as practising Catholics during the period to 1660, although Philip Sherwood, a royalist officer in the Civil War, aroused suspicions concerning his religious allegiance. He belonged to a well-known Catholic family. His father, Dr John Sherwood who lived in Abbey House until his death in 1621, was described later by Anthony Wood as 'an eminent practitioner .... in the City of Bath .... much resorted to by those of the Roman Catholic religion, he himself being of that profession.' Dr Sherwood's own father and mother were devout papists; his brother, Thomas, emerged as an Elizabethan martyr for his faith; and three other brothers became Catholic priests. Furthermore, four of his seven sons were all converted to the Catholic faith - Thomas (who joined the Society of Jesus), Robert and William (both of whom entered the Benedictine Order) and John (who was a practising Catholic in Ireland). There is no direct evidence that Philip followed his brothers' example, just as there is no evidence for widespread recusancy in the Bath area between 1627 and 1660. It is nevertheless a fact that Sherwood, with his particular family background, became a permanently hostile opponent of the Puritan faction on Bath Corporation.

The Restoration of Charles II in 1660 provided Catholics with something of a twelve-year truce, during which restrictions were eased, fines remained largely uncollected and travel without licences became increasingly possible. Nevertheless, the non-attendance of individuals at Anglican services was still noted and, in 1662, twelve 'reputed papists' were reported by local churchwardens at the Archdeacon's visitation. These were - (from the Abbey) Berkeley Carne, Elizabeth Carne and Ann Long; and (from St James's parish) John Hockley, Ann Hockley, Ann Rawlee, Elizabeth Rawlee, Margaret Combes, Frances Nevill, Philippa Dolton, Winifred Sloper and Katherine Kemish. Although these numbers were small, the very presence of Catholics in their midst aroused in some local people the fear of conspiracy. In 1667, for instance, crowds of Protestant dissenters around Bath were reported to have demonstrated against the lenient treatment afforded to Catholics in the vicinity. William Prynne, Member of Parliament and Recorder for Bath, wrote about a 'great and scandalous meeting' of Papists in Bath - although a local reporter dismissed the story as nothing more than 'a dozen simple women and three or four inconsiderable men, who were at their beads'. This is no evidence for the existence of a Catholic meeting place within the city at this stage.

During the 1670s, anti-Catholic feeling mounted considerably in the country at large, reaching a climax in 1678 when allegations of a Popish Plot to assassinate the king were circulated. Regulations against Catholics were, therefore, quickly tightened as recusants were again prosecuted and fined for non-attendance. Eight Bath Catholics were named in a nationwide report of 1680 - and nine were listed by the Grand Jury in Bath in 1683. The 1680 lists included Thomas Gibbs, a brewer and eldest son of Thomas Gibbs, innkeeper of *The Golden Lion*, whereas the 1683 list included a cook, a tailor, a joiner, a musician and a cloth worker. However, the only name which is common to both lists *and* the list of 1662 is that of Berkeley Carne.

The Carnes had undoubtedly emerged as the city's most prominent Catholic family. Berkeley, a lodging house keeper, had married Elizabeth Speke of Cheney Court in Wiltshire, who also came from a long-standing Catholic family. Their children Francis and Mary, who had both been baptised in Bath Abbey, were both included in the 1683 list of reputed Papists. Francis later emerged as something of a colourful character - a lodging house keeper, owner of a small theatre built at the end of Vicarage Lane and, surprisingly, Master of King Edward's Free School. The latter appointment was made personally by James II - himself a Catholic - during his visit to the city in 1687, when William Baker, who had been Master since 1681, was summarily dismissed by the king. Known locally as a keen Presbyterian at heart, Baker had been assistant minister of the Abbey just before the Restoration in 1660. Francis Carne, on the other hand, fitted well into the king's plan to appoint Catholics to positions of influence in both the army and local affairs. Indeed, his Declaration of Indulgence of that year had granted Catholics the right to hold public office (from which they had previously been barred). Carne's triumph, however, was short-lived. Baker was quickly reinstated to the mastership in 1688 following the invasion by William of Orange in 1688, which saw James II flee into exile.

As Bath grew in fame as a health resort towards the end of the century, it is probable that many of the Catholic visitors to the spa were lodged in Bell Tree House, which stood at the corner of Binbury Lane and Beau Street. Once the rectory of St James's Church, it was in part a lodging house and in part a Benedictine chapel where, by the turn of the century, the Catholic mass was celebrated illegally by a resident priest. Bell Tree House therefore began to act as a Catholic mission in the heart of the city, serving also the needs of many villages in the locality. From the 1740s, it became the residence of a Catholic bishop and, from 1753, the chapel was mentioned quite openly in *The Bath Guide* - almost forty years before the Catholic Relief Act officially recognised Catholic places of worship! Nevertheless, it should be stressed that, even as late as 1692, an official survey found just 176 Roman Catholics in the whole diocese of Bath and Wells, compared with 5,856 nonconformists and 145,464 Anglicans.

SOURCES USED IN CHAPTER 14

1. Printed material:
Bates-Harbin, E.H. (ed.): *Quarter Sessions Records*, vols. 1, 2 & 3 (1907-8)
Besse, Joseph: *A Collection of the Suffering of the People called Quakers, vol. 1* (1753)
Birch, Kerry J: *The Baptists of Bath, 1752-1851* (1986)
Birch, Kerry J: 'Richard Gay of Haycombe' in *The Baptist Quarterly*, vol. 32, (8) (1998)
Britton, J: *The History and Antiquities of Bath Abbey Church* (1825)
Chapman, Henry: *Thermae Redivivae: the City of Bath Described* (1673)
Fawcett, Trevor: *Voices of Eighteenth-Century Bath* (1995)
Hamilton, Meg: *Bath before Beau Nash* (1978)
Hylson-Smith, Kenneth: *Bath Abbey: a History* (2003)
Hunt, William: *The Somerset Dioceses, Bath and Wells* (1885)
Jackman, Derek: *Baptists in the West Country* (1953)
Lewcun, Marek: 'The Clay Tobacco Pipe-Making Industry of Bath' in *Bath History*, vol. 5 (1994)
Matthews, A.G: *Calamy Revised* (1934)
Matthews, A.G: *Walker Revised* (1948)
McClure, N.E., *The Letters and Epigrams of Sir John Harington* (1930)
Morland, Stephen C: *The Somerset Quarterly Meetings of the Society of Friends, 1668-99* (Somerset

Record Society, 1978)

Morrill, John (ed.): *Reactions to the English Civil War, 1642-1649* (1982)

Murch, J: *History of the Presbyterian and General Baptist Churches in the West of England* (1835)

Plumtree, E.H: *The Life & Times of Thomas Ken, Bishop of Bath & Wells* (1899)

Rawlinson, Richard: *The History and Antiquities of the Cathedral Church of Salisbury and the Abbey Church of Bath* (1719)

St Michael's Churchwardens' Accounts (Proceedings of the Somerset Archeological & Natural History Society, 1880, pt 2)

Shaw, W.D: *A History of the English Church during the Civil Wars, 1640-1660*, vol. 2 (1900)

Sims, Alison: *Pleasures and Pastimes in Tudor England* (1999)

Stieg, Margaret: *The Parochial Clergy in the Diocese of Bath and Wells, 1625-85* (unpublished, 1970)

Stieg, Margaret: *Laud's Laboratory: The Dioceses of Bath and Wells in the Early 17th Century* (1982)

Stokes, James & Alexander, Robert (eds.): *Records of Early English Drama, Somerset,* Vol. 1 (1991)

The Journal of the Friends' History Society, vol. 51 (1965-67)

Underdown, David: *Revel, Riot and Rebellion, 1603-1660* (1985)

Ward, Ned, *A Step to the Bath with a Character of the Place* (1700)

Warner, Richard, *The History of Bath* (1801)

Warrington, John (ed.): *The Diary of Samuel Pepys*, vol. 3 (1953 ed.)

Williams, J.A: *Bath and Rome: the Living Link* (1963)

Williams, J.A., *Post-Reformation Catholicism in Bath*, vol. 1 (1975)

Wood, John: *A Description of Bath*, 2 vol. (1765)

Wroughton, John: *A Community at War: the Civil War in Bath &North Somerset* (1992)

Wroughton, John: *The Stuart Age, 1603-1714* (1997)

Wroughton, John: *From Civil War to Age of Reason: Bath Abbey, 1600-1800* (1997)

Wroughton, John: *An Unhappy Civil War: the Experiences of Ordinary People* (1999)

2. Documentary material:

Bath Record Office:	Bath Chamberlain's Accounts, 1568-1734
	Bath Council Minute Books, No. 1
Bodleian Library:	Rawlinson MSS, Charles Paman's Letter Book
British Library:	Additional MSS, Letter from John Ford, 1661
	Harleian MSS, Petition to Queen Elizabeth, 1583
	Thomason Tracts, 1643, 1646, 1648
Public Record Office:	Calendar of State Papers Domestic, 1667, 1683, 1693
Somerset Record Office:	Bath Abbey Vestry Minutes, 1684-1732
	St James's Churchwardens' Account Book, 1654-1770
	Diocesan Records - Comperta, 1615, 1638;
	Chapter Act Books, 1638-39
Wiltshire Record Office:	North Somerset Friends' Monthly Meeting Book, vol.1, 1667-1688 vol. 2, 1688-1712

CHAPTER 15

Entertainment

Decline of Public Entertainment under the Puritans, 1600-1660

There is no doubt that leisure activities in the nation at large underwent a major transformation from the middle of the sixteenth century as the Puritan revolution began to establish its grip. The traditional culture of the poorer sort, including their parish revels (i.e. wakes to celebrate the foundation of the local church), popular games, processions and festivals were a source of constant attack from clergy and magistrates alike since the time of the Reformation. Puritan preachers increasingly expressed their disapproval of Saints' Days and mystery plays, which smacked of 'Popery and superstition'; all forms of revelling, which not only undermined parental authority, but also caused young people to neglect their work and religion; dancing, which gave women a dangerous amount of sexual freedom; and festivals of any kind, which merely encouraged the formation of disorderly crowds and attracted both idlers and vagrants. Furthermore, an Act of 1541 had summarised existing bans on tennis, dice, cards, bowls and other 'unlawful games', chiefly because these all encouraged a great deal of gambling. With the rapid extension of poverty and unemployment towards the end of the sixteenth century, local leaders became more and more concerned about the state of public order and the need for firm control over all popular activities, which had an undermining effect on discipline.

Health resorts like Bath were particularly vulnerable to the assembly of large numbers of poor people attracted by the city's apparent affluence. The local Puritan elite, which commanded a majority in both the Bath Corporation and elsewhere in the county, was therefore totally opposed to all activities which encouraged the formation of unruly crowds, such as animal baiting, fairs and performances by travelling players. As early as 1603, a proclamation had been read in the city prohibiting fairs, while the county Quarter Sessions at Wells in 1608 had ordered that 'all **bull-baitings and bear-baitings** be immediately, throughout the whole county of Somerset, utterly forbidden and suppressed'.

Their failure to eliminate these activities in the county as a whole is underlined partly by the reissue of this order in 1612 and 1624 and partly by a petition of the Grand Jury to the Assizes meeting at Bath in 1638. In this petition, the scarcity of corn (which resulted in high

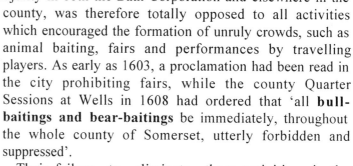

(left) *This 16th-century woodcut of an animal-baiting session in Germany gives a good idea of the horrors of the 'sport'. The bear on the right is not in fact cuddling the dog, but rather crushing it to death. Animal baiting in Bath took place not in arenas like this, but in the courtyards of inns. (By courtesy of the Bridgeman Art Library)*

prices) was partly blamed on 'a late practice of gathering great companies of unruly people at bull-baitings', thus causing excessive quantities of ale to be brewed. The poor were thus encouraged to spend more than they could afford, so that 'many thefts' were committed after their departure. In Bath itself, entries in the chamberlain's accounts indicate that occasional bear-baitings had taken place during the latter part of the sixteenth century. Payments were made to Lord Warwick's bearward in 1576, Lord Dudley's in 1594 and the Queen's in 1602. In addition to these visits by travelling troupes, local people had arranged their own entertainment on at least one occasion in 1577, when a subsidy of twelve pence was given by the corporation 'to the baiting of John Chapman's bear'. From 1602, however, it set its face firmly against such activities, even though individuals still tried to indulge themselves whenever the back of authority was turned. William Powell was therefore censured by the Bishop in 1606 not only for 'keeping a baiting bull', but also for 'being present at the baiting of the said bull at Bath and Bathwick', during which the animal was killed.

The same restrictive policy was also applied to **travelling players** and other entertainers, who had been a regular feature of the social calendar in Bath throughout the Elizabethan period. The production of mystery or miracle plays had been a long-standing tradition in the city - particularly at St Michael's Church where small touring troupes of players occasionally performed the story of the creation or other religious episodes on a temporary stage in the large space outside the North Gate. The churchwardens, for instance, paid the Players of Gloucester, who accompanied by a group of mummers, to perform in this way. The final reference to such productions, however, was in 1601 when the city chamberlain paid 'the drum players' for performing 'before the mystery'.

Other public amusements had included a 'bag pipe player' (1569), acrobats (1578,1589), school plays (1583, 1601), a blind organ player (1616), the fencers and musicians who celebrated the proclamation of James 1 in 1603 and the 'Waits of Bristol', who performed for the visit of the Earl of Pembroke in 1601 (as they had done on previous occasions). Many cities - though not Bath until later in the seventeenth century - boasted such groups of official musicians, who wore the city livery, performed at official functions and were available for outside hire. However, as local authorities began to restrict increasingly the many bands of strolling performers who wandered the countryside, at least one more privileged group found itself favoured with a short-lived reprieve. For whereas an Act of Parliament in 1598 had forbidden 'all fencers, bearwards, common players of interludes and minstrels wandering abroad', certain troupes of theatrical players were given exemption from this ruling, if they had been licensed by a high-ranking patron (such as the Queen or Lord Chamberlain). These well-organised touring companies each had a small repertoire of two or three plays, which they performed in guildhalls (if they were lucky), inn courtyards or open market places. Without a licence, each player would be treated as a vagabond and would therefore be 'stripped naked from the middle upwards and openly whipped till his body be bloody'.

In Bath, most companies were paid a flat-rate fee by the corporation for their performance. However, a different system operated for visits by the most prestigious company of all - The Queen's Players, of which Shakespeare was a member. On these occasions, the performers themselves first made a collection from the audience ('the gathering') and then the corporation, from city funds, made up the amount to the pre-arranged fee. Thus, in 1581, the chamberlain paid 19s 4d to make up what 'was gathered at the bench' to a total of 26s 4d. Among groups of players performing in

Bath, The Queen's Players were by far the most regular, attending almost annually between 1583 and 1607. Other groups included The Lord Admiral's, The Lord of Derby's, The Lord of Worcester's, The Lord Chamberlain's, The Lord of Pembroke's, the Earl of Hertford's, the Lord of Leicester's, the Lord of Oxford's and many more - including a troupe belonging to the Master of the Revels. Although in some years as many as six different companies had visited the city, this practice suddenly ended in 1612 when the final payment was made. Nevertheless, the Queen's Players returned to the city for one last time six years later when they were permitted to hire the Town Hall for 3s 4d, even though the Corporation clearly withheld its usual fee.

Much of the traditional colour of popular entertainment had therefore passed from the local scene by 1620, just as traditional festivals (the crowning of the Autumn King, processions at Pentecost and Rogationtide, the Crowning of the King of Bath at Whitsuntide and the Midsummer Eve festival) had largely disappeared by the second half of the sixteenth century. But although the Puritan elite saw such popular gatherings as a danger to both order and morality, they were nevertheless keen to retain some elements of **civic ritual** as a means of emphasising lessons in authority and obedience. In Bath, therefore, formal processions were still maintained at the coming of the Assizes; trumpeters were engaged to herald royal visits; bonfires were lit to celebrate the birth of royal princes in 1630 and 1634; ceremonial presentations were made to distinguished visitors (such as the brace of pheasants and sugar loaf given to the Archbishop of York in 1634); beer and cakes were regularly offered to the freemen of the city at Whitsuntide, and a splendid banquet was arranged for officers and deputy lieutenants at the annual muster of the trained bands.

Colour and ritual, therefore, did not entirely disappear, but the focus of attention was henceforth centred on the symbols of authority (judges, councillors, army officers and visiting dignitaries) with the crowd as passive observers on the outside. Gradually, too, the Puritans added special celebrations of their own to emphasise their religious and political beliefs, especially during the years of royalist occupation when they wanted to make political points to their oppressors. Gunpowder Treason Day (5th November) replaced Hallow'e'en as a later autumn celebration, followed a few days later by Crown Nation Day (17th November), commemorating the anniversary of Queen Elizabeth's accession. These occasions, which enabled them to express not only their longing for a return to the so-called 'glorious days' of Queen Elizabeth but also their hatred of 'Popery', gave local citizens the chance to celebrate through bonfires, fireworks and the ringing of church bells.

Pastimes and Pleasures, 1603-1714

In spite of Puritan controls on public entertainment and mass gatherings, the citizens of Bath were not totally deprived of recreational activities during the seventeenth century (particularly from 1660). Indeed, as a child of the Age of Enlightenment, Richard Warner listed in somewhat disparaging terms in 1801 the many amusements at their disposal - amusements which, he said, 'suited the grossness and simplicity of the time'. They included 'the pranks of mountebanks *[quacks who performed tricks and dispensed cures from a temporary platform]*; the feats of jugglers, tumblers and dancers; the jests of itinerant mimes and mummers and the dangerous amusement of quintaine'. The latter, which perhaps related more to the sixteenth century, was originally played on horseback. It involved striking hard a target at one end of a revolving crossbar and then moving away quickly to avoid being hit on the head by the

(right) *A contemporary drawing of a game of real tennis in progress on a court designed for the purpose. The ball is being served onto the sloping roof at the side and thence across the 'net' (a piece of string) . In the field outside, boys, who cannot afford to play the proper game, are plaing handball instead.* (Taken from J.A. Comenius, Orbis Sensualiun Pictus,1672 edtn., *by permission of the British Library: ref - 1607.2351)*

bag of sand attached to the other end. These older amusements, said Richard Warner, were 'diversified occasionally by the pageant and the masque or the elegant pastimes of bull-baiting, cock-fighting, cock-scaling, pig-racing, bowling, football, grinning through a horse collar and swallowing scalding frumenty *[hulled wheat boiled in sweetened milk].*'

However, even in the more restrictive atmosphere of first part of the seventeenth century, visitors to the health resort clearly found plenty to do. In the 1630s, for instance, Sir Edmund Verney admitted that 'we pass our time as merrily as pain will give us leave' - although in his case, that probably did not mean **tennis**. Nevertheless, this had become a popular sport in the sixteenth century, thanks in part to the enthusiasm of Henry VIII who had no fewer than four courts at Whitehall. Royal or 'real tennis', which is the type under discussion, was normally played indoors on a special court and involved serving the ball (made of sheepskin and stuffed with sawdust) with a racquet (made of yew with cat-gut strings) onto the sloping roof, which ran along one side of the court, and thence across the net (see illustration). Poorer people, who also took up the game in great numbers, often played in the fields, using a piece of string instead of a net and their hands instead of a racquet (hence the term 'handball'). There was at least one tennis court in Bath, which is shown on Speed's map of 1610 and again on Overton's map of 1668. Although the court was no longer used for tennis by the end of the century (it did not feature on Gilmore's map of 1694), it was occasionally used for meetings (the Quaker, William Penn, preached there in 1687). The leaseholder of the 'tennis court' was given permission in 1686 to open a door from the court into one of the slipways which led into the bath. In the meantime, a **fives** court had been opened just outside the West Gate.

One sport which did appeal to both residents and visitors alike was **bowling**, in which the player tried to get his bowl as near to the jack as possible. One visitor to Bath in 1634 noted that there were actually two bowling greens near the Abbey - 'one of them is curiously and neatly kept where only Lords, Knights, Gallants and Gentlemen of the best rank and quality do daily meet in seasonable times to recreate themselves for both pleasure and health'. This more exclusive area, known as the Inner Green, was situated on the site of the old Abbey orchard. It was still very much in evidence in 1700, when Ned Ward visited the city. He later described how, on one evening, he had witnessed 'a great match at bowling' between a team of 'Courtiers' (including visiting merchants, bankers and clergy) and a team of local 'Citizens'. As usual, it provided a fine opportunity for gambling - 'Ten guineas to five, I uncover the

A section of Joseph Gilmore's map of 1694, showing the location of the sites used for entertainment.

1 = Kingsmead, 'the pleasant green meadow' where Celia Fiennes found good walks and 'cakehouses'.
2 = The Fives Court, opened towards the end of the century * 3 = The Cock Pit, which was used for cockfighting.
4 = The site of the Theatre or Play House, opened in 1705 * 5 = Animal-baiting took place in the first part of the century
within the courtyards of inns such as The Bear * 6 = The New Bowling Green, opened in the latter part of the century.
7 = Site of the Outer Bowling Green until its closure in 1677, when the Gravel Walks (on left of map) were laid out.
8 = The more exclusive Inner Bowling Green * 9 = Site of Harrison's Assembly Rooms (opened in 1709) with walks down
to the river * 10 = The Guildhall, where balls and plays weree staged * 11 = Site of the first Pump Room, opened in 1706.

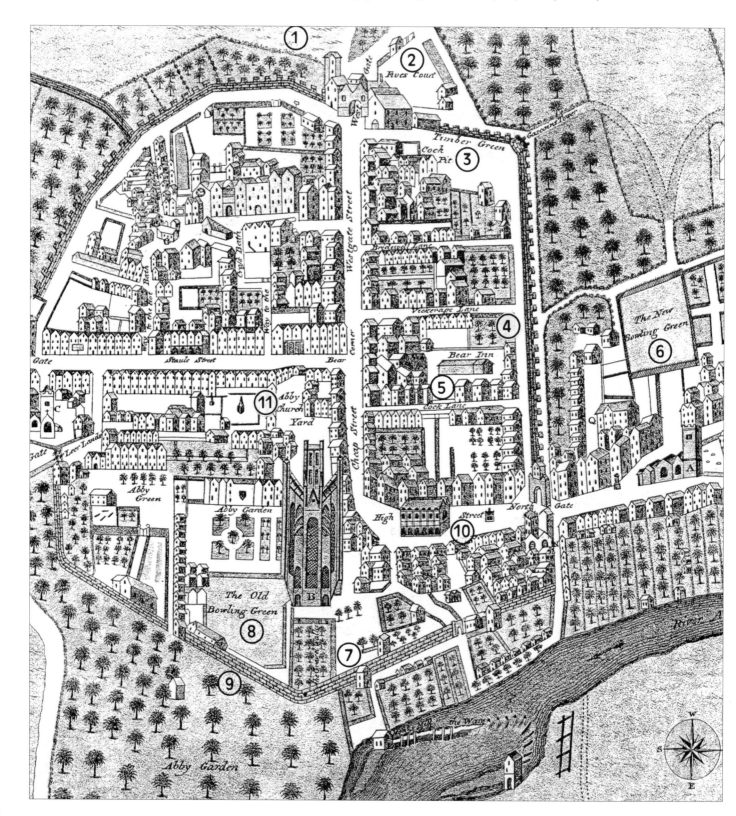

jack', shouted one competitor, 'another swearing he knew the ground to an inch and would hold five pound his bowl came in'. As far as the match itself was concerned, Ward noted that 'the Citizens won the Courtiers' money - and the Courtiers swore to be revenged on their wives and daughters'. Charles Cotton made the apt comment that 'a bowling green is a place where three things are thrown away besides the bowls - *viz.* time, money and curses'.

The other green, known as the Outer Green, had been levelled out of part of the Litton - a large open space, which had previously been the churchyard of the old Priory. This somewhat rougher green had been set aside for the use of ordinary people with a skittles alley also attached alongside. As early as 1608, Lionel Cranfield (the merchant, who later became the Earl of Middlesex) paid four pence on a visit to Bath to play **skittles** (also known as 'pins' or 'clash') - either in that alley or in one of several based in local inns. For many years, the corporation rented out this Outer Green at twenty shillings a year to a selected leaseholder, who then charged players a fee for its use. However, when Walter Werratt's lease came up for renewal in 1677, it was resolved that whereas in future he was able 'to enjoy [the] pleasure of the skittles alley', he was 'not to enjoy the bowling green'. Although the Outer Green, therefore, was closed to make way for other facilities (see below), a 'New Bowling Green' was opened shortly afterwards outside the North Gate, near St Michael's Church, for the use of ordinary people [in the area where Green Street is today].

Meanwhile, according to John Wood, the area just south of the Litton was also used for a variety of popular sports, including 'smock-racing, pig-racing, playing at football and running with the feet in bags' - not to mention 'jigging on a stage' for prizes. There were two types of **football** being played. The first tended to be played by groups of youngsters in any small space where they could kick a ball (as on the Litton). This is described by a French visitor to England, César de Saussure:

> Another amusement, which is very inconvenient to passers-by, is football. For this game a leather ball filled with air is used and is kicked about with the feet. In cold weather you sometimes see a score of rascals in the street kicking at the ball, and they will break panes of glass and smash the windows of coaches - and also knock you down without the slightest compunction; on the contrary, they will roar with laughter.

A contemporary drawing of a game of football in progress. The boy second from the right seems to have kicked the ball, but the others are seeking to gain possession of it with their hands. (Author's collection)

A much more serious and dangerous form of the game, however, was played as a popular ingredient of the traditional Shrovetide games. These, having being abolished by the Puritans, were revived in Bath as elsewhere after 1660. According to John Wood, writing in 1742, football of this type was played on the Ham meadow as part of 'the common sports of Shrove Tuesday. It provided an ideal opportunity for local hooligans to voice their protest against authority or to settle old scores. Bearing no resemblance to the modern-day game, it featured large numbers of youths who fought both literally and vigorously to gain possession of the ball. In 1583, Philip Stubbes described the game like this:

> As concerning football playing: I protest unto you it may rather be called a friendly kind of fight than a play or recreation; a bloody and murdering practice than a fellowly sport or pastime. For doth not everyone lie in wait for his adversary though it be upon hard stones...so that by this means, sometimes their necks are broken, sometimes their backs, sometimes their legs, sometimes their arms, sometimes one part thrust out of joint, sometimes the noses gush out with blood, sometimes their eyes start out.

Once the ball had been seized, the runner had no thought of passing it, but rather relied on his friends to protect him by simply attacking any opponents who came near. This tactic caused Henry Packham to note in 1612 that one person had been maimed 'who never saw the ball'.

Wood also included, as one of the Shrove Tuesday sports, '**cock-threshing**', which he said was a 'barbarous and unmanly custom'. It was also referred to in passing by Dr Robert Peirce, the Bath physician, in his *Memoirs*. The person, he said, who put forward theories without facts to support them was like the man who 'set up a Shrove-Tuesday cock for everyone to throw at, without so much as paying two pence for three throws'. The sport was explained further by de Saussure, who aptly observed that there was 'cruelty and even ferocity in some of the pastimes of the people':

> [Cock-threshing is an amusement which] is fortunately only permitted on the last four days of Lent. A cock is taken and fastened by a long cord to a stake and, for a few pence, anyone may throw a short, heavy wooden club at him - and he becomes the property of the man who kills him...But so many clubs are thrown about that you run the risk of receiving one on your head.

By the eighteenth century (until the practice was banned in about 1756), it seems that in Bath the cockerels were initially placed in pots, which would have offered them protection only until the pots broke.

Delight in various forms of **animal baiting** continued throughout the century, in spite of the best efforts of the Puritans to abolish it. As early as 1634, George Chapman was given a grant of land outside the East Gate 'to make dog kennels' (it is known that several of the Chapman family were involved in baiting), while four years later John Pinckin and his friends were admonished when they 'caused a bull to be baited'. In 1648, a group of Bath residents, led by former councillor Henry Chapman, even organised a weekly bull-baiting session outside just outside the city's area of jurisdiction and in defiance of the magistrates. Bear-baiting involved tying the bear to a rope, which was fixed to a post, and then letting loose large English mastiffs to do the baiting - although the bear, it has to be stated, did its best to defend itself by mauling the dogs.

Towards the end of the century, **cockfighting** had also become a popular activity in Bath with the erection of a cockpit in Saw Close. This would probably have been an octagonal enclosure, surrounded by benches, to which spectators paid an entrance fee of a penny. It is clear that some local people specialised in breeding cocks for both cock-threshing and cockfighting - including William White , whose lease in 1684 for a property in the old churchyard of St Mary de Stall included a 'cock loft'. At the heart of all these sports was the people's love of gambling with large bets placed on the outcome of each contest - a fact noticed by von Uffenbach, a German visitor to England in 1710:

> In the afternoon we went to see the cockfighting. This is a sport peculiar to the English...The building is round like a tower and inside it is just like a theatre as all round it there are benches in tiers, on which the spectators sit. In the middle is a round table covered with mats, on which the cocks have to fight. When it is time to begin the persons appointed to do so bring in the cocks hidden in two sacks and then, before they have seen the birds, everyone starts to shout their wagers...Then the cocks are taken out of the sacks and fitted with silver spurs...and are thrust at each other until they get angry. Then one should just see how they peck at each other, and especially how they hack with their spurs...There is nothing so amusing as when one cock seems quite exhausted and there are great shouts of joy and terrific bets and then, though he seemed to be quite done for, he suddenly recovers and masters the other...The people become as heated about their wagers as the cocks themselves

Quite apart from all these sports and pastimes, the period from 1660 also saw the revival of a number of **public festivities**. Occasions such as the King's Birthday or the Fifth of November presented a great opportunity for fireworks, bonfires and merrymaking in the streets - as did the coronation of Charles II in 1661 (see page 208), the safe return of William III from Ireland after his victory at the Boyne in 1690, the rout of the French fleet in 1692 and the discovery of a Jacobite plot to assassinate the king in 1696. The birthday of Charles II in 1664, for instance, was celebrated in style with bonfires, fireworks, ringing of church bells, volleys of muskets and musical entertainment - the corporation paying for bread for the soldiers and beer and cakes for themselves 'while the bonfires were burning'.

Two of the **traditional fairs** were also revived - the Orange Fair in February and the Cherry Fair in June. Held in the market place outside the Guildhall, these colourful (and sometimes riotous) occasions brought along entertainers as well as traders in livestock and general merchandise. Even greater excitement was generated by the old custom of '**Processionings**'. Held every three years in September, the practice continued until well into the nineteenth century, being vividly described by Rowland Mainwaring in 1838.

(right) *The frontispiece of* **The Compleate Gamester** *by Charles Cotton (1680 edtn.), which highlights the endless opportunities for gambling in a place such as Bath - including billiards, cards, dice, backgammon and cockfighting. (By permission of the British Library: ref - 7915.aa.26)*

The mayor and corporation would emerge from the Guildhall and proceed down the river in a decorated barge, accompanied by a band of musicians. In 1669 for instance, the corporation paid Messrs Gay and Gibbs sixpence each for 'rowing the boat on Procession Day' - while a further sum of three shillings was spent on 'beer on Procession Day'. Followed by a large crowd of local people, the official party would disembark further down river and would then commence their perambulation of the city boundaries along the line of the modern Marlborough Buildings.

A similar event was held in the various parishes on **Rogation Sunday** (the fifth Sunday after Easter), when a procession of clergy, churchwardens and congregation with cross and banners would perambulate the bounds of the fields and streets in their respective parishes. This provided a traditional method of preventing subsequent property disputes by ensuring that ancient boundaries were not forgotten. In the sixteenth century at least, the curate of the parish would have been required to offer prayers in the fields, before stating out loud 'cursed be he who removeth the bounds and doles *[markers]* of his neighbours' fields'. The day ended with a communal meal and somewhat rowdy festivities - which was one reason for the ban imposed of such events by the Puritans, who also felt that they were based far more on superstition than on true religion.   .

The Rise of the Leisure Resort, 1675-1714

The period after the Restoration in 1660 marked the gradual rise to prominence in England of a number of 'leisure towns', including Bath. As Angus McInnes has pointed out, these were often spa towns complete with their coffee houses, parks, gardens, shops offering a wide range of luxury goods, and specialists (surgeons, apothecaries, milliners, perfumers and tailors) providing everything that was needed for personal display and grooming. These towns therefore presented 'a miniature London season'. In the immortal words of Ned Ward, describing Bath after a visit in 1700: 'In a word, 'tis a valley of pleasure, yet a sink of iniquity - nor is there any intrigue or debauch acted at London, but is mimicked there'. McInnes, in analysing the reasons for this development, points to the decline of Puritanism; the spread of 'Renaissance ideas of gentility'; the growth of overseas trade which brought new luxuries - tea, coffee, spices and fine fabrics - onto the English market; the calmer atmosphere from 1660, after the disruption of the Civil War; the rapid increase in the number of middle and upper class people with wealth to spare; and the rise of entrepreneurs, like Richard Nash, who were prepared to organise a programme for 'the company' *[i.e. the visitors who had assembled in Bath for the season]*. In short, 'the arts of civilised living took root'.

Bath Corporation became increasingly aware from 1674 of the need to provide a series of pleasant walks for the recreation of visitors to its rising spa. One important location for development was the Litton [the area which was eventually to become known as Orange Grove] - hence the decision in 1677 to close down the Outer Bowling Green (see above). Trevor Fawcett and Marta Inskip have traced out the various stages in this conversion, commencing in 1675 when formal walks lined with rows of sycamore trees were laid out east of the Abbey next to the Inner Bowling Green. Then, in 1693, the council resolved that 'the walks in the Bowling Green be gravelled' - a task which was completed in the following year with sixty loads of gravel (hence the name, **the Gravel Walks**). At the same time, 'the three great elms' in the remaining part of the old green were 'cut down and sold' and five young elms (purchased in Bathford) planted in their place with suitable protection provided by hawthorns. The

area around was then properly levelled, returfed and regularly maintained by cutting the grass and watering the perimeter banks with a 'watering pot', which had been bought specially.

This corner of the city quickly became a popular meeting place for gentle recreation and polite conversation. To increase the attraction, booths had been set up by 1700 along the southern edge of the walks, selling a range of fancy goods. Known as 'raffling shops', they also ran a type of lottery in which customers, having paid a set fee, either drew lots or threw dice for the prizes on offer. Ned Ward, after bathing one day during his visit, 'went to walk in the Grove - a very pleasant place for diversion'. He entered one of the raffling shops and apparently gained a real bargain by purchasing a snuff box for a guinea (even though he claimed it was 'worth four'). He also commented that in one of the walks were 'several sets of nine-pins' *[skittles]*, looked after by an attendant who took the players' fees. Needless to say, these had become something of a centre for gambling with bets of a guinea most common - 'Tipping all nine for a guinea', said Ward, ' is as common there as two farthings for a porringer of barley broth at the Hospital Gate in Smithfield'.

The atmosphere of gossip and intrigue, which often prevailed in the leisure spa, apparently showed itself in the Gravel Walks, where 'on the several of the trees was hung a lampoon on the marriage of Mr ----, a drug monger, and the famous Mrs----, an old B---- of London'. Visitors to the Walks were also serenaded from time to time by the City Waits or minstrels, a small band of musicians which had been formed with the rise of the leisure resort towards the end of the century. They expected a tip, of course, for their efforts both there and at the various inns and lodging houses where they greeted new arrivals with their music. Ned Ward was totally disgusted by this tactic: 'In the morning', he complained, 'we were saluted by the whole fraternity of cat-gut scrapers and could not get rid of them without the assistance of an angel *[a gold coin]*'. Musical entertainment of a different kind was occasionally provided by morris dancers - the corporation rewarding them with much thirst-quenching in 1707 at a cost of five shillings.

As interest in the resort grew, particularly after the visits of Queen Anne in 1702 and 1703, the corporation became increasingly anxious to continue the development of the area around the Gravel Walks. Between 1702 and 1705, therefore, it began to authorise the building of seven individual shops to replace the raffling booths on the edge of the Walks. The shops, leases for which were granted chiefly to members of the council, were no more than twelve feet deep and were fronted by a new paved walk some ten feet wide. This pavement was eventually extended round the corner from the eastern end of the range - following the line of the City Wall - into what became known as Terrace Walk.

Celia Fiennes, during her visit to the city in 1698, found a number of other spots for healthy walks and good conversation. She particularly liked Kingsmead 'a pleasant green meadow, where are walks round and cross it' - not to mention the 'several little cakehouses where you can have fruit syllabubs and summer liqueurs to entertain the company that walk there'. She also discovered that in wet weather the place to walk was inside the Abbey, 'which is lofty and spacious - and much company walks there'. Antony à Wood, on his visit in 1676, also noticed considerable numbers walking in the Abbey - partly for leisure and partly as a short cut from the baths to the bowling greens (the route outside being totally blocked by the houses which had been built right up against the northern wall of the Abbey). He complained that many of the inscriptions on the flattened headstones inside had been worn out 'by the often pushing of people over them to the bowling green'.

The city's first Assembly Rooms, standing just outside the city walls - see map on p. 196. A painting by William Blackmore. (By courtesy of the Victoria Art Gallery, Bath & North East Somerset Council)

Yet another pleasant walk was provided by the building of the city's first **Assembly Rooms** in 1709. According to Richard Warner, there was by then an urgent need for a civilised place in which 'the company could drink their tea and divert themselves with cards'. Thomas Harrison, a London trader, provided the solution when he persuaded John Hall (the owner of property to the south-east of the Abbey) to lease him land on which to erect a two-storey building at a cost of £1,000. Situated just outside the city wall and opposite Terrace Walk, the development included a delightful walk (for the exclusive use of those clients who had paid a one guinea subscription) down to the river through beautiful gardens and avenues of lime trees. Harrison's Walks, as they were called, amounted in fact to Bath's first-ever pleasure garden. The Rooms themselves provided space for taking light refreshment, socialising, buying luxury items, joining in the fun of a ball (a proper ballroom was in fact added in 1720) and, above all, indulging in the most popular activity of all - gambling.

Harrison was supported wholeheartedly by Richard Nash, who had arrived in Bath in 1705 and whose task it was (at least in part) to persuade the company to visit the Rooms. There was, however, one slight problem to the achievement of this aim. Bath Corporation, which had initially opposed the scheme, not only refused permission for any access to be made through the city wall, but had actually built the wall higher to block out daylight from the windows. Harrison's supporters were so infuriated that they threatened retaliation - as was made clear at a meeting of the council's sub-committee which met in 1711 to resolve the dispute : 'it is reported for a certainty', read the subsequent minute, 'that the persons of quality and gentry now residing in this city have threatened and are resolved to pull down...the new wall that was erected upon the borough wall'. The dispute was grave enough to go to the Court of Chancery for a decision. Eventually reason eventually prevailed; access was provided; and Harrison's Rooms gained immense popularity.

Meanwhile, the corporation had itself contributed to these developments by opening the first proper **Pump Room** next to the King's Bath in 1706. This enabled the wealthier sort, who had been prescribed by doctors to take the waters, to do so in comfort. It also provided another gathering place in which visitors could socialise before going on to Bath's other attractions later in the morning. Evening

The Pump Room in Bath, which was opened in 1706 next to the King's Bath. Notice the elegant social scene both inside and outside the building - and the two types of sedan chair. A drawing published by George Sperren in 1737 - by courtesy of Bath & North East Somerset Library and Archive Service (Bath Central Library)

entertainment was provided in part by the opening of a small **theatre** in Upper Borough Walls in 1705. Built by George Trim and funded, according to John Wood, by subscriptions from 'people of the highest quality', it provided a much more satisfactory venue than the Guildhall, where plays had traditionally been staged. Although the city no longer enjoyed the benefit of the numerous touring troupes, which had visited Bath in Elizabethan times, there was something of a revival after 1660 (the corporation, for instance, contributing to the costs of 'the players in the Town Hall' in 1674). However, Bath's new company provided an opportunity for a number of more unusual attractions to emerge. Trevor Fawcett has pointed, for example, to the establishment in the city of Martin Powell's puppet show from about 1709, featuring marionettes which stood two feet tall and performed various plays in a miniature theatre. Many of these entertainments, of course, were strictly seasonal.

Another main source of evening entertainment was **the formal ball**, often given privately by 'ladies of quality'. In 1696, it was reported from Bath that 'our city is very full and balls every night in the Town hall'. Two years later, Celia Fiennes also commented on the 'very fine Hall, which they use for the balls and the dancing'. It was, however, left again to Ned Ward to give us a more vivid account of such events. 'The Hall', he said, 'is a very spacious room and fitted for that purpose. During the ball, the door is kept by a couple of brawny beadles to keep out the mobility, looking as fierce as the uncouth figures *[the statues in the Hall]*. A consort of delicate music, vocal and instrumental, performed by good masters. A noble collation of dry sweetmeats, rich wine and large attendance'.

Quite apart from these more formal entertainments, Bath offered an increasing number of places where the company could enjoy relaxation and conversation. There were, of course, many **alehouses** (which were largely used by the poorer people) and

taverns, which offered food and a fine range of imported wines and spirits (including 'canary', a fortified wine from the Canaries; brandy; a kind of gin; and rum). As early as 1628, John Earle had drawn a careful distinction between the alehouse and the tavern: 'A tavern', he said 'is a degree - or, if you will - a pair of stairs above an alehouse, where men get drunk with more credit and apology. It is the busy man's recreation; the melancholy man's sanctuary; the stranger's welcome; the lawman's entertainment; the scholar's kindness; and the citizen's courtesy'. César de Saussure, on a visit to England in 1725, noted the Englishman's addiction to alcohol:

> Debauch runs riot with an unblushing countenance. It is not the lower populace alone that is addicted to drunkenness; numbers of persons of high rank and even distinction are over fond of liquor. All men, even churchmen, have a particular club or tavern, where they meet at least twice in the week to drink together in company.

Saussure had been told that this fondness for alcohol was thought necessary to counter 'the thickness and dampness of the atmosphere' in England. Nevertheless, there is little doubt that drunkenness was a national vice in the latter half of the seventeenth century. Daniel King estimated in 1695 that, throughout the country, no less than 28% of the annual household expenditure was given over to the consumption of beer and ale. [This figure, of course, would include the consumption of the weaker small beer during meals.]

From 1660, however, even taverns were having to compete with the latest attraction offering refreshment - namely, **the coffee house**. The first of these opened in Oxford in 1650, followed by one in London in 1652 and several more in various towns during the 1660s. Bath probably saw its first coffee house by 1679 at *The Turk's Head* near the Guildhall. However, as Trevor Fawcett has shown, this was subsequently moved by Robert Sheyler around 1694 to a new site on the corner of Cheap Street, where it became a somewhat exclusive establishment with entry by subscription only. A more popular coffee house, known as Bengy's, had been opened by at least 1709 by Benjamin Jellicot at the end of Terrace Walk overlooking the

Contemporary drawings of an alehouse (top) - the two men at the back seem to be slightly under the influence of drink, while the one on the right is urinating against the beer barrel; and a tavern (bottom) - with the tapster and the cook in discussion. Unlike the alehouse, the tavern was able to provide food - hence the roasts of meat on spits over the fire. (Author's collection)

Inner Bowling Green (see illustration). Coffee houses offered a great variety of drinks, including chocolate and tea (which Thomas Garry claimed provided a cure for giddiness, breathing difficulties, bad sight, weak stomachs and obesity). They quickly became an exclusive preserve of male society, offering a forum for debate, a reading room for the latest newspapers and pamphlets, an office for conducting business (correspondence was frequently directed there for regular clients) and a place to linger with friends. Saussure observed on his visit that 'what attracts enormously in these coffee houses are the gazettes and other public papers', because 'all Englishmen are great newsmongers'.

The coffee house like the alehouse was a strictly male resort. Many men in fact stayed on throughout the day - a fact which caused Charles II to describe coffee houses as 'a great resort for the idle and the dissolute'. It also caused women in London - furious at the amount of time their husbands wasted there - to launch a petition against 'that black, thick, nasty, bitter, stinking, nauseous puddle water'. They also condemned the men's practice of plying between the coffee house and the tavern: 'like tennis balls between two rackets, the fops (our husbands) are bandied to and fro all day' between the two, coming to the coffee house in their drunken stupor 'for a pennyworth of settle-brain'. Ned Ward was perfectly happy to try out the one in Bath, where he enjoyed meeting several of his friends and passing on the latest gossip from London.

However, the rest of the experience was not to his liking. After taking 'a dish or two of that insipid liquor', he said, 'we adjourned to *The Three Tuns*, where we enlivened our souls with a glass of good Bordeaux and sparkling sherry'.

Ward, like many of the visiting company, greatly enjoyed **gambling**. He described how he and his friends went to *The Royal Oak* tavern (which was just outside the North Gate) for sessions of 'backgammon, tick-tack and loaded dice'. Money was in plentiful supply. 'Bank bills and exchequer notes', he said, 'were as plentiful as fops at the coffee houses'. As Ronald Neale has pointed out, Bath had become by 1706 'an international centre' for gambling with the arrival of fifty known gamesters from London. Gambling was patchily controlled in the city with local justices occasionally imposing heavy punishments both for cheating with marked dice and for running illegal

(above) A coffee house depicted in **Vulgus Britannicus** *(1711) as a centre for debate. Note the newspapers and clay pipes on the table, the boys serving coffee in dishes, the large coffee urn being kept warm over the fire - and the formidable owner behind the counter. (By permission of the British Library: ref - 1490.d.83)*

gaming houses. Dice games were a popular form of gambling - Lady Orkney grumbling in 1711 that the 'rattling of the dice' in Bath totally killed all decent conversation. This minor inconvenience, however, was nothing compared with the bitter disputes that broke out around the gambling table. Some of these, where honour was seriously at stake, resulted in duels - including the one in which Captain Webster (Nash's predecessor as Master of Ceremonies) was killed. He apparently met his challenger at dawn in the Outer Bowling Green, having been accused of cheating the night before.

Tobacco was another indulgence for many of the company. Imported from America from the middle of the sixteenth century, it was still comparatively expensive a hundred or so years later. It was smoked in long clay pipes by the male members of society, who were able to purchase it in Bath from 1632 at any one of sixteen licensed outlets (including six mercers and four apothecaries). Pipes, too, were readily available. As Marek Lewcun has shown, they were in fact made locally both by John Gay, who owned a pipe kiln in Bath in the late 1650s, and by John and Richard Tylee of Widcombe from the mid-1690s. Writers of the time strongly advocated the beneficial effects of tobacco - including the historian, James Howell:

> If moderately and seasonably taken (as I find you always do) 'tis good for many things: it helps digestion, taken a while after a meal; a leaf or two being steeped over night in a little white wine is a vomit *[an emetic]* that never fails in its operations; it is a good companion to one that converseth with the dead - for, if one hath been poring long upon a book, or is toiled with the pen and stupefied with study, it quickeneth him and dispels those clouds that usually overset the brain...Is is good to fortify and preserve the sight, the smoke being let in round the balls of the eyes once a week, and frees them from all rheums *[watery discharges]*.

Sometimes the wealthier members of the community felt the need to break away from the claustrophobic atmosphere of the city by **taking the air** in the countryside around. Several visitors made the point that there was little point in having a coach inside the city itself. Celia Fiennes, for instance, commented that 'there is little use of a coach...for the ways are not proper for coaches; the town is adapted to the bathing and drinking of waters and nothing else'. On the other hand, she admitted after a three-mile ride that 'Lansdown is a very pleasant hill to ride for air and prospect'. Daniel Defoe agreed with her about the congestion of streets in the city centre. 'Sometimes', he said, 'persons of quality who have coaches go up [on the downs] for the air; but very few people care to have coaches here, it being a place where they have but little room to keep them and less to make use of them'. Bearing these problems in mind, the corporation agreed in 1699 to set out part of Bath Common (henceforth known as 'the Ride') 'for gentlemen's coaches and horses to take the air'. At a time when most people could ride a horse, many visitors also took the air by riding on the beautiful downs which surrounded the city.

Nevertheless those without coaches or horses, who were unable or unwilling to walk too far in the city, were able in the latter part of the century to be transported in a hired 'chair', which was supported on poles and carried by two porters. The chairs came in two types - the 'glass chair' (better known as **the sedan chair**), which was enclosed and had windows from which to view the scene; and the baize-covered 'Bath chair', which was open in front. Whereas the former type was used for leisurely trips around the city, the latter was designed to transport visitors seeking health cures from their lodgings to the baths. As Celia Fiennes commented in 1698: 'the company use all the morning the chairs of baize to carry them to the bathing, so they have the chair or sedan to carry them in visits'. The chairmen wore a uniform of blue coat, black breeches, white stockings and cocked hat. Following an Act of Parliament in 1707, sedan chair owners were required to obtain a licence to operate from the mayor at a cost of three shillings (on pain of a 13s 4d fine on default); to paint an identification number on the back so that aggrieved customers could complain more easily; and to charge an approved rate of hire (with a maximum of sixpence for a ride within the walled city, a shilling for a trip to the parishes outside and sixpence for every half-hour's waiting time). Fines were to be imposed for a range of offences, including overcharging and abusive language. It was planned that at least sixty chairs should be available for the ever-increasing size of the company.

(below)   A Plan of Bath, 1723. This shows that the city was still essentially the same city as that depicted on John Speed's map of 1610 - a city largely hemmed in by medieval walls and surrounded by fields and meadows. However, the first sign that the city was ready to burst out its confines is indicated by the development of Trim Street to the north. In 1707 George Trim , a clothier and member of Bath Corporation, was given permission to breach the city walls and establish the street just outside. By courtesy of Bath & North East Somerset Library and Archive Service (Bath Central Library)

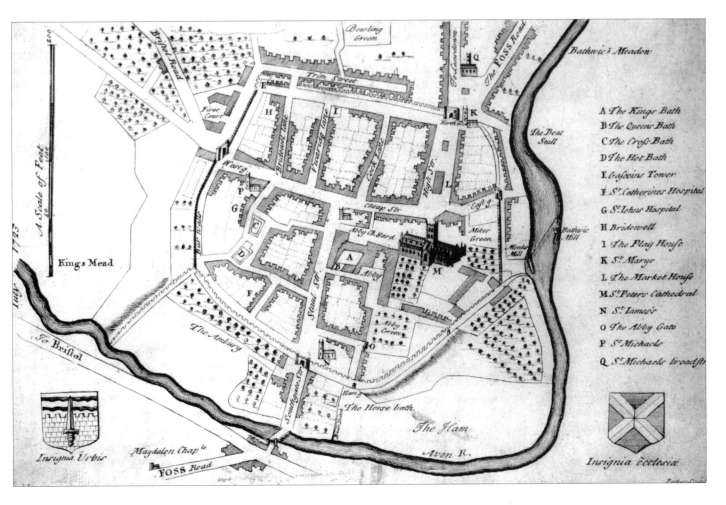

The Coronation of Charles II

23rd April 1661

Celebrations in Bath

A letter from John Ford, Mayor, to William Prynne, MP for Bath.

Whilst the morning was ushered in and welcomed by the bells, the drums beat, calling to such as would demonstrate their good affections to the King, to show themselves armed for the celebrating the day. Whereupon all men that had arms fit for that employment appeared. By this time... myself and the Aldermen, in scarlet, attended by the rest of our Corporation in their gowns, I went to Church, the streets being guarded by these forementioned persons in arms on both sides, leaving a passage for us to pass between, and crying out "God save the King" with great acclamations of joy.

After us followed above four hundred virgins, most in white waistcoats and green petticoats, going two and two, each two bearing aloft in their hands crowns and garlands, made in the form of crowns, bedecked with all manner of rare and choicest flowers. These ushered Mistress Mayoress to the church, who was attended on by the Aldermen's wives, and Common Councilmen's wives, and divers other gentlewomen of the city. These being paired, the soldiers marched after, and having laid by their arms, came into the church, as generally the whole city did, so that our church was never fuller; all persons expressing as much piety towards God as loyalty towards their King. After Mr Masters our minister had given us a most excellent and learned sermon... the sermon being ended, the soldiery again made a guard for us, and we having now the loud music playing before us... we passed from the church to the conduit in the market-place, being also guarded by the way with a company of foot from the parish of Weston, a mile from us, led by Captain Sheppard - and also by a troop of horse, being volunteers, commanded by your nephew Mr. George Clark. Having passed these and come to the conduit, it began to run with claret, where we drank a health to His Majesty, which was seconded with loud acclamations of loyalty, each person crying out "God save the King".

From thence we passed to the Guildhall, where having entertained the gentlemen of our city, and such gentlemen as came out of the country to us, we with the soldiery marched from thence with the loud music playing before us, through every street in our city. In the meantime, the gentlewomen and their virgin attendance were entertained by the Mayoress at home. All which being performed with many volleys of shot, and loud acclamations of joy, the night began to participate of our mirth, which we entertained with bonfires and flying fireworks, prepared by certain persons sent to for that purpose from Bristol, who excellently well performed their undertakings for several hours. Which being done, the people civilly dispersed, and the whole day's work was carried on with great sobriety and temperance, I hope to the great credit of our city.

The Bath Chamberlain's Accounts for 1661 show that the corporation entertained the soldiers who took part in these celebrations with three hogsheads of beer, together with tobacco, bread and cheese; the church bell ringers with bread, cheese and beer; and the maidens with beer. It hired a drum for the occasion and paid 'Thomas Griffin's boy' for 'playing before the maids'. Furthermore, it invested heavily in 'gold streamers' for the streets and the gilding of the crown and the fleur-de-lis at the King's Bath. During the festivities, serious damage was caused to two houses overlooking the Queen's Bath, when fireworks fell onto the flat roofs and melted the lead

SOURCES USED IN CHAPTER 15

1. Printed material:
Borsay, Peter: *The English Urban Renaissance: Culture and Society in the Provincial Town, 1660-1770*
          (1989)
Chapman, Henry: *Thermae Redivivae: the City of Bath Described* (1673)
Chapman, Mike: *An Historical Guide to the Ham and Southgate Area of Bath* (1997)
Clark, Peter & Slack, Paul: *Towns in Transition, 1500-1700* (1976)
Collinson, John: *History of Somersetshire*, vol.1 (1791)
Cotton, Charles: *The Compleat Gamester* (1680 edn.)
Cunliffe, Barry: *The City of Bath* (1986)
Davis, C.E: *Mineral Waters of Bath. The Bathes of Bathe's Ayde in the Reign of Charles II* (1883)
Defoe, Daniel: *Tour of the Whole Island of Great Britain*, vol. 2 (ed. Ernest Rhys, 1927)
Fawcett, Trevor: 'Chair transport in Bath: the Sedan era' (in *Bath History*, vol. 2, 1988)
Fawcett, Trevor: *Bath Entertain'd: Amusements, Recreations and Gambling at the Eighteenth-Century*
          Spa (1998)
Fawcett, Trevor & Inskip, Marta: 'The Making of Orange Grove' in *Bath History*, vol.V (1994)
Fawcett, Trevor & Bird, Stephen: *Bath: History and Guide (1994)*
Gurr, Andrew: 'The Theatre and Society' in *The Oxford Illustrated History of Tudor & Stuart Britain* (ed.
          John Morrill, 1996)
Hamilton, Meg: *Bath before Beau Nash* (1978)
Hart, Roger: *English Life in the Seventeenth Century* (1970)
Hart-Davis, Adam: *What the Tudors and Stuarts did for Us* (2002)
James, P.R: *The Municipal Records of Bath* (unpublished, 1942)
Lewcun, Marek: 'The Clay Tobacco Pipe-Making Industry of Bath' in *Bath History*, vol. 5 (1994)
McInnes, Angus: *The English Town, 1660-1760* (1980)
Morris Chris (Ed.): *The Illustrated Journeys of Celia Fiennes, 1685-c1712* (1982)
Neale, Ronald: *Bath: a Social History, 1680-1850* (1981)
Page, W. (ed.): *Victoria County History of Somerset*, vol. 2 (1911)
Peirce, Robert: *History and Memoirs of the Bath* (1713 edn.)
Saussure, César de: *A Foreign View of England in the Reigns of George I and George II* (1902 edn., ed.
          Mme van Muyden)
Sims, Alison: *Pleasure and Pastimes in Tudor England* (1999)
Smith, Alan: *The Emergence of a Nation State, 1529-1660* (1984)
Waller, Maureen: *1700: Scenes from London Life* (2000)
Ward, Ned: *A Step to the Bath* (1700)
Warner, Richard: *The History of Bath* (1801)
Wickham, L.G (ed.): *A Relation of a Short Survey of Twenty-six Counties, 1634* (1904)
Wilson, F.M: *Strange Island* (1955; for the account in translation by von Uffenbach)
Wood, Anthony à: *Monumental Inscriptions in the Churches of Bath* (1881)
Wood, John: *Essay Towards a Description of Bath*, vol. 2 (1765 edtn.)
Wroughton, John: *A Community at War: the Civil War in Bath & North Somerset* (1992)
2. Documentary material:
Bath Record Office: Bath Chamberlain's Accounts, 1568-1734
                    Bath Council Books, Nos. 1, 2 & 3 (1631-1715)
                    Act for Repairing, Amending and Enlarging the Highways,
                    1707 [with regulations to control the hire of chairs]

Index